The Bank Valuation Handbook

Second Edition

The Bank Valuation Handbook

Second Edition

A Market-Based Approach to Valuing A Bank

Hazel J. Johnson

A Bankline Publication

IRWIN
Professional Publishing®

Chicago • London • Singapore

Irwin Professional Book Team

Publisher: *Wayne McGuirt*
Acquisitions editor: *Mark Butler*
Marketing manager: *Brian Hayes*
Project editor: *Christina Thornton-Villagomez*
Production supervisor: *Laurie Kersch*
Prepress Buyer: *Jon Christopher*
Compositor: *Hendrickson Creative Communications—HCC*
Typeface: *10.5/12.5 Times*
Printer: *Quebecor Book Press, Inc.*

⬤ **Times Mirror**
◤ **Higher Education Group**

Library of Congress Cataloging-in-Publication Data

Johnson, Hazel.
    The bank valuation handbook/Hazel J. Johnson.—2nd ed.
       p. cm.—(A bankline publication)
    Includes bibliographical references and index.
    ISBN 1–55738–795–8
    1. Banks and banking—Valuation—United States. 2. Fair value—
Accounting.   I. Title.   II. Series
HG1707.7.J64   1996
332.1'068'1—dc20

                         95–33417
                             CIP

Printed in the United States of America
1 2 3 4 5 6 7 8 9 0 Q 2 1 0 9 8 7 6 5

In Loving Memory of
Ida W. Kelly and Lucille V. Johnson

Contents in Brief

CHAPTER 1
The Growing Emphasis on Market Valuation

CHAPTER 2

The Difference between Book Value and Market Value

CHAPTER 3
Time Value of Money

CHAPTER 4
Market Valuation Models for the Balance Sheet

CHAPTER 5
Embedded Options

CHAPTER 6

Measuring the General Effect of Interest Rate Changes

CHAPTER 7

The Impact of Changing Interest Rates on the Market
Value of Specific Bank Balance Sheet Categories

CHAPTER 8
Market Valuation Models for Off-Balance-Sheet Items and Derivatives

APPENDIXES

List of Figures

List of Tables

PREFACE

When the first edition of *The Bank Valuation Handbook* was published in 1992, the banking community was only beginning to realize the impact that market valuation would have on the industry. Since that time, the market value disclosure required by Financial Accounting Standard (FAS) No.107 has expanded to full market value accounting (MVA) for portions of the securities portfolio (FAS No.115), impaired loans (FAS No.114 and FAS No.118), derivatives held for trading purposes (FAS No.119), and mortgage servicing rights (FAS No.122). All of these pronouncements require an understanding of market valuation principles.

The increasing waves of mergers add to the need for better market valuation of commercial banks. Consolidation in the industry will be further enhanced by the 1994 passage of the Riegle-Neal Interstate Banking and Branching Act, effective in 1997. Under provisions of this law, entire banks or portions of branch networks can be acquired across state lines.

Bank valuation in market value terms has never been more important. The financial theory to establish reasonable estimates of market value has long been developed. *The Bank Valuation Handbook* is built on present value and options theory, but it goes far beyond merely explaining the relevant theories. It is a step-by-step, hands-on guide to market valuation. The input information that is required is readily available from a bank's internal systems including the general ledger, securities, loan, and deposits systems. *The Bank Valuation Handbook* has a specific model for virtually every line item on the balance sheet and includes examples of its implementation.

The revised edition of the book includes coverage of Financial Accounting Standard Nos. 114, 115, 118, 119, and 122. In addition, the revised edition includes an entirely new chapter on the valuation of off-balance-sheet exposures and derivative instruments, including unused loan commitments, letters of credit, loans transferred with recourse, when-issued securities, and interest rate swaps, futures, and forwards.

Companion software facilitates implementation of the concepts described in *The Bank Valuation Handbook*. A description of Bank Valuation Software is provided in Appendix B. Bank Valuation Software is available through Global Bank Research (502-423-0760).

The Bank Valuation Handbook bridges the gap between theory and practice and is a complete reference for all issues that relate to the market valuation of commercial banks.

Hazel J. Johnson, Ph.D., C.P.A.

The Bank Valuation Handbook

Second Edition

CHAPTER 1

THE GROWING EMPHASIS ON MARKET VALUATION

INTRODUCTION

Financial institutions can no longer ignore the issue of market valuation. The experiences of the 1970s and 1980s taught bank analysts that the financial statements for a commercial bank in that era did not necessarily reflect the viability of the institution. The classic example of this deficiency is the experience of savings and loan associations (S&Ls). In this beleaguered industry during the 1970s, the true economic value of large portfolios of low-yielding, fixed-rate mortgage loans declined to such an extent that many S&Ls were fundamentally insolvent. At the same time, their financial statements did not suggest financial distress. Market valuation techniques help to correct this deficiency.

Consolidation of the banking industry is another reason why market valuation is critical. In a number of large mergers, hindsight makes it clear that the acquiring bank paid an inflated price for the acquired firm because problems with the loan portfolio or operational issues were not completely factored into the analysis. Sound market valuation techniques can help to reduce the number of surprises in these business combinations, thereby improving the efficiency of each merger and, collectively, of the industry as a whole.

Regulatory agencies now stress the need for market valuation of financial assets and liabilities. Beginning with fiscal years ended after December 15, 1995, all institutions must include disclosures with respect to the fair value of financial assets and liabilities.[1] Other market valuation requirements affect the securities portfolio, the loan portfolio, off-balance-sheet items, and fee-generating activities. Market valuation concepts have long been a part of the securities

1

industry and other financial services industries but are a relatively recent phenomenon in banking circles.

WHEN BOOK VALUE WAS SUFFICIENT

After the bank reforms of the 1930s, commercial banks operated in a fairly stable, protected environment. The Banking Act of 1933 (frequently referred to as Glass-Steagall):

➤ Forced commercial banks to divest themselves of their investment banking affiliates.
➤ Prohibited interest payments on demand deposits.
➤ Established government authority to regulate interest rates on time deposits.

Commercial banks were considered special institutions that controlled a major share of the money supply because only they could offer demand deposits. Also, the country's monetary policy was implemented primarily through commercial banks. The Federal Reserve (Fed) used the discount rate (the rate it charges banks to which it lends in its capacity of lender of last resort), the reserve requirement (the share of bank deposits that must be set aside in Fed accounts), and open market operations (purchases and sales of government securities which, in turn, represent a significant component of commercial bank asset portfolios) to control the money supply and the pace of economic growth.

For several decades, the Fed was successful in maintaining stability in the system. After the reforms of 1933, its monetary policy was geared primarily to preventing another reoccurrence of the Great Depression and the banking crisis that had accompanied it. During World War II, the Fed helped to finance the war effort by buying government securities and by intervening in the credit markets to keep interest rates well under 3 percent on Treasury issues. Of course, the money supply swelled, but price controls kept wages and prices in check. Even after World War II, the Fed kept interest rates low to accommodate the Treasury and to encourage maximum employment in accordance with the Employment Act of 1946. Of course, the Treasury-Federal Reserve Accord of 1951 gave the Fed more flexibility (independence from the Treasury) with respect to monetary policy. Nevertheless, interest rates remained low and stable. U.S. Treasury bond yields before the 1960s were maintained well below 5 percent, a level lower than the rates in any other major industrialized country, including Japan, Germany, the United Kingdom, France, and Italy.

The net effect of the special status of commercial banks and pre-1960s monetary policy was that:

> ➤ Banks enjoyed low-cost sources of funds.
> ➤ The interest rate spread (the difference between the average earned on earning assets and the average rate paid on interest-bearing liabilities) was predictable.
> ➤ There was little or no difference between the book value and market value of bank assets and liabilities.

Since cash flows were fairly predictable and interest rates were stable, book value was a very good approximation of market value.

A CHANGING ENVIRONMENT

The banking system's stability was shaken by several factors beginning in the 1960s. After the Korean Conflict (1950–1953), the U.S. fiscal budget was in surplus for two years (1956 and 1957) between 1954 and 1960. The cumulative deficit during this period was only $16.7 billion. The war in Vietnam and the domestic reforms embodied in the Great Society initiatives of the 1960s created a large demand for loanable funds on the part of the federal government.

Federal expenditures for defense and for payments to individuals increased dramatically. Table 1–1 shows that defense expenditures went from $48.1 billion in 1960 to $81.9 billion only eight years later, a 70 percent increase. Payments to individuals rose even faster. This portion of the federal budget grew from $24.2 billion to $49.8, for a 106 percent increase. The net effect of these increases is that the level of federal budget deficits also rose. The average deficit had been $2.4 billion per year from 1954 through 1960 [($16.7 billion)/7]. After this period, the federal budget was never again in surplus, with the deficit reaching $6.5 billion in 1964, then $27.8 billion in 1968, and $54.9 billion by 1978. This huge increase in demand for loanable funds by the federal government was a destabilizing factor in the previous stable interest environment.

The foreign trade situation also contributed to the changing financial landscape. The U.S. trade balance had been consistently positive during the 1960s with exports exceeding imports by an average of $4.6 billion per year from 1961 through 1970. During the 1970s, however, two oil crises revealed energy-related vulnerability in the U.S. economy and worked to shift this trade surplus into trade deficit. What had been a $4.6 billion average surplus became an $8.9 billion average trade deficit from 1971 through 1979. This compounded the inflationary effect of large federal budget deficits. Inflation went from an average of 1.3 percent in the four-year period from 1961 through 1965 to 11.0 percent in 1974.

Table 1–1.

FEDERAL BUDGET EXPENDITURES FOR DEFENSE AND PAYMENTS TO INDIVIDUALS, 1960 AND 1968

	Current Dollars	Constant Dollars[1]
Defense		
1960	$48.1	$192.1
1968	$81.9	$254.8
Total increase	70.3%	32.6%
Average annual increase	6.9%	3.6%
Payments to Individuals		
1960	$24.2	$73.2
1968	$49.8	$128.0
Total increase	105.8%	74.9%
Average annual increase	9.4%	7.2%

[1]   Represents the equivalent in 1982 dollars, after adjusting for inflation.
Note: All amounts are in billions of dollars.
Source: Global Bank Research, based on data from U.S. Office of Management and Budget, *Historical Tables; Budget of the United States Government,* 1990.

The economy was hit hard by the increases in crude oil prices and the general inflationary trend that accompanied the oil price hikes. The Fed was faced with a new economic dilemma often referred to as *stagflation,* inflation that occurs simultaneously with stagnant economic growth. During the 1960s and 1970s, the Fed had pursued a relatively easy money policy to keep interest rates low in hopes of spurring the economy. This resulted in additions to the money supply which, in turn, served to further fuel inflation. In October 1979, the Federal Reserve announced that it would no longer target interest rates but instead would focus on growth in the money supply. In the process, interest rates would be allowed to find their own level.

THE NEW REALITIES OF COMMERCIAL BANKING
With the inflation that began in the 1960s and the shift in Fed policy, commercial banking would never be the same. The stable interest rate environment was gone and the bank deposit base changed dramatically.

Interest Rates and the Corporate Sector

Figure 1–1 shows the volatility of interest rates that has occurred since the 1960s. After the 1979 shift in Fed policy, the average annual discount rate went from 7.5 percent in 1978 to 10.3 percent in 1979 and to 13.4 percent in 1981. The prime lending rate rose from its 1978 average of 9.1 percent to a high of 18.9 percent in 1981.

The foundations of commercial banking were badly shaken. The predictable cost of funds and the stable interest rate spread were gone forever. The traditional customer base of high-quality corporate clients was threatened. The interest-free demand deposit was not attractive to corporate treasurers. The negotiable certificate of deposit (CD), which had been free from interest rate

Figure 1–1.

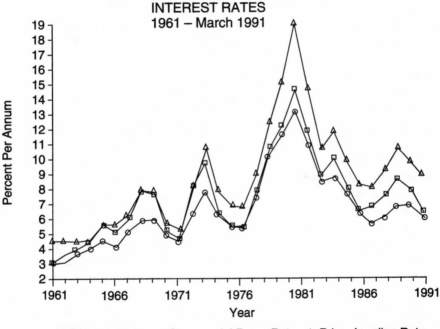

INTEREST RATE VOLATILITY

INTEREST RATES
1961 – March 1991

○ Discount Rate   □ Commercial Paper Rate   △ Prime Lending Rate

Source: Global Bank Research, based on data from U.S. Department of Commerce, *Survey of Current Business*, April 1991, and *Business Statistics 1961–1988*, 1989.

restrictions (Federal Reserve Regulation Q) since 1970, helped to keep large corporate clients inhouse. This instrument was issued in minimum denominations of $100,000 and paid competitive, market rates of return. Negotiable CDs outstanding grew at an average annual rate of 24 percent from 1969 to 1979. This was a much more expensive source of funds, however.

At the same time, corporate treasurers were not at all satisfied with the loan rates available to them. Commercial paper became a viable alternative to short-term commercial bank loans for large, creditworthy corporations. When the average prime lending rate went to 18.9 percent in 1981, the commercial paper rate was 14.8 percent, 410 basis points lower. Even more compelling, this commercial paper rate was only 140 basis points higher than the discount rate. Commercial paper outstanding grew at an average annual rate of 13 percent from 1969 to 1979. This was, indeed, a good substitute for short-term bank loans.

Thus, commercial banking was altered in two ways:

➤ A source of low-cost funding was significantly reduced.
➤ The market for blue-chip corporate loans was seriously eroded.

Competition for Consumer Deposits
While interest rates soared during the late 1970s and early 1980s, small depositors did not have a satisfactory outlet for their savings in the commercial banking system. Savings accounts that paid 5 percent interest were hardly competitive when the rate of inflation exceeded 10 percent. An investment in Treasury bills required a minimum investment of $10,000 and jumbo CDs required an even larger $100,000. Thus, the deposit regulations put in place in 1933 to ensure stability in the banking industry became a source of major instability because small savers were faced with an investment alternative that yielded a negative real rate of return.

As a result of this situation, a new financial services industry rose from the turmoil of the 1970s. The money market mutual fund accepted small deposits and pooled these funds to invest them in money market instruments that did earn the market rate of return: Treasury bills, negotiable CDs, commercial paper, and bankers' acceptances. This industry has grown faster than any other financial services industry. From $2 billion under management in 1974, money market mutual funds hold more than $500 billion today. The banking industry and, indeed, all depository institutions were seriously threatened: The small investor, who had historically been a solid source of low-cost funding, had found a superior alternative to bank deposits.

Deregulation

Legislation in 1980 and 1982 relieved some of the competitive pressure on commercial banks but also increased the amount of competition among depository institutions.[2] The Depository Institutions Deregulation and Monetary Control Act of 1980:

➤ Called for the phaseout of all Reg Q deposit interest rate ceilings by 1986.

➤ Gave all depository institutions the power to issue interest-bearing transactions accounts, called NOW accounts (negotiable order of withdrawal), to individuals and nonprofit organizations.

➤ Increased the limit on federal deposit insurance coverage from $40,000 per account to $100,000.

➤ Gave savings and loan associations (S&Ls) the power to issue credit cards.

➤ Gave S&Ls the power to offer commercial real estate loans and consumer loans, each up to 20 percent of total assets.

➤ Gave mutual savings banks (MSBs) the power to make business loans and to offer demand deposit accounts to those business clients.

➤ Effectively eliminated state usury laws (loan rate ceilings) for mortgage, business, and agricultural loans.

In 1982, the powers of depository institutions were expanded even further. The Garn-St Germain Depository Institutions Act:

➤ Permitted all depository institutions to issue money market deposit accounts (MMDAs) to compete directly with money market mutual funds.

➤ Permitted federal, state, and local governments to own NOW accounts.

➤ Gave S&Ls the power to further diversify their loan portfolios (up to a maximum percentage of total assets) into commercial real estate loans (40 percent), secured and unsecured commercial loans (5 percent), commercial leasing (10 percent), and consumer loans (30 percent).

The provisions of these acts made it easier for banks to attract deposit funds through NOW accounts and MMDAs. Furthermore, since loan rates also were deregulated, the bank's balance sheet was effectively freed of any interest rate constraints. It is also true, however, that a bank's interest rate spread is no longer protected by legislation. Interest rates earned and paid are now less predictable. This means that the market value of assets and liabilities is no longer necessarily equal to book value.

Also contributing to the uncertainty of interest rates and value is the fact that S&Ls and MSBs can compete with commercial banks in the areas of demand deposit accounts, business loans, credit cards, and consumer loans. For some time, mutual funds and securities firms have competed by offering bank-like services such as cash management accounts that are effectively checking accounts. The deregulation of the early 1980s virtually ensured more intense competition among providers of financial services. This competition, in turn, means that banks must respond by adjusting the price of bank services, that is, interest rates. Both the climate of variable interest rates and the necessary response to competitive forces render the book value of bank assets and liabilities less meaningful.

THE DEBATE OVER MARKET VALUE
VERSUS BOOK VALUE

Despite the changes in the commercial banking industry, some observers believe that market value accounting (MVA) is either not necessary or may in fact destabilize the banking industry. In particular, the loan portfolio contains financial assets for which there is, at best, a thin market. These MVA opponents argue that historical cost is preferable for several reasons.

Intent to Hold an Asset until Maturity

Opponents of MVA suggest that if a bank intends to hold an asset until it matures, the market valuation of that asset is not relevant since it has no impact on the cash flows to the investing bank.

This argument ignores the realities of the savings and loan industry during the early 1980s. High market interest rates caused the economic value of the loan portfolios of many S&Ls to decline below the value of the institutions' liabilities, rendering the S&Ls economically insolvent. Under these circumstances, the institutions themselves were so weak that they did not have the ability to hold the assets until maturity.

The argument also ignores the practice of evaluating certain bank managers on the basis of performance of the securities portfolio on an MVA basis. The asset/liability management committee (ALCO) is always evaluating the bank's position in light of market conditions with respect to interest rates, loan demand, and liquidity needs. MVA only enhances this process. In this context, however, intent to hold an asset until maturity has little relevance.

Transactions Price versus Going Concern

Opponents of MVA point to the illiquidity of the typical loan portfolio and suggest that it is difficult to obtain a market valuation for many financial assets held by banks. Whatever market values are obtainable may not reflect the true benefit of the asset to the bank. For example, a single observable market transaction may not accurately reflect the aggregate cash that would be received when attempting to sell an entire loan portfolio. In selling the entire portfolio, significant, though perhaps unquantifiable, discounts from book value and other transactions costs may be necessary. Thus, MVA could actually distort the portfolio value. Book value is closer to a going concern valuation.

Proponents of MVA acknowledge the illiquidity of some assets held in bank portfolios. When transactions prices are either not available or not relevant, the better alternative is to use discounted cash flow methods. Referring again to the S&L example, if discounted cash flow accounting had been used for the mortgage loan portfolios, the severity of the crisis within the industry would have been recognized sooner and billions of taxpayer dollars would have been saved. Also note that markets for securitized assets have developed to such an extent that the parameters for market valuation are now much more readily available. For example, mortgage-backed securities trade in a healthy secondary market, and securities backed by credit card loans and automobile loans also have emerged.

Financial Stability

Since changes in the market value of assets and liabilities would ultimately affect current and retained earnings, opponents of MVA suggest that the public may misinterpret or overreact to the variability of earnings and equity. This increased volatility could lead the public to withdraw funds on a massive scale and destabilize the banking industry that is at the heart of the country's payments and credit allocation systems.

MVA proponents counter this argument by noting that the federal deposit insurance system is in place to prevent such bank runs and that the Federal Reserve System as lender of last resort would act to shore up the system if necessary. Moreover, those institutions that are known to be sound on an MVA basis will generate even more confidence on the part of depositors and investors. Indeed, the market discipline that would result from MVA could, in the long run, reduce the moral hazard associated with the investment of federally insured deposits.

THE CHANGING FACE OF COMMERCIAL BANKING

At one time, a commercial bank was just that. Loans were made primarily to businesses for short periods of time, giving the bank a maturity structure of assets that was similar to the maturity structure of liabilities. This is no longer the case.

The Asset Portfolio

After World War II, banks began to make more loans backed by real estate. Many real estate borrowers were mortgage companies that carried their own customers' loans until mortgages could be set up. Also, banks began to make mortgage loans directly, that is, to make conventional mortgage loans for which banks assumed the ultimate risk. Growth in these loans (with original maturities of 15 to 30 years) and construction loans (with typical original maturities from 18 months to three years) coincided with major construction in the United States during the post-World War II years.

Also after 1946, commercial banks sought to further diversify their loan portfolios with consumer installment loans. Expanding branch networks helped to reach the ultimate consumers. Establishing relationships with appliance and automobile dealers also helped. In dealer relationships, banks purchased loans or paper from the dealers after consumers had made their purchases of these durable, high-ticket items. Banks also began to provide inventory financing directly to durable goods dealers. Through floor planning, manufacturers' invoices for durable goods were paid by the bank, with the loans being repaid when consumers purchased the items. Credit cards are another way that banks have expanded loans to both consumers and businesses.

Over time, bank asset portfolios have become (1) more dominated by loans, and (2) more concentrated in long-term loans. With these shifts from short-term, self-liquidating loans to long-term investments, market valuation is no longer optional because long-term asset values are far more sensitive to changing interest rates than the values of short-term assets.

Figure 1–2 provides a breakdown of financial assets for all U.S. banks in 1964 and 1991. Holdings of cash (vault cash, due from other banks, and reserves at the Federal Reserve) declined from 7.3 percent of total financial assets to 1.4 percent. Investment securities represented one-third of assets in 1964, but only 20.8 percent by 1991. The share devoted to the loan portfolio increased from 47.9 to 59.2 percent. These aggregate changes point to the reduced liquidity of commercial banks: the composition of the categories is particularly illuminating.

Figure 1–2.

THE COMPOSITION OF COMMERCIAL BANK FINANCIAL ASSETS, 1964 AND 1991

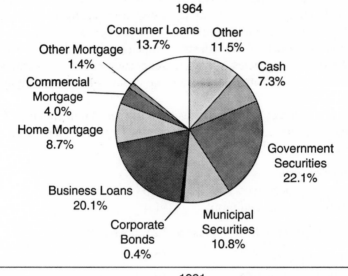

1964

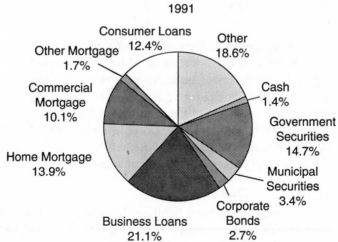

1991

Source: Global Bank Research, based on data from Board of Governors of the Federal Reserve System, *Flow of Funds Accounts; Financial Assets and Liabilities*, various issues.

The most stable categories have been business loans and consumer loans. Business loans went from 20.1 to 21.1 percent of assets. Consumer loans decreased slightly from 13.7 to 12.4 percent.

Other categories reflect substantial change, however. In 1964, the industry portfolio contained 22.1 percent in government securities, but by 1991 that share was down to 14.7 percent. This decline was in the area of Treasury securities, as the holdings of government agency securities actually increased from 1.7 to 8.9 percent. Agency securities have a higher rate of return than Treasuries and have helped the industry compensate partially for a higher cost of funds. Most of the agencies, however, are mortgage-backed securities whose values are almost as sensitive to interest rate changes as the underlying mortgage loans.

Holdings of direct mortgage loans have increased tremendously. In 1964, the industry portfolio contained 14.1 percent in mortgage loans, with the following breakdown:

Home mortgages	8.7%
Commercial mortgages	4.0
Other (multifamily and farm)	1.4

By 1991 direct mortgage loans represented 25.7 percent:

Home mortgages	13.9%
Commercial mortgages	10.1
Other	1.7

Together, mortgage-backed securities and direct mortgages went from 15.8 percent of the industry balance sheet to 34.6 percent in 1991.

To suggest that bank portfolios, with such a heavy concentration in mortgage-related investments, should not be examined from a market value standpoint is to ignore the experience of the savings and loan industry. It is also to ignore an important current issue with respect to stability in the banking industry. In the late 1980s and early 1990s, real estate loans were the single greatest source of loan losses and the cause of many bank failures.

Bank Liabilities

Changes in the composition of bank liabilities have been equally dramatic. At one time, commercial banks accepted large amounts of noninterest-bearing demand deposits and relatively low-yielding savings and time deposits. But as treasurers of nonfinancial corporations became more sophisticated, these money managers sought higher-yielding, short-term investments to replace demand deposits. The result was a severe reduction in demand deposit balances held by corporations.

The negotiable CD was the banks' response to this deposit drain. Its development is a testament to the ability of the banking industry to successfully manage market valuation issues. In 1960, the first bankers certificate was offered by the Overseas Division of First National City Bank. The $1 million certificate issued to Union Bank of Switzerland was described as marketable. However, Union Bank found that the market for the new instrument was nonexistent.

Walter Wriston, head of the overseas division, suggested to Discount Corporation, a government securities dealer, that it make a market in the new certificates. Discount Corporation was willing to do so if First National City provided the dealer with a $10 million unsecured loan to finance the operation. First National City overlooked its long-standing rule of not lending to securities dealers on an unsecured basis, and the market for bankers certificates was born.

On February 20, 1961, First National City announced the new bankers certificate to be sold in units of not less than $1 million with Discount Corporation agreeing to make a market. Walter Wriston would go on to become president and later chairman of the nation's largest bank, now known as Citibank. The new negotiable CD would become an extremely important instrument in U.S. money markets, second only to the Treasury bill. Its enthusiastic reception helped banks regain much of the funding that had been lost.

The birth of the negotiable CD enabled banks to manage their liabilities by offering higher interest rates to attract deposits. Other short-term borrowed funds assisted in this liability management. Figure 1–3 shows the change in the composition of bank liabilities from 1964 to 1991. In 1964, 49.5 percent of all bank liabilities was attributable to checkable deposits, all noninterest-bearing since NOW accounts were not permitted until 1980. Another 35.4 percent came from small time and savings accounts, all subject to Reg Q interest rate ceilings. Large time deposits (including negotiable CDs) were 8.7 percent of the total. Both short-term and long-term borrowed funds (federal funds purchased, repurchase agreements, and bonds) constituted only 1.6 percent. Only the large time deposits and borrowed funds (10.3 percent of the total) were, in any sense of the word, interest-sensitive.

By 1991, checkable deposits had declined to 16.6 percent of total liabilities and a share of these, of course, were interest-bearing NOW accounts. Small time and savings accounts and large time deposits increased to 40.6 percent and

Figure 1–3.

THE COMPOSITION OF COMMERCIAL BANK
LIABILITIES, 1964–1991

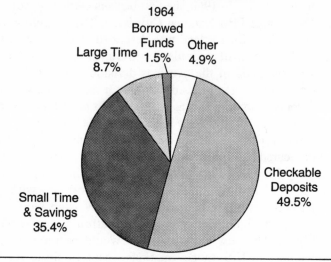

1964

Borrowed
Funds   Other
Large Time 1.5%   4.9%
8.7%

Checkable
Deposits
49.5%

Small Time
& Savings
35.4%

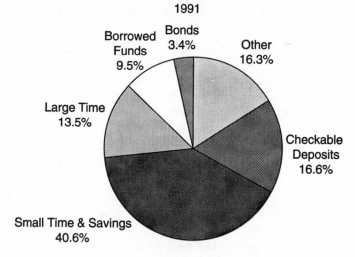

1991

Borrowed Bonds
Funds   3.4%   Other
9.5%   16.3%

Large Time
13.5%

Checkable
Deposits
16.6%

Small Time & Savings
40.6%

Source: Global Bank Research, based on data from Board of Governors of the Federal Reserve
System, *Flow of Funds Accounts; Financial Assets and Liabilities*, various issues.

13.5 percent, respectively. The most dramatic increase, however, is in the borrowed funds categories. Short-term and long-term borrowed funds went from 1.6 percent in 1964 to 12.9 percent in 1991. Together, the most interest-sensitive instruments (large time deposits and borrowed funds) increased from 10.3 to 26.4 percent of total liabilities.

Both interest rates and bank liabilities (particularly borrowed funds and large time deposits) are extremely sensitive to market conditions. Thus, a market valuation of these obligations is appropriate. Furthermore, the investors in bank liability products should be better informed with respect to the market value of bank assets.

THE MERGER TREND

The commercial banking industry in the United States is undergoing a major consolidation. Passage of the Riegle-Neal Interstate Banking and Branching Efficiency Act of 1994 assures that the brisk pace of consolidation will continue. The structure of the U.S. banking system will approach those of its major trading partners. Of course, the concepts of market valuation are critical to an efficient industry consolidation.

International Comparisons

When the banking system of the United States is compared to the systems in other industrialized countries, the contrasts are striking. Two points are clear:

> ➤ The amount of total assets in the U.S. banking system is smaller than the total in the Japanese system but larger than the others in the comparison.
> ➤ The average bank size in the United States is smaller than in any other country analyzed.

Total assets. Figure 1–4 shows the relative proportions of bank assets in seven industrialized countries including the United States. Japanese bank assets alone are almost half of the total and the United States represents over 25 percent. The other shares range from 3.3 to 8.7 percent. Taken in the aggregate, the U.S. banking system is the second largest banking system in the world.

Average size. Even with a large share of total banking assets, U.S. banks operate at a competitive disadvantage because their average size is so much smaller. Consider the following breakdown of average bank size for these countries in 1989.

	Banks	Assets ($ billions)
United States	12,689	$ 0.26
United Kingdom	47	15.55
Canada	10	39.50
Germany	264	2.54
France	8	129.13
Switzerland	34	14.44
Japan	145	36.69

Figure 1–4.

BANK ASSETS OF SELECTED
INDUSTRIALIZED COUNTRIES
1989

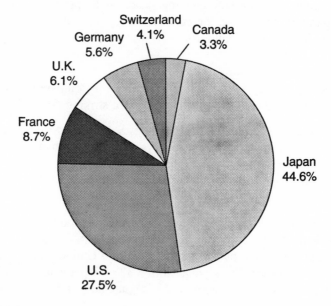

Note: Data for Switzerland is for 1987.
Sources: Global Bank Research, based on data from *Bank Profitability; Statistical
Supplement; Financial Statements of Banks 1981–1989*, Organization for
Economic Cooperation and Development, 1991; and *International Financial
Statistics*, International Monetary Fund, Yearbook 1990.

The average size of U.S. banks is 10 percent the size of the average German bank, 0.2 percent the size of the average French bank, and somewhere in between these percentages for the banks in the other countries. This significant size difference is important because a growing share of banks operating in the United States are foreign banks that compete directly with U.S. domestic banks. To the extent that U.S. banks are smaller and less able to offer a full range of services, domestic banks will continue to lose market share on their own turf.

Difference in size is also important because industrial firms operate increasingly in a global environment. The future international competitiveness of the United States will depend in large measure on the ability of small- and medium-size firms to sell their goods and services abroad. Large banks in Japan have helped Japanese industrial firms to compete and to expand internationally. Likewise, U.S. banks assist U.S. firms. The amount of assistance can be limited by the size of the bank, however, because a smaller bank's loan portfolio can more easily become overly concentrated in one industry. Furthermore, it is not clear that foreign banks always have the same commitment to U.S. firms as U.S. banks.

Population per bank. The relative small size of U.S. banks is not attributable to lack of banking assets in this country, but to the large number of banks. The number of banks in the United States is almost 50 times the number in Germany and almost 90 times the number in Japan. The populations of these countries are also smaller than the U.S. population but not so much as to justify the difference in the number of institutions. Figure 1–5 shows that the population per bank in the United States is 20,000 people. Switzerland has the next smallest population per bank at 192,000 people, 10 times the U.S. figure, and France has the highest at more than 7 million people per bank, 350 times the U.S. average.

Population per bank branch. Figure 1–6 also shows that availability of banking services has not necessarily been compromised by the smaller number of banks because the population per bank branch among the six countries shown is remarkably similar. In the United States, France, the United Kingdom, and Switzerland, the population per bank branch is between 4,000 and 5,000 people. In Japan and Germany, the number is no more than twice this level. Thus, the convenience and availability of banking services need not be compromised in a banking system of larger institutions.

The Pace of Consolidation
Bank mergers in the United States are accomplishing the needed consolidation. As recently as 1975, U.S. banks numbered more than 14,000. The number of

Figure 1–5.

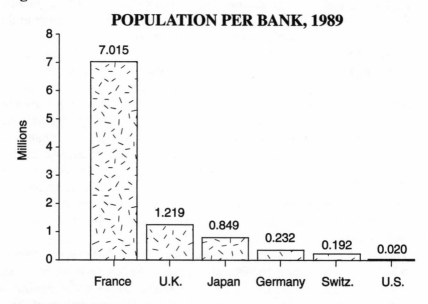

POPULATION PER BANK, 1989

Note: Data for Switzerland is for 1987.
Sources: Global Bank Research, based on data from *Bank Profitability; Statistical Supplement; Financial Statements of Banks 1981–1989*, Organization for Economic Cooperation and Development, 1991; and *The World Bank Atlas 1990*, The World Bank, 1990.

banks was relatively stable even in light of the difficult economic conditions produced by the hyperinflation of the early 1980s. However, the number began to decline precipitously in the mid-1980s. By 1994 the number of U.S. banks was down to 10,592. Early consolidation in the industry resulted primarily from bank failures that rose from less than 20 per year in the 1940 to 1980 period to more than 200 per year by the late 1980s. Since that time, the failure rate has declined significantly to 72 in 1992 and only 42 in 1993. In fact, the banking industry posted record profits in 1993.

Nevertheless, the industry continues to shrink. As illustrated in Figure 1–7, the level of merger activity has increased from less than 100 in 1975 to a high of 800 in 1988 to a current average of approximately 500 per year. It has been projected that this merger and acquisition trend will end only when the number of U.S. banks is closer to 5,000. The consolidation process has been made easier by enactment of the first federal law that permits nationwide banking.

Figure 1–6.

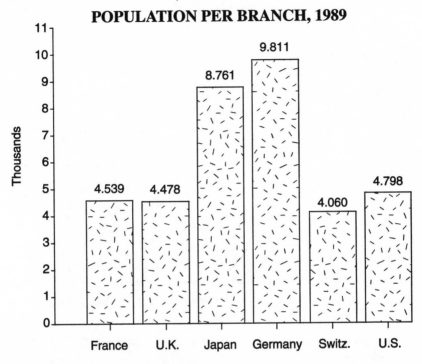

POPULATION PER BRANCH, 1989

Note: Data for Switzerland is for 1987.
Sources: Global Bank Research, based on data from *Bank Profitability; Statistical Supplement; Financial Statements of Banks 1981–1989*, Organization for Economic Cooperation and Development, 1991; and *The World Bank Atlas 1990*, The World Bank, 1990.

The Interstate Banking Act

The Riegle-Neal Interstate Banking and Branching Efficiency Act of 1994 was passed after many earlier versions of this legislation had been defeated. The major provisions of the act involve:

➤ Interstate bank holding company acquisitions.
➤ Interstate bank mergers.
➤ De novo interstate bank branching.
➤ Foreign bank interstate branching.
➤ Interstate bank agency.

Figure 1–7.

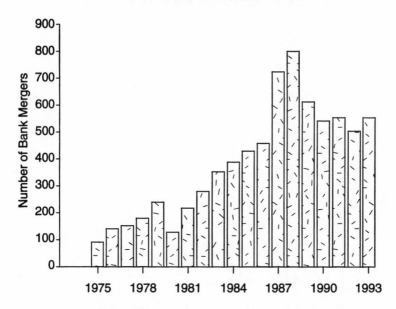

U.S. BANK MERGERS

Source: Global Bank Research, based on data from *FDIC Statistics on Banking*,
various years.

Interstate bank holding company acquisitions. Beginning in September
1995, a bank holding company (BHC) may acquire banks located in any state.
States may not prohibit or opt out of these interstate BHC acquisitions.
However, individual states may establish a minimum age of local banks (up
to five years) that are subject to interstate acquisition by out-of-state BHCs.
(For purposes of this provision, the home state of a BHC is the state in which
its banking subsidiaries have the largest amount of deposits as of the later of
July 1, 1966, or the date on which the company became a BHC.)

To qualify, the acquiring BHC must be adequately capitalized and managed. Even if the BHC is qualified for the acquisition, the Federal Reserve
Board (FRB) may not approve the acquisition if:

➤ After the acquisition, the BHC will control more than 10 percent of
U.S. insured depository institution deposits.

➤ The BHC already has a depository institution affiliate in the host state and, after the acquisition, the acquiring BHC will control 30 percent or more of the insured depository institution deposits of the host state.

Even if the 30 percent limitation is exceeded, the FRB may approve the acquisition if the host state has established a higher limit. At the same time, a state may limit the share of deposits held within the state by any bank or BHC as long as the limitation does not discriminate against out-of-state banking organizations.

The FRB also will consider the extent of compliance with the CRA. Notwithstanding these stipulations, the act gives the FRB the authority to approve an acquisition if the target bank is in default (or in danger of default) or if the FDIC is providing assistance for the acquisition.

Interstate bank mergers. Beginning June 1997, national and state banks may merge across state lines, thus creating interstate branches. However, such mergers may not take place if the home state of one of the banks has enacted, prior to June 1997, legislation that prohibits or opts out of interstate bank mergers. However, any such law will not affect mergers approved prior to the effective date of the prohibitive legislation.

States may opt in prior to June 1997 and may establish a minimum age (up to five years) for local banks permitted to participate in interstate mergers. Both home states of the merging banks must have adopted early prohibitive legislation. A host state may not discriminate against out-of-state banking organizations in this legislation with the exception of establishing a nationwide reciprocity rule.

Such mergers can be undertaken by both affiliate banks and independent banks. Mergers also may involve the acquisition of individual branches of a bank, instead of the entire bank, only if the state in which the branches are located permits such acquisitions by statute.

Also applicable in interstate bank mergers are the provisions specified in connection with interstate bank holding company acquisitions:

➤ 10 percent and 30 percent concentration limitations.
➤ Higher limits permitted by state law.
➤ Different limits that do not discriminate against out-of-state banking organizations.
➤ CRA compliance.
➤ Approval of mergers involving a troubled institution.

In reviewing potential mergers, the appropriate federal regulators must determine that each participating bank is adequately capitalized and that the resultant bank will be adequately capitalized and well managed. Furthermore, nothing in the act affects the applicability of antitrust laws or the ability of states to charter, supervise, regulate, and examine banks within their state boundaries.

After the merger is complete, the resultant bank may continue to operate those offices that had been in operation prior to the merger. The resultant institution also may acquire additional branches in any location where the acquired bank previously could have established and acquired branches.

The branches of an out-of-state bank will be subject to the host state laws, whether the out-of-state bank has a national charter or a state charter. If the out-of-state bank is a national bank, the Office of the Comptroller will enforce applicable state laws for national banks in the host state. If the out-of-state bank is a state-chartered bank, the branches will be subject to the same laws as other state banks in the host state. However, the branches of an out-of-state, state-chartered bank may not engage in any activity not permissible for a bank chartered in the host state.

De novo interstate bank branching. A national or state bank may, with appropriate federal approval, establish a de novo branch in a state outside its home state in which it previously has not maintained a branch.[3] However, the host state must have enacted legislation that applies to all banks and specifically permits all out-of-state banks to branch de novo into the host state. All state and federal laws that apply to an existing branch also apply to a de novo branch.

Foreign bank interstate branching. Essentially, foreign banks are permitted to engage in interstate bank mergers and establish de novo interstate branches to the same extent and on the same conditions as national and state banks. However, federal regulators may require a foreign bank to establish a U.S. subsidiary to branch interstate if the regulators determine that they can verify the foreign bank's compliance with capital adequacy guidelines only through the use of a separate subsidiary. Also, any branch of a foreign bank will continue to be subject to CRA requirements unless the branch receives only deposits that are permissible for an Edge Act Corporation.[4]

Interstate bank agency. Beginning one year from enactment of the legislation, a bank may receive deposits, renew time deposits, close loans, service loans, and receive payments on loans and other obligations as agent for any bank or thrift affiliate, whether the affiliate is located in the same state or a different state than the agent bank. However, a depository institution may neither conduct, as agent, an activity that it is prohibited from conducting as a principal, nor have an agent conduct for it any activity that it is prohibited from conducting as principal. Also, if an out-of-state bank is not prohibited by statute from operating a branch in a host state, a savings institution affiliate located in the host state may act as agent for the bank.

The permissible merger activity implied by the Interstate Banking Act will require more market valuation. Each bank, bank branch, and bank facility will be subject to assessment of its true value in this era of consolidation.

REGULATORY ATTENTION TO MARKET VALUATION

For several years now, regulatory bodies have taken on the issue of market valuation of financial assets and liabilities. Included in this group is the Securities and Exchange Commission (SEC), the U.S. Treasury Department, and the Financial Accounting Standards Board (FASB).

Securities and Exchange Commission

The SEC has authority to prescribe accounting standards for all companies whose securities are publicly traded. The agency's position is that the balance sheet should be presented with full market value accounting for all marketable securities. Marketable securities excludes real estate, plant and equipment, intangible assets, and loans. Essentially, the SEC would like to see the securities portfolio of all firms, including commercial banks, marked to market instead of being reported at book value in the financial statements. Likewise, related liabilities, such as the firm's own bonds payable would be marked to market. Changes in the value of these assets and liabilities would be recorded either as gains or losses in the firm's income statement or as changes in retained earnings.

The SEC position is that securities brokers and dealers, mutual funds, and pension funds already report on a market value basis. Thus, it is reasonable that other financial firms do the same. Furthermore, if MVA had been in place, perhaps it would have provided an early warning as to the savings and loan crisis.

U.S. Treasury Department

The Financial Institutions Reform, Recovery, and Enforcement Act of 1989 (FIRREA) directed the Treasury Department to investigate, review, and evaluate the feasibility of MVA for depository institutions. After its review was completed in 1991, the Treasury concluded that comprehensive MVA, though advantageous, was not currently feasible. Carrying all assets and liabilities on the balance sheet at their estimated fair market value would make the performance of the institution more transparent to investors. This practice also would discourage gains trading, that is, selling appreciated assets for the sole purpose of realizing a gain and improving earnings of the current period.

The Treasury Department suggested, however, that since many of the asset categories do not have active secondary trading markets, the discounted cash flow approach could be manipulated by the reporting institution. This would only increase uncertainty as to the true condition of the institution and complicate the auditing process. A second consideration was the cost of implementing a full MVA accounting system. It was felt that such a requirement would be particularly costly for the smaller institutions.

In light of these considerations, the Treasury Department concluded that requiring comprehensive MVA would be premature and that the appropriate standard would be supplemental disclosure of market values in footnotes to the financial statements or memoranda items within shareholder or regulatory reports. Once the supplemental disclosure process is refined and better understood by institutions, regulators, auditors, and investors, comprehensive MVA could then be reevaluated.

Thus, both the Treasury Department (under a previous administration) and the SEC have agreed that MVA should be incorporated in some way in the financial statements of commercial banks. However, the Treasury Department report was prepared in response to a request by the U.S. Congress and is, therefore, of an advisory nature. The SEC has authority to prescribe accounting treatment, but generally looks to the private sector to generate the actual accounting standards, subject to SEC oversight.

Financial Accounting Standards Board

The FASB is the most authoritative private-sector policy-making body with respect to accounting methods. Its statements of Financial Accounting Standards (FASs) are the vehicles through which generally accepted accounting principles (GAAP) are communicated. In May 1986, FASB began a review of the issue of financial instruments. In December 1991, FAS No. 107, "Disclosures about Fair Value of Financial Instruments," was released. This statement requires disclosure of the fair value of all financial instruments (both assets and liabilities recognized and unrecognized in the balance sheet) in the financial statements of all firms (including commercial banks).

Compliance dates. FAS No. 107 is effective for all financial statements issued for fiscal years ending after December 15, 1992, with one exception. Entities with total assets less than $150 million had until December 15, 1995, to comply. The provision for small companies is to permit them to develop cost-effective means to estimate fair values of assets and liabilities. Earlier compliance, however, is encouraged.

Definitions. The following definitions of financial instruments address both on- and off-balance-sheet liabilities:

➤ A contractual obligation to (1) deliver cash or another financial instrument to a second party or (2) exchange other financial instruments on potentially unfavorable terms with a second party.

➤ A contractual right to (1) receive cash or another financial instrument from a second party or (2) exchange other financial instruments on potentially favorable terms for the first party.

Fair value is defined as:

➤ The amount at which a financial instrument could be exchanged in a current transaction between willing parties, other than in a forced or liquidated sale.

If a quoted price is available for an instrument, the fair value to be disclosed for that instrument is the product of the number of trading units of the instrument multiplied by that market price. If quoted prices are not available, management may base its best estimate of fair value on:

➤ The quoted market price of a financial instrument with similar characteristics.

➤ Valuation techniques such as present value of estimated future cash flows, option pricing models, or matrix pricing models.

Excluded Financial Instruments. Certain financial instruments are excluded from coverage by FAS No. 107:

➤ Employers' and plans' obligations for pension benefits, other postretirement benefits including health care and life insurance benefits, employee stock option and stock purchase plans, and other forms of deferred compensation arrangements. (See FAS Nos. 35, 87, 106, 43, and APB Opinions Nos. 25 and 12.[5])

➤ Substantially extinguished debt and assets held in trust in connection with an effective defeasance (refinancing) of that debt. (See FAS No. 76.)

➤ Insurance contracts, other than financial guarantees and investment contracts. (See FAS Nos. 60 and 97.)

➤ Lease contracts. (See FAS No. 13.)

➤ Warranty obligations and rights.

➤ Unconditional purchase obligations. (See FAS No. 47.)

➤ Investments accounted for under the equity method. (See APB Opinion No. 18.)

➤ Minority interests in consolidated subsidiaries.
➤ Equity investments in consolidated subsidiaries.
➤ Equity instruments issued by the entity and classified in
   stockholders' equity in the balance sheet.

Financial Statement Disclosure. Each firm must disclose the fair value of assets and liabilities either in the body of the financial statements or in the accompanying notes. In addition, the methods and assumptions used to arrive at these values also must be disclosed.

Of particular importance for commercial banks, the fair value of deposit liabilities may not include the value of long-term relationships with depositors, frequently referred to as core deposit intangibles. These intangibles do not qualify as financial instruments. Also, the fair value of those deposit liabilities with no specified maturities is the amount payable on demand as of the date of the balance sheet.

In the event that it is not practicable (achievable without excessive costs) to estimate the fair value of a financial instrument, other disclosures are required:

➤ Information relevant for estimating fair value such as carrying
   amount, effective interest rate, and maturity.
➤ The reasons why estimating fair value is not practicable.

Table 1–2 provides the sample disclosure format for commercial banks included in FAS No. 107. This example includes data for both the current balance sheet and a comparative balance sheet for the prior year. The FAS presents this as a guide only; other methods may be used as long as they satisfy the requirements of the statement. In addition, it is left to the bank's management to develop the valuation techniques most appropriate for that institution.

The Investment Portfolio and FAS No. 115
The emphasis on mark-to-market concepts was strengthened significantly by FAS No. 115, "Accounting for Certain Investments in Debt and Equity Securities." Issued in May 1993, this statement has been effective for fiscal years after December 15, 1993. Basically, FAS No. 115 requires distinctions in the securities portfolio among:

➤ Investment portfolio—held-to-maturity.

Table 1–2.

FAS No. 107
SAMPLE DISCLOSURE FOR COMMERCIAL BANKS

	19X2		19X1	
	CA[1]	FV[2]	CA[1]	FV[2]
Financial Assets:				
Cash and short-term investments	$XX	XX	$XX	XX
Trading account assets	XX	XX	XX	XX
Investment securities	XX	XX	XX	XX
Loans	XX		XX	
Less: allowance for loan losses	<XX>		<XX>	
	XX	XX	XX	XX
Financial Liabilities:				
Deposits	XX	XX	XX	XX
Securities sold not owned	XX	XX	XX	XX
Long-term debt	XX	XX	XX	XX
Unrecognized Financial Instruments:[3]				
Interest rate swaps:				
In a net receivable position	XX	XX	XX	XX
In a net payable position	<XX>	<XX>	<XX>	<XX>
Commitments to extend credit	<XX>	<XX>	<XX>	<XX>
Standby letter of credit	<XX>	<XX>	<XX>	<XX>
Financial guarantees written	<XX>	<XX>	<XX>	<XX>

1   Carrying amount

2   Fair value

3   Carrying amounts represent accruals or deferred income (fees) associated with unrecognized financial instruments. Interest rate swaps and other derivative instruments entered into as trading activities are included in "trading account assets" or "securities sold not owned."

Source: Author's adaptation of Financial Accounting Standards Board. "Statement of Financial Accounting Standards No. 107: Disclosures about Fair Value of Financial Instruments," December 1991, p.13.

➤ Trading portfolio.
➤ Available-for-sale portfolio.

The new classification of held-to-maturity (HTM) is the category in which most investment securities historically have been recorded. Under FAS No. 115, to classify securities as held-to-maturity, banks must have positive intent and the ability to hold to maturity. This classification of securities is not marked-to-market; instead, the securities are recorded at amortized cost. Only realized gains and losses are recorded (upon sale), with recognition in the income statement.

The trading portfolio is unchanged in its interpretation. This portfolio of securities is actively traded with the objective of generating profits on short-term price changes. While there is no predetermined classification for particular classes of securities, mortgage-backed securities held for sale in connection with mortgage banking activities must be reported in the trading portfolio. Trading securities are marked-to-market, with unrealized gains and losses being recorded in the income statement for the period.

The available-for-sale (AFS) portfolio contains all securities that cannot be classified as either part of the HTM or trading portfolios. AFS securities are mark-to-market, with unrealized gains and losses not recorded in income, but reflected in a separate component of stockholders' equity.[6]

FAS No. 115 suggested that, generally, the sale of HTM securities would generate skepticism on the part of external auditors and regulators as to the appropriateness of the classifications. However, there are some situations in which the sale of HTM securities would generate no such skepticism. Specifically, the appropriateness of classifications does not become suspect if:

➤ The securities were within three months of maturity.
➤ 85 percent of principal had been repaid.
➤ There was significant deterioration in the issuer's creditworthiness or change in the structure of the security.
➤ There was a change in the tax status of the securities.
➤ A major business combination or divestiture occurred.
➤ Significant increase in regulatory capital requirements necessitated downsizing.
➤ There was a significant increase in risk weights involved in regulatory risk-based capital requirements.

However, certain reasons for sale are not considered justification for selling HTM securities:

> Changes in market interest rates and accompanying prepayment risk.
> Changing liquidity needs.
> Increased attractiveness of alternative investments.
> Changes in funding sources and terms of funding.
> Shifts in foreign exchange rates.
> Asset/liability management considerations.

FAS No. 115 classifies securities as either debt or equity securities. Debt securities represent a creditor relationship with the issuer, while equity securities represent an ownership interest.

Examples of debt securities are U.S. Treasury securities, U.S. government agency securities, municipal securities, corporate bonds, convertible debt, commercial paper, and all securitized debt instruments. In addition, the category of debt security includes (1) preferred stock that either must be redeemed by the issuer or is redeemable at the option of the investor and (2) a collateralized mortgage obligation (CMO) (or other instrument) that is issued in equity form but is required to be accounted for as a nonequity instrument in the issuer's statement of financial position. Excluded from the category of debt securities are option contracts, financial futures contracts, forward contracts, lease contracts, and loans receivable arising from consumer, commercial, and real estate lending activities of financial institutions.

The equity classification includes common, preferred, or other capital stock. Rights to acquire an ownership interest are also considered equity securities, including warrants, rights, and call options on equities. In addition, the category includes rights to dispose of equities, such as put options on equities.

During the first quarter of 1995, FASB decided to amend FAS No. 115 to require that interest-only strips and excess servicing receivables be accounted for as securities and to indicate that any security whose contractual terms do not entitle the holder to recover its investment by holding it to maturity cannot be designated as HTM.

The scope of application of FAS No. 115 may expand. Early in 1995, FASB received requests from the insurance industry to undertake a project that would permit reporting the fair value of liabilities associated with AFS securities reported under FAS No. 115. This area of study will be considered by the FASB in the future.

MVA and the Loan Portfolio: FAS Nos. 114 and 118

In May 1993, market value accounting (MVA) was expanded to certain elements of the loan portfolio through FAS No. 114, "Accounting by Creditors for

Impairment of a Loan." This statement is effective for fiscal years beginning after December 15, 1994. In October 1994, FAS No. 114 was amended by FAS No. 118, "Accounting by Creditors for Impairment of a Loan—Income Recognition and Disclosure," also effective for fiscal years that began after December 15, 1994.

The two statements apply to all categories of loans with the following exceptions:

> Large groups of smaller-balance homogeneous loans.
> Loans recorded at fair value or at lower-of-cost-or-market.
> Leases.
> Debt securities.

The statement does not provide guidance with respect to the identification of impaired loans. Instead, an institution is expected to follow its normal credit review procedures. Also, the normal provisions for loan loss are not affected by the statement.

The definition of impairment revolves around changes in the cash flows as originally contracted. There has been impairment if:

> It is probable that all payments of principal and interest will not be collected.
> There are delays in timing of the collection of all payments of principal and interest.

Probable is interpreted to mean likely to occur. Insignificant differences in either payments or timing of payments do not create an impairment.

The present value of future cash flows is used to arrive at the measurement value. This value is based on the best estimate of the amount and timing of future cash flows, under reasonable and supportable assumptions. These cash flows then are discounted at a rate that is the contractual rate adjusted for premiums, discounts, deferred fees, or other considerations. Alternatively, the measurement value may be the (1) observable market price of the loan or (2) fair value of collateral for collateral-dependent loans. (A collateral-dependent loan is defined as one for which repayment is generated solely from sale or operation of the collateral.) In the event that foreclosure is probable, measurement value must be set at the fair value of collateral.

Loan impairment is measured as the excess of the amount of recorded investment over the measurement value. The loan impairment is provided for as bad debt expense for the period.

Off-Balance-Sheet Items and Derivatives Disclosure: FAS Nos. 105 and 119

In March 1990, FASB issued FAS No. 105, "Disclosure of Information about Financial Instruments with Off-Balance-Risk and Financial Instruments with Concentrations of Credit Risk," effective for fiscal years that ended after June 15, 1990. This FAS statement addressed the issues of:

➤ Off-balance-sheet items with market risk or credit risk.
➤ Concentrations of credit risk for all financial instruments.

Credit risk is defined as "the possibility that a loss may occur from the failure of another party to perform according to the terms of a contract." Market risk is "the possibility that future changes in market prices may make a financial instrument less valuable or more onerous."[7]

Required disclosures for financial instruments with off-balance-sheet risk are:

➤ Face, contract, or notional amount.
➤ Nature and terms of the financial instruments, including, but not limited to, credit and market risk of the instruments, cash requirements, and accounting policies for the instruments.

Required disclosures of credit risk of off-balance-sheet financial instruments are:

➤ The amount of accounting loss that would be incurred if a counterparty completely failed to perform.
➤ The policy with respect to collateral.

In terms of concentrations of credit risk for all financial instruments, the disclosures must include:

➤ Information about the (shared) activity, region, or economic characteristic that identifies the concentration.
➤ The amount of accounting loss that would be incurred if parties of the relevant financial instruments failed completely to perform.
➤ The policy with respect to collateral.

FAS No. 105 provides illustrations that would give rise to off-balance-sheet risk of accounting loss due to either credit risk or market risk. Examples of off-balance-sheet financial instruments that represent market risk for the *issuer* or *seller* include[8]:

➤ Repurchase agreement accounted for as a sale by the issuer.
➤ Covered or naked put option on stock.
➤ Covered or naked put option on interest rate contracts.
➤ Call option on stock, foreign currency, or interest rate contracts.
➤ Fixed-rate loan commitments.
➤ Interest rate caps.
➤ Interest rate floors.

Examples of off-balance-sheet financial instruments that represent market risk for *both counterparties* (seller and buyer) include:

➤ Interest rate swaps on the accrual basis.
➤ Interest rate swaps, marked-to-market.
➤ Financial futures contracts used as hedges.
➤ Financial futures contracts not used as hedges.
➤ Forward contracts used as hedges, marked-to-market.
➤ Forward contracts not used as hedges, marked-to-market.
➤ Forward contracts, not marked-to-market.

In October 1994, in the wake of numerous financial crises directly tied to the use of the derivatives, FASB issued FAS No. 119, "Disclosure about Derivative Financial Instruments and Fair Value of Financial Instruments," effective for fiscal years that ended after December 15, 1994. As is true for all FASs, this statement was preceded by deliberations about the cost and benefits of increased disclosure requirements. Early in 1994, FASB set out the following concepts as the basis for a policy with respect to derivative financial instruments:[9]

➤ All free-standing derivative instruments should be recognized and measured at fair value.
➤ Special accounting should be provided to net some gains or losses that are perceived to be related to other positions recognized in earnings in the same period.
➤ Designation should be a basis for special accounting (with the result that special accounting is elective).
➤ Changes in fair value not recognized in earnings might be recognized as a separate component of equity (that is, comprehensive income) or with related assets and liabilities.
➤ Special accounting should be provided for instruments that manage cash flow exposures as well as those that manage exposures to changes in value.

➤ Special accounting should be provided for exposures from firmly committed and forecasted transactions.

➤ Risk reduction (as opposed to risk management) should not be a criterion for special accounting.

➤ Special accounting should be provided for a range of risk-management techniques, including dynamic portfolio management.

However, in October 1994, the Board could not agree on the policy that had been drafted on the basis of these concepts.

In their November 1994 meeting, the Board agreed that all derivatives must be classified as either "for trading" or "other than trading." Those derivative instruments classified as for trading must be valued at fair value with changes in values recognized in earnings in the period in which the changes occur. Those held for purposes other than trading would also be measured at fair value, with changes in values not recognized in current earnings, but instead recognized in a separate component of equity until realized. Realized gains and losses would be reported in earnings.

The final version of the statement, FAS No. 119, differentiates between trading purposes and other than trading purposes. However, only derivative securities designated for trading are subject to market valuation. Entities that either hold or issue derivative financial instruments are required to disclose in either *the body or footnotes of the financial statements:*

➤ Average fair value of the derivative instruments during the period.[10]

➤ End-of-period fair value.

➤ Classification as an asset or a liability.

➤ Net gains or losses from trading disaggregated by class, business activity, risk, or other category consistent with the management of the derivatives.

➤ Where net gains and losses are reported in the income statement.

Entities trading other (nonderivative) financial instruments also were encouraged to disclose average fair market value of these assets or liabilities.

If the derivatives are held for purposes other than trading, the required disclosures under FAS No. 119 are:

➤ Objectives for holding or issuing the derivatives.

➤ Context needed to understand the objectives.

➤ Strategies to achieve the objectives, including the classes of derivatives used.

➤ How each class of derivatives is reported in the financial statements.
➤ Policies for recognizing and measuring the derivatives.
➤ Upon income or loss recognition, where this recognition is reported in the financial statements.
➤ For derivatives used as hedges:
  • Anticipated transactions being hedged.
  • Description of the classes of derivatives used in hedges.
  • Amount of hedging gains or losses that are deferred.
  • Transactions that give rise to recognition of gains or losses.

FAS No. 119 defines a derivative as a futures, forward, swap, option contract, or other financial instrument with similar characteristics. Examples of other financial instruments with similar characteristics include:

➤ Interest rate caps (similar to options).
➤ Interest rate floors (similar to options).
➤ Fixed-rate loan commitments (similar to options).
➤ Certain variable-rate loan commitments (similar to options if rate adjusts lag changes in market rates).
➤ Commitments to buy stocks or bonds (similar to forward contracts).
➤ Forward interest rate agreements (similar to forward contracts).
➤ Interest rate collars (similar to forward contracts).

Those instruments similar to option contracts generally permit the holder or owner to benefit from favorable changes in the price of the underlying instrument without significant exposure to loss from unfavorable price changes, often in exchange for an up-front fee. Those instruments similar to forward contracts generally provide both a benefit from favorable price changes and exposure to loss from unfavorable price changes, usually with no up-front payment.

FAS No. 119 also amended FAS No. 105 to require a distinction between financial instruments with off-balance-sheet risk held for trading purposes and those held for purposes other than trading. For those held for trading purposes, the instruments must be measured at fair value with gains or losses recognized in earnings for the period. FAS No. 119 also extended this disclosure to derivative financial instruments without off-balance-sheet risk.

FAS No. 119 amended FAS No. 107 to prohibit combining, aggregating, or netting the fair value of derivative financial instruments with the fair value of nonderivative instruments or with the fair value of other derivative instruments.[11] FAS No. 119 also amended FAS No. 107 to require a summary table of fair values in the event that disclosures are made in more than one footnote, including a clear distinction between assets and liabilities. Lastly, FAS No. 119 amended FAS No. 107 to require a distinction between financial instruments held or issued for trading purposes and those held or issued for purposes other than trading.

Mortgage Servicing Rights and FAS No. 122

The Board has reconsidered certain aspects of the accounting for mortgage servicing rights as specified by FAS No. 65, "Accounting for Certain Mortgage Banking Activities." In June 1994, Exposure Draft E129 was issued, "Accounting for Mortgage Servicing Rights and Excess Servicing Receivables and for Securitization of Mortgage Loans: an Amendment to FASB Statement No. 65." The final statement, issued in May 1995 was FAS No. 122: "Mortgage Servicing Rights," effective for fiscal years after December 15, 1995. The issue of excess mortgage servicing rights was omitted and comprehensive treatment of securitization was deferred for later consideration. FAS No. 122 applies to an entity that (1) acquires mortgage servicing rights through either the purchase or origination of mortgage loans and (2) sells or securitizes those loans with servicing rights retained. FAS No. 122 requires that the entity allocate the total cost of the mortgage loans to:

➤ The mortgage servicing rights.
➤ The loans (without the mortgage servicing rights).

This allocation is based on relative fair values, if it is practicable to estimate these values. If loans are originated or purchased with a definitive plan to sell or securitize, then the allocation is based on relative fair values at the date of purchase or origination.[12] In the absence of such a definitive plan, the allocation is based on relative fair values at the date of sale. If it is not practicable to estimate the fair values, the entire cost is allocated to the mortgage loans with no cost allocation to the mortgage servicing rights.

With respect to impairment of servicing rights, capitalized mortgage servicing rights will be evaluated based on their fair values. The valuation of servicing rights can be based on one of several techniques:

➤ Discounted cash flow.
➤ Option-adjusted spread or other option models.
➤ Fundamental analysis.
➤ Matrix pricing.

The techniques must be consistent with fair market value and include assumptions with respect to mortgage market participants. At a minimum, an entity will stratify its capitalized mortgage servicing rights based on one or more of the predominant risk characteristics of the underlying loans. These characteristics may include:

> Loan type.
> Loan size.
> Loan rate.
> Date of origination.
> Loan term.
> Geographic location.

The amount of impairment recognized will be the amount by which the capitalized mortgage servicing rights for each stratum exceed the fair values of the servicing rights. Impairment will be recognized through a valuation allowance. Disclosures in the financial statements must include methods and assumptions used to estimate fair market value of mortgage servicing rights and impairment. In addition, the characteristics used to develop strata must also be disclosed.

Other important elements of FAS No. 122 are:

> The statement applies to transactions in which a mortgage banking enterprise sells or securitizes mortgage loans with servicing rights retained.
> Impairment evaluations will apply for all mortgage servicing rights retained.
> An entity that has purchased mortgage servicing rights prior to the effective date may continue to apply its accounting policies for stratifying those mortgage servicing rights.
> Early application is encouraged.
> Retroactive capitalization of originated mortgage servicing rights will be prohibited.

The Regulatory Trend
The trend toward MVA is clearly emerging in accounting standards. FAS No. 107 requires disclosure of the market value of all financial assets and liabilities and, as amended by FAS No. 119, a designation of whether the financial instruments are held for trading or other than trading purposes. The value of impaired loans must be reported on a market value basis as outlined in FAS No. 114 and FAS No. 118, with a reduction in market value reflected as bad debt expense. Any securities available for sale must now be carried at their market value according to FAS No. 115. FAS No. 119 requires the market valuation of deriv-

atives held for trading purposes. Under provisions of FAS No. 122, mortgage servicing rights must be carried at market value, with impairment reflected in a valuation account. Furthermore, based on the deliberations of FASB that have not yet been codified in final statements, MVA will affect every aspect of the banking industry—balance sheet positions, off-balance-sheet positions, and fee-generating activities.

THE BENEFITS OF MARKET VALUATION

The regulatory focus on market value accounting is significant and growing. The bank merger phenomenon begs for improved valuation techniques. The composition of bank asset and liability portfolios and the exposure to interest rate risk make a strong sense of market valuation concepts a prerequisite for assessing a commercial bank.

The following are benefits of market valuation:

➤ Market valuation of assets and liabilities results in a better estimate of the true value of bank equity. Ultimately, economic equity is the barometer of the institution's value and solvency.

➤ Regulators can more easily identify those banks whose capital is impaired and begin any necessary corrective action sooner.

➤ Market valuation discourages transactions intended solely to improve accounting returns. For example, market value accounting discourages gains trading, (i.e., selling appreciated assets while retaining depreciated assets merely to increase reported earnings).

SELECTED REFERENCES

Board of Governors of the Federal Reserve System. *Flow of Funds Accounts; Financial Assets and Liabilities,* Washington, DC: Federal Reserve System, various issues.

Cleveland, Harold and Thomas Huertas. *Citibank 1812–1970.* Cambridge: Harvard University Press, 1985.

Federal Deposit Insurance Corporation. *FDIC Quarterly Banking Profile.* Washington, DC: FDIC, First Quarter 1992.

Financial Accounting Standards Board of the Financial Accounting Foundation. *Statement of Financial Accounting Standards No. 107: Disclosures about Fair Value of Financial Instruments.* Norwalk, CT: FASB, 1991.

Financial Accounting Standards Board of the Financial Accounting Foundation. *Statement of Financial Accounting Standards No. 105: Disclosure of Information about Financial Instruments with Off-Balance-Sheet Risk and Financial Instruments with Concentrations of Credit Risk.* Norwalk, CT: FASB, 1990.

Financial Accounting Standards Board of the Financial Accounting Foundation. *Status Report No. 263, Financial Accounting Series No. 148–A.* Norwalk, CT: FASB, April 10, 1995.

Johnson, Hazel J. *Financial Institutions and Markets: A Global Perspective.* New York: McGraw-Hill, 1993.

Karr, Albert. "Regulators Expected to Drop Plan Pegged to Market Value of Securities," *The Wall Street Journal,* November 10, 1994, p. B5.

McGough, Robert. "Blood Will Run in the Streets: Will Market Value Accounting Bring Down the Banks?" *Financial World* 161, no. 10 (May 12, 1992), pp. 16–19.

Office of Management and Budget, Executive Office of the President of the United States. *Historical Tables; Budget of the United States Government; Fiscal Year 1990.* Washington, DC: U.S. Government Printing Office, 1989.

Organization for Economic Cooperation and Development. *Bank Profitability; Statistical Supplement; Financial Statements of Banks 1981–1989.* Paris: OECD, 1991.

Taub, Stephen. "Banking on the New Merger Wave." *Financial World* 160, no. 22 (October 29, 1991), pp. 11–12.

U.S. Department of Commerce, Bureau of Economic Analysis. *Business Statistics, 1961–1988.* 26th ed., Washington, DC: U.S. Government Printing Office, 1989.

U.S. Department of Commerce, Bureau of Economic Analysis. *Survey of Current Business,* 71, no. 4 (April 1991).

U.S. Department of the Treasury. *Modernizing the Financial System: Recommendations for Safer, More Competitive Banks.* Washington, DC: U.S. Government Printing Office, 1991.

ENDNOTES

1 For institutions with at least $150 million in assets, the effective date of this disclosure requirement was for fiscal years ending after December 15, 1992.

2 Other features of the legislation changed the regulatory structure of the system. For example:

- ➤ Member and nonmember banks were subject to the same reserve requirements set by the Federal Reserve.
- ➤ All depository institutions (commercial and savings banks, S&Ls, and credit unions) were now entitled to services by the Federal Reserve, but also were subject to the Fed's reserve requirements.
- ➤ Federal regulators were given more financial and geographic flexibility for rescuing failed savings banks and S&Ls, making it possible for financial and nonfinancial firms to purchase thrifts on more favorable terms.

3 A de novo bank or branch is a newly chartered bank or branch, as opposed to an existing office acquired through acquisition.

4 An Edge Act Corporation is chartered by the Federal Reserve, owned by state or national banks, may operate interstate branches, accepts deposits outside the United States, and invests in non-U.S. firms. The Edge Act subsidiary buys and sells notes, drafts, and bills of exchange, complementing the international banking activities of the parent bank.

5 The Accounting Principles Board (APB) was the predecessor of the FASB.

6 In November 1994, federal bank regulators (Federal Deposit Insurance Corporation, Office of the Comptroller of the Currency, Office of Thrift Supervision, and the Federal Reserve) elected not to require an adjustment for unrealized gains and losses (AFS category) in the calculation of regulatory capital. Note that a series of interest rate increases during 1994 generated large losses for all participants in the fixed-income securities industry.

7 See Financial Accounting Standards Board of the Financial Accounting Foundation, *Statement of Financial Accounting Standards No. 105*, p. 3.

8 FAS No. 105 also provided examples for off-balance-sheet financial instruments that created credit risk. Those have not been included here.

9 See Financial Accounting Standards Board, *Status Report No. 263*.

10 Averages based on daily values are preferred.

11 The only exception that is permitted is the netting allowed under FASB Interpretation No. 39, *Offsetting Amounts Related to Certain Contracts*.

12 A definitive plan can be based on a commitment to sell the loans prior to origination (or within a reasonable time after origination), including estimates of selling price.

CHAPTER 2

THE DIFFERENCE
BETWEEN BOOK VALUE
AND MARKET VALUE

INTRODUCTION

For some assets and liabilities, the book value closely approximates the market value. In other cases, certain factors may give rise to a difference between book value and market value:

➤ Time to maturity.
➤ Contractually fixed interest rates (coupon, loan, deposit, or borrowing rates).
➤ Call provisions in bond indentures.
➤ Possible loan prepayments.
➤ Interest rate caps and floors.
➤ Off-balance-sheet treatment.

The changes in market value as the result of interest rate changes are also related to these factors. The extent to which these factors affect market value depends on characteristics of the financial instrument. In this chapter, these characteristics are examined to facilitate the valuation process. In addition, the role of the commercial banking industry in the markets for certain of these instruments is discussed to evaluate market depth and the availability of market quotations. The following sections examine these balance sheet categories:

Assets

➤ Cash and cash items.
  • Vault cash.

- Due from banks.
- Due from Federal Reserve.
- Cash items in collection.

➤ Temporary investments.
  - Interest-bearing time deposits in other banks.
  - Federal funds sold.
  - Term federal funds sold.
  - Securities purchased under agreement to resell.

➤ Investment securities.
  - U.S. Treasury securities.
  - U.S. government agency securities.
  - Tax-exempt securities.
  - Other investment securities.

➤ Bond trading account.
➤ Loans.
  - Commercial loans.
    - Commercial loans—fixed rate.
    - Commercial loans—variable rate.
    - Commercial loans—tax exempt-fixed rate.
    - Commercial loans—tax exempt-variable rate.
    - Commercial loans—lease financing.
    - Commercial loans—nonaccrual.
  - Real estate loans.
    - Residential mortgage loans—fixed rate.
    - Residential mortgage loans—variable rate.
    - Commercial mortgage loans—fixed rate.
    - Commercial mortgage loans—variable rate.
    - Construction loans—fixed rate.
    - Construction loans—variable rate.
    - Real estate loans—nonaccrual.
  - Consumer loans.
    - Credit card loans.
    - Installment loans—direct-fixed rate.
    - Installment loans—direct-variable rate.
    - Installment loans—dealer-fixed rate.
    - Installment loans—dealer-variable rate.
    - Consumer loans—lease financing.

- Securities loans.
- Overdrafts.
➤ Reserve for loan loss.
➤ Bank premises and equipment.
➤ Other real estate owned.
➤ Investments in subsidiaries.

Liabilities

➤ Deposits.
- Noninterest-bearing transactions accounts.
  - Correspondent deposits.
  - Commercial deposits.
  - Consumer deposits.
  - Public funds.
  - Trust deposits.
  - Official checks.
  - Other transactions accounts.
- Interest-bearing transactions accounts.
- Small time and savings accounts.
  - Savings accounts.
  - Time deposits < $100,000.
  - IRA accounts.
    · IRA—fixed rate.
    · IRA—variable rate.
- Large time deposits.
  - Nonnegotiable time deposits ≥ $100,000.
  - Negotiable CDs.
  - Foreign deposits.
    · IBF deposits.
    · Eurodollar time deposits.

➤ Short-term borrowed funds.
- Federal funds purchased.
- Term federal funds purchased.
- Securities sold under agreement to repurchase.
- Commercial paper.
- Treasury tax and loan account.
- Other short-term borrowed funds.

> Long-term borrowed funds.
  - Subordinated notes and debentures.
  - Other long-term borrowed funds.

Equity

> Preferred stock.
> Common equity.
  - Common stock.
  - Capital surplus.
  - Undivided profits.

CASH

The *cash* category includes extremely liquid assets that are either cash or convertible into cash within a day or so. This category is often referred to as *primary reserves.*

Vault cash is maintained on bank premises to meet day-to-day transactions needs such as cashing checks. Vault cash is the most liquid asset the bank holds. *Due from banks* and *due from the Federal Reserve* are the next most liquid assets that a commercial bank holds. These are demand deposit accounts in other commercial banks and at the Federal Reserve Bank. Vault cash and due from the Federal Reserve satisfy the bank's minimum reserve requirement.

Cash items in collection are primarily checks deposited by bank customers for which the customers have been given credit, subject to withdrawal restrictions until the checks clear. The clearing process often is accomplished through a bank-owned clearinghouse association. Funds are generally available to the bank on a same-day or next-day basis.

Essentially, all of these cash categories are available on a same-day or next-day basis at the carrying value. Thus, there are no factors that can cause the market value of these assets to differ from book value.

TEMPORARY INVESTMENTS

Temporary investments are also quite liquid, but they differ from cash in that they are not necessarily immediately available. The investments are intended to earn a reasonable rate of return on what is essentially excess liquidity. These funds are considered *secondary reserves.*

Interest-bearing time deposits in other banks are large deposits for predetermined periods of time. Generally the maturities are relatively short, but they are not due on demand as are due-from-bank accounts.

Federal funds sold are unsecured advances of immediately available funds in deposits at Federal Reserve Banks and at larger correspondent banks. Most of these transactions are reversed the next day (i.e., they are overnight transactions). Some are for longer periods of time, however. *Term federal funds sold* are for periods up to 90 days, but most often for no more than seven days.

Securities purchased under agreement to resell are contracts to purchase securities and to later reverse the transaction with both prices and dates specified. Reversal usually occurs on the following day. The securities are most often U.S. Treasury securities but may be government agency securities.[1] Thus, the transaction is essentially a collateralized loan. From the standpoint of the securities dealer, this is a *repurchase agreement* or *repo*. From the perspective of the other party, this is a *reverse repo*.

These investments are not payable on demand. Technically, this factor causes a difference between book and market value. Practically, however, the time to maturity is so short that the difference is relatively small.

INVESTMENT SECURITIES

The investment securities category of assets is an important component of the bank's balance sheet, second only to loans in the amount of resources devoted to it. As a result, the value of the investment portfolio has a major impact on the bank's market value. Investment securities are held for income purposes, rather than to manage excess liquidity (as in the case of temporary investments).

U.S. Treasury Securities

Treasury securities are interest-bearing obligations of the United States government with maturities ranging from three months to 30 years. They are issued to finance government budget deficits (i.e., the excess of expenditures over tax receipts). *Treasury bills* have original maturities from 91 to 365 days, *Treasury notes* from 1 to 10 years, and *Treasury bonds* from 10 to 30 years. Treasury securities are primarily fixed-rate instruments sold on an interest-paying basis, with the exception of T-bills that are sold on a discount basis.

Commercial banks are major holders of these securities, but the commercial bank share of Treasuries has declined significantly over time. Figure 2–1 shows that the share dropped from almost 25 percent in the late 1960s to less than 10 percent currently. The Treasury market is broadly held, extremely liquid, and efficient. Market quotes are easily obtainable. However, because many of the instruments are long-term, fixed-coupon bonds, market values are sensitive to changes in market rates, giving rise to potentially significant differences between book value and market value.

Figure 2–1.

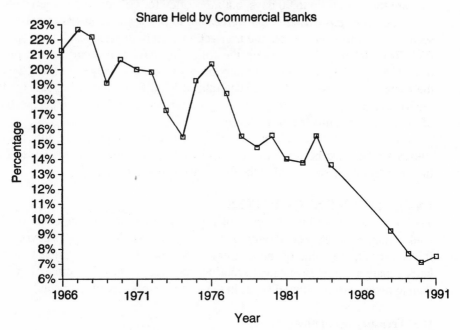

Source: Author's graphic based on data from Board of Governors of the Federal Reserve
       System, *Flow of Funds Accounts; Financial Assets and Liabilities*, various issues.

U.S. Government Agency Securities
Agencies affiliated with the U.S. government also issue securities. Their primary purpose is to facilitate secondary market trading of loans in important public
policy areas such as housing and education. These are the agencies (and the
secondary markets in which they operate):

➤ Federal National Mortgage Association (Fannie Mae), established as
   a government agency in 1938 but now a federally chartered stock-
   holder-owned corporation (residential mortgages insured or guaranteed by federal agencies).

➤ Government National Mortgage Association (Ginnie Mae), established in 1968 (residential mortgages guaranteed by the Department
   of Veterans Affairs or by the Federal Housing Administration).

➤ Federal Home Loan Mortgage Corporation (Freddie Mac), established in 1970 (conventional residential mortgages).

➤ Student Loan Marketing Association (Sallie Mae), publicly traded corporation established in 1972 (guaranteed student loans).

➤ Federal Agricultural Mortgage Corporation (Farmer Mac), established in 1987 (farm credit).

The securities issued by these agencies are either *pass-through certificates* or *pay-through bonds*. Both types of securities are securitized assets (i.e., ownership interests in collections of loans—usually mortgages—with similar characteristics).

For pass-through certificates, the entire cash flow from the loans is dedicated to payment of principal and interest to the investors. Ginnie Mae pass-through certificates are the most popular, but certificates issued by the Federal Home Loan Mortgage Corporation and the Federal National Mortgage Association are also widely held. One disadvantage of pass-through certificates is that the actual life of the certificate may be shorter than the stated maturity because borrowers often pay off the underlying loans early when interest rates decline.

A pay-through bond is a mortgage-backed bond that is collateralized by a pool of mortgages. An example of a pay-through is a *collateralized mortgage obligation* or *CMO*. Like pass-throughs, the cash flows from the underlying mortgage pool are devoted exclusively to servicing the bonds. The difference is that CMOs are issued in maturity classes to minimize the uncertainty of the timing of payments.

In a CMO, the regular principal and interest payments made by borrowers are separated into different payment streams, creating several bonds that repay invested capital at different rates, or in different *tranches*, to meet the needs of investors. There are often four tranches:

➤ The first pays off interest and principal rapidly.

➤ The second pays interest only until the earlier tranches are repaid completely, then pays both interest and principal.

➤ The third pays variable interest based on an index, typically the London Interbank Offered Rate (LIBOR) even though the underlying mortgages are fixed-rate loans.

➤ The fourth, called an *accrual bond* or *Z-bond*, pays no interest or principal until all other tranches have been retired.

The first tranche is best for investors who desire a quick payoff; the accrual bond is most attractive to investors who want protection from early, unexpected repayments on the underlying mortgages.

Commercial banks hold an even larger share of government agency securities than Treasury securities. Figure 2–2 shows that the bank share, though diminished from earlier years, is still a significant 20 percent of the market. This market, too, is deep and very liquid, making market quotes easy to obtain.

The market value of agency securities is affected by the fact that they are long-term, frequently fixed-coupon instruments. In addition, the possibility of prepayment of the mortgages underlying pass-through certificates also affects market valuation.

Tax-Exempt Securities

Local, county, and state governments issue municipal bonds to finance public utilities, school construction, roads, transportation systems, and industrial development. In most cases, the interest income from these bonds is exempt from federal income taxation.

Figure 2–2.

U.S. GOVERNMENT AGENGY SECURITIES

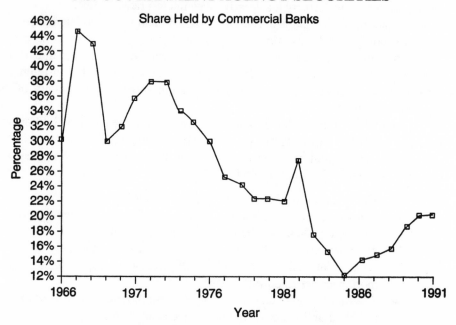

Source: Author's graphic based on data from Board of Governors of the Federal Reserve System, *Flow of Funds Accounts; Financial Assets and Liabilities*, various issues.

General obligation municipal bonds, also called *GO bonds*, are backed by the issuer's full faith credit and taxing authority. These bonds are normally issued to finance nonrevenue-producing public projects such as schools, roads, and public buildings. In contrast, *revenue bonds* are not backed by the issuer's full faith and credit but by the revenues from an income-producing project such as a toll bridge, highway, hospital, or other public facility built with the proceeds of the bond issue. Only these revenues are devoted to paying interest and principal on the bonds. An important classification of revenue bonds is the *industrial revenue bond* or *IRB*. A private corporation is responsible for IRB payments of interest and principal.

Commercial banks once held more than half of all tax-exempt securities outstanding (see Figure 2–3). However, the Tax Reform Act of 1986 eliminated the tax exemption for private purpose bonds and reduced the tax benefits of

Figure 2–3.

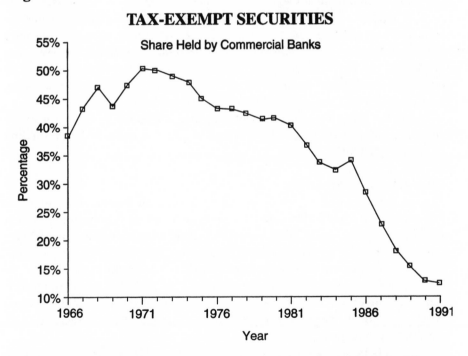

Source: Author's graphic based on data from Board of Governors of the Federal Reserve System, *Flow of Funds Accounts; Financial Assets and Liabilities*, various issues.

public purpose bonds issued by entities that raise more than $10 million through bond issues per year. Commercial bank holdings dropped dramatically after that date. Households, property and casualty insurance companies, and mutual funds are also major investors in tax-exempt bonds. Because of their necessarily regional nature, tax-exempt bonds are not as widely traded as Treasury or government agency securities. Thus, obtaining a market quote may be more difficult.

Some tax-exempt bonds are *callable*; that is, the issuer has the right to redeem all or part of the bond issue before maturity. The bonds may not be called, however, before the first *call date* that is specified in the bond indenture (the written agreement identifying the terms and conditions of the bond issue). Call provisions benefit bond issuers because they make it possible to refinance the issue should interest rates decline significantly. Often callable tax-exempts give the investor call protection for 10 years (i.e., the first call date is 10 years after the date of issuance). Further, the indenture may require that the issuer pay a call premium (an amount over par value) on call.

When the interest rate environment is such that it becomes clear that the bonds will be called on the first call date, the issuer may arrange an advance refunding. In an *advance refunding*, the issuer floats new bonds at lower rates of interest and turns the proceeds over to a trustee to buy Treasury issues or other high-quality debt as collateral. On the first call date of the original issue, the trustee converts the collateral into cash and retires the original issue.

Market valuation of tax-exempt securities is affected by time to maturity and fixed interest rates. In addition, call provisions and advance refunding influence valuation.

Other Investment Securities
The last category of investment securities contains all investment instruments that may not be classified as either Treasury, government agency, or tax-exempt securities. This includes CMOs issued by private securities firms, now 80 percent of the total CMO market, and foreign government bonds. In general, commercial banks may invest only in those securities rated as investment grade, or having bond ratings in the top four categories—AAA, AA, A, or BBB. Further, banks may invest no more than 10 percent of capital and surplus in this category of bonds. Investments in equity securities other than Federal Reserve stock are strictly prohibited.

Largely because of the popularity of private CMOs, the commercial share of corporate and foreign bonds outstanding has increased significantly as shown in Figure 2–4. In the late 1960s, commercial banks owned less than 2

Figure 2–4.

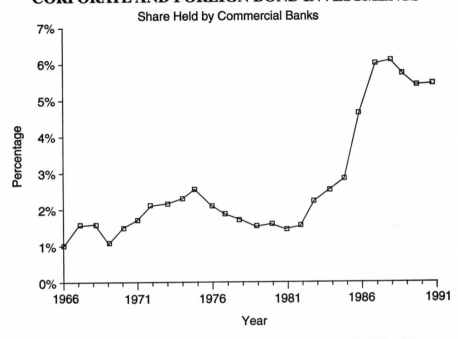

CORPORATE AND FOREIGN BOND INVESTMENTS
Share Held by Commercial Banks

Source: Author's graphic based on data from Board of Governors of the Federal Reserve
System, *Flow of Funds Accounts; Financial Assets and Liabilities*, various issues.

percent of these instruments. By 1991, bank investments constituted more than
5 percent of the market. The most significant investors are insurance companies
and pension funds.

Markets in these securities are much less liquid than U.S. Treasury and
government agency markets. In most cases, however, a market quote is obtainable. The market value of corporate and foreign bonds is affected by time to
maturity (most are long-term), fixed coupon rates, and call provisions.

BOND TRADING ACCOUNT
A bond trading account contains securities managed by commercial banks that
buy or underwrite U.S. government securities and other securities for resale to
other banks and to the general public. These securities are maintained in an
account separate from the bank's investment securities portfolio and the securi-

ties are held for brief periods of time. The bank's profit is derived from the difference between the price the bank pays for the bonds and the price at which they are later sold. The 1933 Glass-Steagall Act permits national banks to underwrite (buy and sell in the primary market) U.S. government securities and general obligation bonds of state and municipal governments.

Although there is no general federal provision for banks to engage in securities underwriting, Section 20 of the Glass-Steagall Act allows commercial banks to be affiliated with other firms that are *not principally engaged* in the corporate securities business. This has been interpreted by the Federal Reserve to mean that a Section 20 subsidiary of the bank may derive no more than 10 percent of its revenues from securities dealings. Section 20 subsidiaries are permitted not only to underwrite government and GO securities but also to underwrite and deal in:

➤ Commercial paper.
➤ Mortgage-backed securities.
➤ Municipal revenue bonds.
➤ Securitized assets.
➤ Corporate bonds.
➤ Corporate equities.

All of these securities must be marked-to-market. This means that there is no difference between the book value and market value of the securities. Technically, there is a possibility that future changes in market interest rates will materially affect the market value of the portfolio before it is liquidated, particularly if the instruments are long-term with fixed-rate coupons. Since the securities are held for only brief periods of time, however, the probability of this occurring is low.

LOANS

Loans are the largest category of assets in the bank's portfolio. The terms and conditions of specific types of loans can lead to substantial differences between market and book value.

Commercial loans

Commercial loans are made to business enterprises for varying reasons and in several forms. Essentially business clients need loans for:

➤ Working capital (short-term).
➤ Long-term purposes.

The forms of commercial loans include:

> ➤ Bullet loan.
> ➤ Working capital line of credit.
> ➤ Term loan.
> ➤ Revolving line of credit.
> ➤ Asset-based loan.

The market values of these loans depend on loan maturity, whether cash flows are received in the interim, and whether the loan rate is fixed or variable.

Loan maturity. A business requires *working capital loans* to sustain itself through its *operating cycle* (i.e., the length of time that it takes for the firm to produce its final product, sell to its customers, and collect proceeds of the sale in cash).

Inventory is necessary to either manufacture a final product or to stock wholesale goods for subsequent retail sales. To the extent that the business enterprise extends credit to its own customers, more time elapses between the sale and actual cash collection. The enterprise may obtain trade credit from its vendors, but trade credit may not be available for any more than 30 days. The difference between the level of current assets (cash, accounts receivable, and inventory) and current liabilities (accounts payable and other accruals) is *net working capital.*

If there are major seasonal fluctuations in net working capital, there is also a fluctuating portion of the firm's short-term assets that should be financed with short-term loans. However, if net working capital is fairly consistent over the course of a year, there is a permanent working capital need that should be financed with long-term funds.

Seasonal working capital loans are repaid from the proceeds of sales and/or accounts receivable collections (i.e., out of liquidity). While banks may require that their commercial customers secure the seasonal loans with inventory or accounts receivable, often collateral is not required because the risk level is usually low as long as the clients' liquidity levels are sufficient. Longer-term loans are repaid from the bank customer's future profitability.

Fixed versus variable rates. Banks may offer loans at either fixed or variable rates of interest. A fixed-rate loan removes uncertainty for the borrower. Should interest rates increase, the borrower's debt-servicing cash flow is unaffected. However, the lending bank sustains an opportunity cost because it is unable to reinvest at the higher rates. At the same time, for competitive reasons, banks often permit more timely adjustments of deposit interest rates. These conditions can have significant, adverse implications for bank profitability. Further, if the loans are long-term, fixed loan rates mean that the market value of the loan portfolio may not equal book value and deteriorates when market interest rates increase.

Variable-rate loans relieve this pressure for the commercial bank. Actually, the pressure is not eliminated, it is simply shifted to the borrower. As a result, borrowers are willing to pay a higher interest rate for fixed-rate loans than for their variable-rate counterparts, particularly if interest rates are expected to increase. Variable rates also mean that the market value of the loan portfolio is very close to book value and does not change as dramatically when market interest rates change.

Floating-rate commercial loans are fairly common, especially when compared to consumer loans. Further, many commercial loans that are technically fixed are short-term enough to expose the bank to minimal interest rate risk. The bank's CD rate or average cost of funds frequently serves as a base rate. Alternatively, the London Interbank Offered Rate (LIBOR) can be the base. The contractual (loan) rate usually equals the base rate plus 2 percent or less.

If the loan rate is variable, the bank may provide the borrower with a *cap*—an agreed-on maximum with respect to the loan rate regardless of changes in market interest rates. A cap has an intrinsic value much like an option held by the borrower. The lender may also be protected with a *floor*—an agreed-on minimum with respect to the loan rate regardless of changes in market interest rates. The combination of a cap and a floor is called a *collar*. The existence of any of these optionlike features has an impact on the market value of a loan.

Types of loans. A *bullet loan* has a one-time payment at its termination. Bullet loans may be short term or long term. Because no payments are received in the interim, the bullet loan is like a zero-coupon bond. If the loan rate is variable, its market value closely approximates its book value. If the loan rate is fixed, there can be a significant difference.

A *working capital line of credit* is a preapproved credit facility (usually for one year) that enables a bank customer to borrow up to a specified maximum amount at any time during the relevant period of time. In this case, the bank and its client agree on the terms of the arrangement once each year. They mutually agree on the maximum amount of credit that will be available, the interest rate, and the *commitment fee,* which is the rate charged to a bank customer for the unused portion of a line of credit. Interest is charged only on actual borrowings. The commitment fee (usually less than 1 percent per annum) is charged on the part of the credit line that the client does not use. The bank will commonly require the client to reduce borrowings to zero at least once a year to verify seasonality of the financing need. These are short-term loans whose market values will not be materially different from book value even if the loan rate is fixed.

A *term loan* extends beyond 1 year and up to 15 years, with the most common maturities falling between 1 and 5 years. This is the most common form of intermediate bank loan to commercial enterprises. It is appropriate to finance inventory, permanent working capital needs, or plant and equipment. The loan repayment schedule may require monthly, quarterly, semiannual, or annual payments. The loan rate often floats with either the bank's cost of funds, the federal funds rate, LIBOR, or the bank's prime rate. If there is a cap, floor, or collar, the market value of the variable rate loan does not equal its book value. A fixed loan-rate also potentially creates differences between book value and market value because of the time to maturity of the loan.

Revolving lines of credit may extend beyond one year and are, as such, a combination of working capital and term loans. The more strict interpretation as a term loan involves repayment over a period of years. If the purpose of the loan is acquisition of plant or equipment, funds are advanced in full, right away. If the need is related to higher anticipated permanent working capital needs, funds are advanced as needed. In either case, however, the market value of these credit arrangements depends on the timing of anticipated cash flows, the loan rate, and whether there are any optionlike features (caps, floors, or collars).

An *asset-based loan* is any loan secured by the client's assets that are directly related to loan repayment. Loans based on inventory or accounts receivable are considered working capital asset-based loans. Accounts receivable provide the borrower a higher *borrowing base* (the amount a lender is willing to advance against the dollar value of collateral) because receivables are more liquid than inventory. In either case, the loan is repaid as inventory is sold or as receivables are collected.

Loans for leveraged buyouts (LBOs) are asset-based loans to investors who intend to purchase a firm that may hold undervalued assets. Once the firm has been purchased, some of the undervalued assets are sold at prices closer to true value and the proceeds are used to repay the loan.

Most asset-based loans are relatively short term. Thus, given that the collateral has not been impaired, their market value closely approximates book value.

Figure 2–5 illustrates the declining share of total nonfinancial business financing by commercial banks. From a high of more than 20 percent of business financing, commercial banks now provide less than 15 percent of total business borrowings. This trend indicates that the loan products offered to business must be ever more competitive and must necessarily include more option-

Figure 2–5.

COMMERCIAL BANK LOANS AS A PERCENTAGE OF
TOTAL BUSINESS LIABILITIES

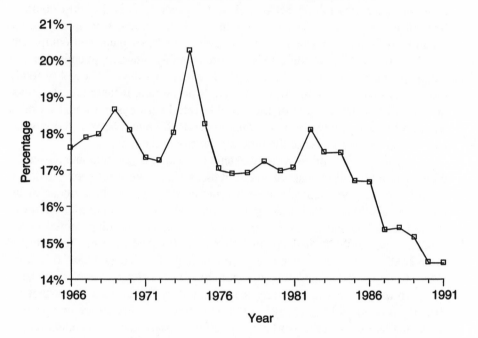

Source: Author's graphic based on data from Board of Governors of the Federal Reserve
System, *Flow of Funds Accounts; Financial Assets and Liabilities*, various issues.

like features to make them attractive to business clients. These enhancements
also can cause a greater divergence of market value from book value.

Nonaccrual loans. When a loan is not being repaid according to the contractual terms, it may be classified as a *nonaccrual loan* or *doubtful loan.* This
classification contains those loans for which full payment of interest and principal are not anticipated and for which periodic interest accrual has ceased. For
regulatory purposes, nonaccrual loans are defined as those for which interest
and principal have not been paid for at least 90 days. The market value of
nonaccrual loans is highly subjective. Some combination of reducing anticipated future cash flows and increasing the discount rate used to find the present
value of the cash flows must be adopted.

Real Estate Loans

Real estate loans are used to purchase or construct homes, apartment buildings, office buildings, shopping centers, and other facilities. They fall into three general categories:

➤ Home mortgages.
➤ Commercial mortgages.
➤ Construction and land development loans.

Home mortgages. Home mortgages are loans made to individuals and families for primary or secondary residences. Original maturities are generally from 25 to 30 years. However, because of resale, the effective maturity is closer to seven years on average. The vast majority of these loans are repaid in monthly installments of principal and interest, with a fixed loan rate. The market value of these assets is very much affected by changes in market interest rates because of their long-term nature. Also, significant decreases in market interest rates prompt prepayments in much the same way that bonds are called when interest rates decline. Prepayment alters the future cash flow stream and, therefore, the market value.

Adjustable rate mortgages (ARMs) do not carry a fixed loan rate. The rates vary with some index, for example, the six-month Treasury bill rate or the lender's internal cost of funds, and often are adjusted every six months. Since an ARM passes along the interest rate risk exposure to the borrower, the market value of the loan is close to the book value.

An *annual cap* provision may be included in an ARM for the benefit of the borrower, however, setting a limit on the increase in the loan rate for any given year. Annual caps often are accompanied by *life of loan caps* that limit the total loan rate increases over the life of the loan. For example, in the case of an 8 percent loan with a 1 percent annual cap and a 5 percent life of loan cap, the interest rate cannot increase more than 1 percent per year and can never exceed 13 percent. The value of this option for the benefit of the borrower affects the market value of the loan and, therefore, causes a difference between market and book value.

A *graduated payment mortgage (GPM)* is a fixed-rate mortgage characterized by early payments that are lower than the later payments. A GPM accommodates the borrower that cannot currently afford the regular fixed-rate payments. For example, the payments may rise each year for the first 10 years and then stay the same until the loan is completely repaid. It is common for this arrangement to be linked with *negative amortization*; that is, an increasing unpaid principal amount in the early years because initial payments are not large enough to cover the interest and principal of a regular amortization schedule. This type of mortgage will be even more affected by changes in market interest rates than regular home mortgages since the principal is not reduced as quickly. A variation of this type of loan is an *adjustable rate graduated payment mortgage* for which the loan rate is adjusted every three to five years. The market value of the adjustable GPM is less volatile than the fixed-rate GPM.

A *balloon mortgage* schedules a loan payoff in a shorter time than a regular mortgage. In the interim, either interest only is paid by the borrower or the loan is structured for retirement in three to five years with interest and principal payments until then. In either case, the borrower maintains a low repayment schedule until the end of the term of the loan and then must pay a large lump-sum payment to retire the loan. In essence, the loan is simply refinanced at the end of the term of the balloon mortgage. Because the principal is repaid in a relatively few number of years, the market value of a balloon mortgage is not as sensitive to market interest rate changes as a regular mortgage.

Home equity loans are in addition to the first mortgage on a residence. A home equity loan may be a second mortgage or a revolving line of credit. During the 1980s, these loans became popular because of rapidly appreciating residential property values. In this environment, home equity (the difference between market value and mortgage balance) grew rather quickly. In addition, the Tax Reform Act of 1986 marked the beginning of a phaseout of tax deductibility of interest on consumer debt. By 1991, only interest on first mortgages and on home equity loans could be deducted from taxable income. These factors have helped to create another large loan market for commercial banks. To protect itself from downturns in the real estate market, a bank lends only 50 to 70 percent of equity. Other factors such as the client's general indebtedness and income also are considered. Since these are also long-term loans, differences between book value and market value are generated whenever the loan rate is fixed.

Figure 2–6 illustrates the importance of the home equity loan in the commercial banking industry. The commercial bank share of the mortgage market had generally been declining since 1980. In 1986, however, this trend reversed largely because of home equity loans. Today, home mortgages are an extremely important part of bank asset portfolios. This implies an even greater concentration of bank assets in long-term investments for which market value can significantly diverge from book value.

In fact, the role of commercial banks in all mortgage markets has grown tremendously as shown in Figures 2–7, 2–8, and 2–9. While the commercial bank share of Treasury, government agency, and municipal securities outstand-

Figure 2–6.

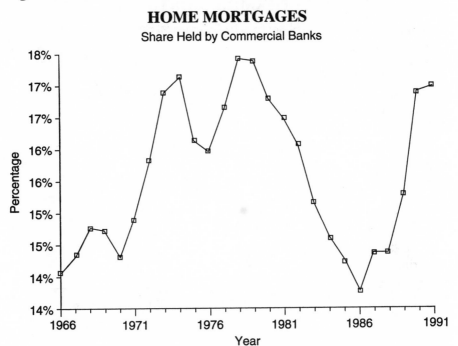

HOME MORTGAGES

Share Held by Commercial Banks

Source: Author's graphic based on data from Board of Governors of the Federal Reserve
System, *Flow of Funds Accounts; Financial Assets and Liabilities*, various issues.

ing has shrunk, the percentage of multifamily, commercial, and farm mortgages held by banks has increased steadily.

Commercial mortgages. The *commercial mortgage loan* is secured by commercial real estate such as an office building, apartment building, or shopping mall and is a highly customized arrangement over a 20- to 40-year term. While the loan rate for most commercial mortgages floats based on an index, some are arranged with a fixed rate.

A *zero-coupon mortgage* is a commercial mortgage with no payments of interest or principal during the term of the loan. Instead, interest accrues at either a fixed or variable rate and is added to the principal of the loan. The rationale for such a loan is that the borrower can finance the project with a small cash flow and the appreciation in property value pays off the mortgage at maturity.

Figure 2–7.

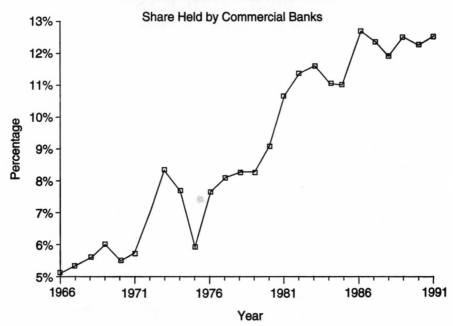

MULTIFAMILY MORTGAGES
Share Held by Commercial Banks

Source: Author's graphic based on data from Board of Governors of the Federal Reserve
System, *Flow of Funds Accounts; Financial Assets and Liabilities*, various issues.

Clearly, for either an amortized commercial mortgage or a zero-coupon mortgage, the market value of the loan can be quite different from its book value because of a fixed loan rate or the volatility of a single future payoff.

Construction and land development loans. These loans are used to complete commercial real estate projects and are a form of interim financing. Funds are advanced to the borrower at specific stages of project completion. These *progress payments* are made, for example, when a certain percentage of the building has been leased to third parties. On completion, the project is funded by permanent mortgage financing from which proceeds the construction and land development loan is repaid. The party providing the permanent financing is referred to as a *take-out lender.*

If the project is an office building or retail facility, an adequate number of tenants is critical to its success. If the project is a development of residential

Figure 2–8.

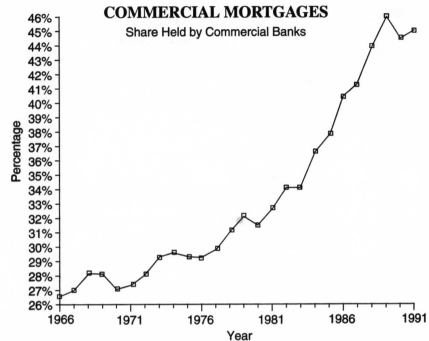

COMMERCIAL MORTGAGES
Share Held by Commercial Banks

Source: Author's graphic based on data from Board of Governors of the Federal Reserve System, *Flow of Funds Accounts; Financial Assets and Liabilities*, various issues.

units, ultimate sales is the key. The bank faces maximum exposure to loan loss when the real estate developer has not preleased or presold the project and there is no take-out commitment.

Since these loans are relatively short-term in nature (usually no more than three years), the most critical factor in determining market value is the viability of the project. This is particularly true given the condition of the commercial real estate market in the early 1990s. However, if the project is viable, there will be relatively little difference between book value and market value of the construction and land development loan.

Consumer Loans

Consumer credit is extended to individuals and households for a wide variety of purposes. Individuals obtain these loans for a number of reasons, including

Figure 2–9.

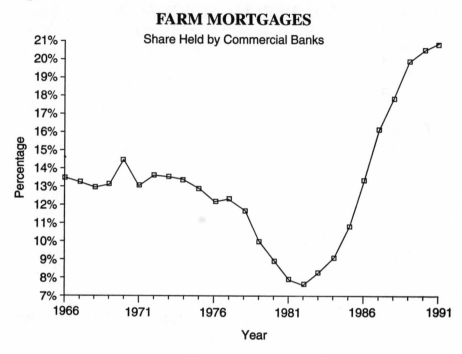

FARM MORTGAGES

Source: Author's graphic based on data from Board of Governors of the Federal Reserve
System, *Flow of Funds Accounts; Financial Assets and Liabilities*, various issues.

durable goods purchases, vacations, medical expenses, and education. The consumer market is another market of growing importance for commercial banks
as illustrated by Figure 2–10. Currently, banks provide almost half of all consumer credit. Generally, consumer loans are more short-term than real estate
loans and their market values deviate less from book value.

Credit card loans. Bank credit cards offer consumers predetermined
maximum amounts of credit. Mastercard and Visa are the most widely held
versions. Service and payment processing are centralized to afford operational
efficiency. Participating banks pay annual fees to the credit card network based
on the number of their active accounts. Banks earn revenues both from their
cardholders and from the establishments that accept the cards. Cardholders pay

Figure 2–10.

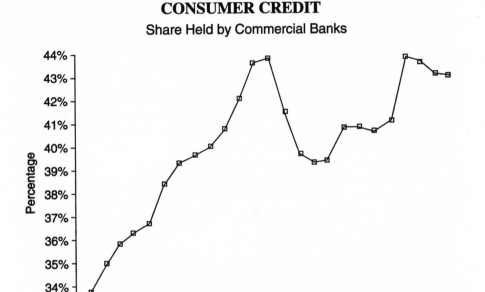

CONSUMER CREDIT
Share Held by Commercial Banks

Source: Author's graphic based on data from Board of Governors of the Federal Reserve System, *Flow of Funds Accounts; Financial Assets and Liabilities*, various issues.

an annual fee and interest on unpaid balances. Vendors that accept the cards receive from 2 to 5 percent less than the face value of the transaction. This percentage off face value represents a discount on the draft, or signed transaction document. The greatest source of credit card income to banks is interest on unpaid balances.

Credit card receivables most often have fixed loan rates. However, the average maturity of the balances is often less than one year. Under these circumstances, the market value of the credit card loans does not differ significantly from book value. In some cases, the loan rate varies with an index and as a result there is almost no difference between market and book. If there are caps and/or floors on the loan rate, this optionlike arrangement causes a difference.

Installment loans. Installment loans are the largest overall category of consumer credit. Typically, the borrower makes monthly payments of interest and principal until the balance is repaid. *Unsecured installment loans* are usually in smaller denominations than secured installment loans. Because of the relatively small size of these loans, often the interest earned is not sufficient to offset the administrative cost and still provide the bank a reasonable profit. Credit cards and revolving lines of credit have become more cost-effective alternatives from the bank's point of view.

Consumers obtain *direct secured installment loans* from their banks, primarily to purchase automobiles. Other collateral includes mobile homes, recreational vehicles, boats, large appliances, and financial assets. These loans mature in four to seven years.

Indirect secured installment loans are generated through dealers (retailers). The consumer completes a credit application that the dealer sends to the bank for processing. On approval, the bank notifies the dealer who, in turn, prepares the relevant loan documents, completes the transaction with the purchaser, and forwards the completed package to the bank. When the bank receives the loan package, the dealer's deposit account is credited and a loan account is established for the purchaser. In addition, if the bank has provided the dealer with floor planning (inventory financing), the wholesale cost of the durable good with accrued interest is deducted from the dealer's account.

The market value of these loans is determined by the loan rate, which is most often fixed, and by the length of time to maturity of the loans. Most of these loans have an original maturity of no more than five years and many may be repaid before this time (especially automobile loans). At any given time, even ignoring prepayments, the average maturity of the portfolio may be as short as three years or less. Technically, there is a difference between market and book values, but the difference usually is small.

Single-payment loans. Single-payment loans make up the smallest category of consumer loans. Customers request these loans for short periods of time, often until another financial transaction occurs. For example, a customer may need a loan until a certificate of deposit matures or may need the down payment for a new home until the current home is sold. From the bank's perspective, the most important consideration is verification of the source of future cash flow for loan repayment. Market value and book value are quite close because of the short time to maturity.

Securities Loans
Securities loans are collateralized by marketable securities. These loans are the

means by which bank customers purchase securities on credit. The Federal Reserve regulates these transactions through Regulation U when the loans are made by banks. The *initial margin* is the amount of cash or eligible securities deposited as partial payment for the securities being purchased. The *equity* in the account is the difference between the market value of the securities and the amount of the loan. The *maintenance margin* is the minimum percentage that equity must always represent of the outstanding loan. The customer's account is marked to market daily. Whenever the market value of the securities declines, the equity declines. If the equity-to-loan ratio declines below the maintenance margin, the bank customer receives a *margin call* or a request for an additional deposit of cash or eligible securities. Because of daily marking to market and the close monitoring of the position, the book value of securities loans closely approximates the market value.

Figure 2–11 shows that commercial bank holdings of securities loans have declined from more than 50 percent in the 1970s to roughly 25 percent. This indicates more involvement in the market by securities firms.

Overdrafts
Overdrafts are checks written by bank clients that exceed the available balance in the respective accounts. Banks are not obligated to pay these checks; when they do pay them, the amounts represent temporary loans that are normally paid quickly. Some clients may have *overdraft protection* in which case the overdrafts are charged to a credit card account or other line of credit. Because of these rapid repayments, the market value of overdrafts is closely approximated by their book value.

RESERVE FOR LOAN LOSS
The *reserve for loan loss* is an accumulated total of provisions for loan loss (charged as expense) over time. As such, it is a contra-asset account or valuation account that reduces the carrying value of the loan portfolio to an approximation of loans thought to be collectible. In market value terms, the reserve is more properly measured as a percentage of the market value of loans, perhaps the same percentage that the book reserve is of the book value of gross loans.

BANK PREMISES AND EQUIPMENT
The bank premises and equipment category includes the bank building, the furnishings and equipment in the bank offices, and automated teller machines. The book value is original cost less accumulated depreciation. These amounts are not

Figure 2–11.

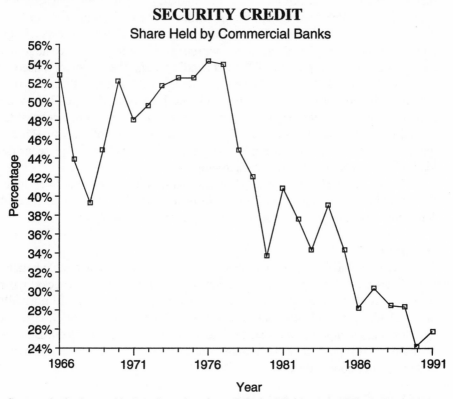

SECURITY CREDIT
Share Held by Commercial Banks

Year

Source: Author's graphic based on data from Board of Governors of the Federal Reserve
System, *Flow of Funds Accounts; Financial Assets and Liabilities*, various issues.

reliable approximations of market value. Professional appraisals of these items
should be obtained.

OTHER REAL ESTATE OWNED
When real estate loans are foreclosed, the property is recorded in this account.
The process begins with the foreclosure. The collateral property is then auc-
tioned with the lending bank usually bidding the amount owed. If no other bid-
ders place higher bids, the bank retains the property and records it in *other real
estate owned (OREO)*. If professional appraisals of the value of the property
are the basis for the entry in OREO and these appraisals are not older than one
year, then book value is a good approximation of market value.

INVESTMENTS IN SUBSIDIARIES

The book value of investments in subsidiaries will generally not be an adequate measure of market value for the same reason that book value of the parent bank is not an adequate measure of market value. An important exception to this general rule is a subsidiary that carries all assets and liabilities at market. This category should reflect the parent bank's percentage ownership interest in the market value of subsidiary equity. The procedures used to value the parent bank may be used to value the subsidiary as well.

DEPOSITS

In general, the time to maturity of deposits is shorter than the time to maturity of assets. From this standpoint, deposit market values are closer to their book values. Of course, the market value of any long-term, fixed-rate instruments can diverge from book value. Also, a penalty for early withdrawal of time deposits is an optionlike instrument with benefits that accrue to the bank.

Noninterest-Bearing Transactions Accounts

Noninterest-bearing transactions accounts are demand deposit accounts that can be withdrawn without notice. Withdrawals can be by check or by automated means, and there is unlimited access in terms of withdrawal and deposit. Several accounts belong in this category.

Correspondent deposits also are called *due from banks*. These are interbank accounts used to clear checks and to settle other transactions such as federal funds sold and purchased.

Commercial deposits belong to businesses. Firms use these accounts to settle their own accounts payable and payroll. If a firm has a line of credit with the bank, often it is able to draw it down by writing checks against a commercial deposit. If the bank requires a compensating balance for loans advanced, the company may maintain the compensating balance in a commercial deposit account.

Consumer deposits include all the checkable accounts other than NOW accounts and money market deposit accounts.

Public funds are those accounts owned by government entities. These include, but are not limited to, cities, counties, school districts, and states.

Trust deposits are used by the bank's trust department, a separate division. This department is essentially a money management area, overseeing assets that belong to other parties. Typical trust department clients are personal trusts and employee benefit trusts, including pension funds. Other activities of this department include settling estates for individuals and acting as a transfer agent for corporate securities. The trust deposits belong to the clients served in this division.

Official checks also are called *cashier's checks* or *treasurer's checks*. These are checks drawn by the bank on itself and signed by a bank official. These accounts are used to disburse loans to customers and to pay the bank's suppliers.

All owners of noninterest-bearing transactions accounts have the right to withdraw the book value of funds without notice and there is no stated maturity date. The market value of these deposits is equivalent to the book value.

Interest-Bearing Transactions Accounts
Before the Depository Institutions Deregulation and Monetary Control Act of 1980, *interest-bearing transactions accounts* had not been permitted since the 1933 Glass-Steagall Act. The only feature that distinguishes these accounts from other checking accounts is the payment of interest. For-profit businesses are prohibited from owning interest-bearing transactions accounts. There are two categories, each with unlimited deposit and withdrawal privileges.

Negotiable order of withdrawal (NOW) accounts are essentially a combination of checking and savings accounts. This account has been permitted since 1980. Although now deregulated, the deposit rate has rarely exceeded 5.5 percent. The *Super NOW* account, authorized in 1983, is a hybrid of checking accounts and money market deposit accounts. The deposit rate for this account changes periodically with the level of money market rates.

Interest-bearing transactions accounts are not subject to any advance notice of withdrawal and have no stated maturity date. These accounts should be valued at book value.

Small Time and Savings Accounts
The category of *small time and savings accounts* contains all deposit accounts excluding transactions accounts and time deposits of $100,000 or more. Individuals hold 98 percent of these instruments. Since the early 1980s, the savings deposit rate ceiling for commercial banks has been the same as for savings and loan associations.[2] Since 1982, commercial banks have been permitted to offer accounts with deposit rates that vary with money market rates. Since 1986, all deposit rates, including small time and savings, have been deregulated. As illustrated in Figure 2–12, this has enabled commercial banks to increase their market of these instruments to almost 60 percent of the total outstanding, competing effectively with savings and loan associations and mutual savings banks.

For valuation purposes, the two relevant subcategories are savings accounts and small time deposits.

Savings accounts. These accounts are interest-bearing and can be maintained in two nonnegotiable forms. The basic savings account pays a fixed rate

Figure 2–12.

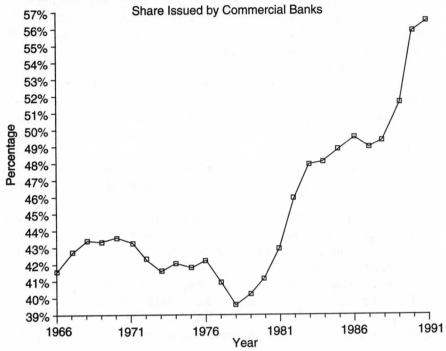

SMALL TIME DEPOSITS AND SAVINGS ACCOUNTS
Share Issued by Commercial Banks

Source: Author's graphic based on data from Board of Governors of the Federal Reserve
System, *Flow of Funds Accounts; Financial Assets and Liabilities*, various issues.

of interest, but there is one form of savings account that pays a variable deposit rate.

The two forms of basic savings account are passbook savings and statement savings. The traditional *passbook savings* account involves a book that is presented to the bank with each deposit or withdrawal and for posting of interest. The *statement savings* account is not evidenced by a passbook; instead, it is accounted for only with computer entries. The customer receives a periodic statement showing all changes in the account since the previous statement: deposits, withdrawals, and interest earned.

The *money market deposit account (MMDA)*, authorized since 1982, is a savings instrument allowing commercial banks to compete directly with money market mutual funds that pay market interest rates and allow withdrawals by check. The MMDA pays an unregulated variable rate of interest as long as the account balance exceeds $1,000. Below $1,000 the deposit rate is the same as for the NOW account. The frequency of deposits and account transfers in person is not restricted. However, MMDA account owners may make only three withdrawals by check and three preauthorized transfers per month.

Savings accounts are interest-bearing deposits that are technically not payable on demand. Practically, however, most banks do permit withdrawal on demand. Further, there is no stated maturity date. Because of these factors, the book value of savings accounts is a good approximation of the market value.

Small time deposits. Deposits for a specified period of time and in amounts less than $100,000 are considered *small time deposits*. The maturities can range from seven days to seven years or longer. There is one important classification that has helped make the commercial banking industry competitive in the consumer deposit market.

The *money market certificate* pays an interest rate tied to the yield on six-month U.S. Treasury bills. Prior to 1983, the instrument was a six-month deposit in a minimum denomination of $10,000. Since deregulation, the minimum deposit is $2,500 for at least seven days.

These small time deposits have a stated maturity date up to seven years and most have a fixed deposit rate. The combination of these factors causes a difference between book value and market. Further, if there is an interest penalty for early withdrawal, this optionlike arrangement, which belongs to the bank, has an impact on market value.

IRA accounts. Individual retirement accounts (IRAs) allow certain individuals to invest up to $2,000 of annual income ($2,250 if the individual has a nonworking spouse) on a tax-deferred basis. This means contributions during a given year may be deducted from taxable income for that year. To qualify for the full tax-deferred amount, an individual must not be covered by a corporate pension plan and must have an annual adjusted gross income of $25,000 or less, or $40,000 or less if married and filing a joint tax return. Beyond these incomes, the permissible amount of tax-deferred investment declines. Any adjusted gross income beyond $35,000 for an individual, or $50,000 for a married couple filing a joint return, disqualifies tax-deferred contributions completely. However, the investment earnings on after-tax contributions to an IRA still qualify for tax-deferred treatment.

When bank customers withdraw funds from IRAs, the amounts withdrawn are subject to full taxation on the tax-deferred contributions and/or investment earnings. Further, if a customer makes the withdrawal before the age of 59.5 years, there is a 10 percent tax penalty.

Despite substantial disincentives to withdraw IRA funds, it is possible for bank customers to do so. In addition, the customers have the ability to transfer the IRA deposits into IRA accounts at other institutions without incurring tax liabilities or penalties. Lastly, to make their deposits attractive to investors, some banks offer their clients the option of withdrawing funds without interest penalties once per year. Thus, the IRA accounts must be considered in terms of their inherent characteristics of short-term versus long-term maturity and fixed versus variable rate. For those IRA deposits with a variable deposit rate, book value approximates market value. For those with a fixed rate, book and market can differ. If optionlike arrangements are offered to clients, these, too, affect market value.

Large Time Deposits

Before the 1970s, commercial banks were the only financial institutions that offered time deposits of $100,000. Then savings institutions (savings and loan associations and mutual savings banks) began to offer them. After the federal deposit insurance limit per account was increased from $40,000 to $100,000 in 1980, this process was enhanced by securities firms that placed client funds with those depository institutions offering the highest rates. Many savings and loan associations grew rapidly by attracting these *brokered deposits* and the market share issued by commercial banks declined as illustrated in Figure 2–13. After the Financial Institutions Reform, Recovery, and Enforcement Act of 1989 (FIRREA), this trend reversed dramatically. FIRREA prohibited capital-deficient S&Ls from accepting brokered deposits. Since then the share of large time deposits issued by commercial banks has grown again to approximately 80 percent of the total. Investors in large time deposits include nonfinancial corporations, households, pension funds, the foreign sector, and money market mutual funds.

There are three basic categories of large time deposits:

➤ Nonnegotiable time deposits ≥ $100,000.
➤ Negotiable CDs.
➤ Foreign deposits.

Nonnegotiable deposits ≥ $100,000. These deposits often are evidenced by *certificates of deposit (CDs)*. These *jumbo CDs* can carry either fixed or variable interest rates. Maturities range from seven days to seven years or more. Most of these instruments are sold at face value with interest accruing to maturity. Some are offered on a discount basis, similar to T-bill pricing. Jumbo CDs are subject to penalties on early withdrawal ranging from partial to complete loss of interest. Ownership may not be transferred prior to maturity.

Negotiable CDs. Negotiable CDs are simply jumbo CDs that may be traded on secondary markets, usually in round lots of $1 million. There is an

Figure 2–13.

LARGE TIME DEPOSITS

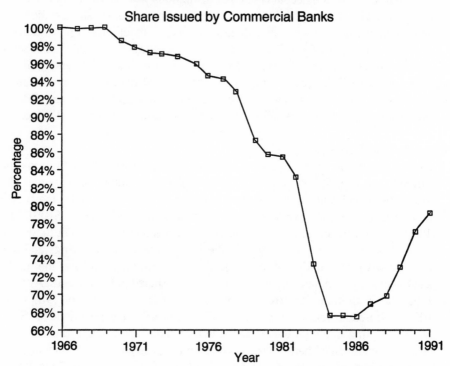

Source: Author's graphic based on data from Board of Governors of the Federal Reserve
System, *Flow of Funds Accounts; Financial Assets and Liabilities*, various issues.

active secondary market for negotiable CDs at the 25 largest U.S. banks. Issuing banks, however, may not repurchase their own instruments or redeem the instruments prior to maturity. The deposit rate is normally fixed and accrued interest is paid at maturity. Maturities range from 14 days to 12 months, with an average of 3 months.

Foreign deposits. Foreign deposits are commonly classified as IBF deposits and Eurodollar time deposits.

An international banking facility (IBF) is the equivalent of an offshore banking facility within a domestic bank. An offshore banking facility is usually a shell operation in a foreign country that accepts deposits and makes loans, not subject to U.S. reserve requirements or deposit insurance premiums and unrestricted by the host country government through taxes, interest rate ceilings, or foreign exchange availability. In 1981, the Federal Reserve Board authorized U.S. domestic banks and U.S. offices of foreign banks to operate IBFs free of reserve requirements and deposit insurance premiums. To qualify for this treatment, IBFs must accept deposits from and make loans to foreign customers, other IBFs, and IBF parent banks only.

Operationally, an IBF is simply a separate set of bookkeeping records. To maintain the separation of IBF activities and regular bank functions, none of the deposits are negotiable. To prevent the use of IBF accounts as normal transactions accounts, all deposits must be at least $100,000.

Eurodollar time deposits are held in banks outside the United States, either foreign banks or overseas affiliates of U.S. banks. This market became particularly important in the 1960s as interest rates for negotiable CDs in the United States were constrained by Regulation Q. As inflation pushed the rates available on T-bills beyond the rates permissible on CDs, the viability of the new negotiable CD market was threatened. Negotiable, dollar-denominated CDs issued overseas, initially in London, were not subject to Reg Q and permitted bank deposits to remain competitive with T-bills. The Eurodollar market grew quickly and has remained popular even after Reg Q ceilings on these deposits were abolished in 1970.

All of these large time deposits have the potential for differences between book value and market value.

➤ The fixed-rate, long-term instruments are most likely to exhibit such differences. Nonnegotiable time deposits ≥ $100,000 are included in this category.

➤ Negotiable CDs often are fixed-rate instruments, but on average have a short time to maturity. Differences here are relatively small.

➤ IBF deposits and Eurodollar time deposits exhibit relatively little difference between book and market because either they are quite short term or the deposit rate is variable.

SHORT-TERM BORROWED FUNDS

Federal funds purchased, term federal funds purchased, and *securities sold under agreement to repurchase* are accounts that correspond to the asset accounts classified as temporary investments. Commercial banks are net borrowers in these short-term markets as shown in Figure 2–14. Once banks were the only participants in the market, but now securities firms, savings and loan

Figure 2–14.

FEDERAL FUNDS PURCHASED AND SECURITIES SOLD UNDER AGREEMENT TO REPURCHASE (NET)

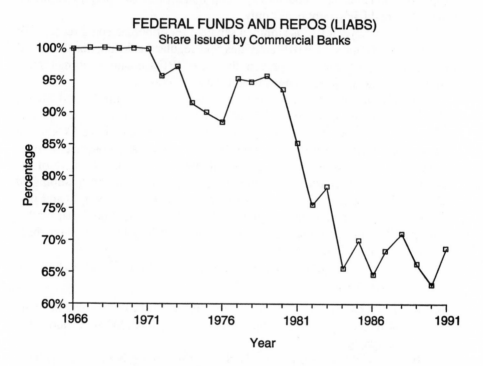

FEDERAL FUNDS AND REPOS (LIABS)
Share Issued by Commercial Banks

Source: Author's graphic based on data from Board of Governors of the Federal Reserve System, *Flow of Funds Accounts; Financial Assets and Liabilities*, various issues.

associations, and mutual savings banks, account for a quarter of the net liabilities in the market.

These are short-term liabilities, overnight in some cases. Their market value differs from book value only slightly because of time to maturity.

Commercial paper is issued by corporations that are large and creditworthy. Commercial bank holding companies and bank affiliates issue commercial paper, but not the banks themselves. Usually issued on a discount basis, commercial paper is sometimes issued in an interest-bearing form. Maturities range from 2 to 270 days, but the secondary market is most active in 30-day paper.

The secondary market for commercial paper is not as well developed as for negotiable CDs. Because of its short-term nature, any small differences between book value and market value are attributable primarily to time to maturity.

The *Treasury tax and loan account (TT&L)* is an account balance maintained by the U.S. Treasury Department. Federal withholding taxes and tax receipts are held in this account. Because the balance is due on demand, there is no difference between book value and market value.

LONG-TERM BORROWED FUNDS

Long-term borrowed funds is a category of liabilities likely to exhibit the greatest difference between market and book because its average time to maturity will be longer than that of deposits and short-term borrowings. *Subordinated notes and debentures* are long-term obligations that can be counted toward regulatory capital as long as these conditions are met.

➤ The original weighted-average maturity must be at least seven years.
➤ Claims of subordinated debt holders must have a lower priority than deposits, that is, be subordinated to deposits.

Subordinated debt is traded often on secondary markets. Thus, market quotes may be obtainable. If the debt is not publicly traded, however, the estimated market value depends on time to maturity and whether the bond rate is fixed or variable.

Over time, bonds have become a significant source of funding for commercial banks. These bonds are now more than 5 percent of total corporate bonds outstanding as shown in Figure 2–15. This generally increasing trend suggests that market values for these bonds will be perhaps more readily available in the future than they have been in the past.

EQUITY

The book value of equity for the bank is the sum of:

➤ Preferred stock.
➤ Common stock.
➤ Capital surplus.
➤ Undivided profits.

Preferred stock is a hybrid between subordinated bonds and common stock. Preferred stockholders receive a fixed dividend (a fixed amount, as is paid to debtholders) in the form of a nondeductible dividend (as is paid to common shareholders). The priority of preferred shareholders' claims on the bank's

Figure 2–15.

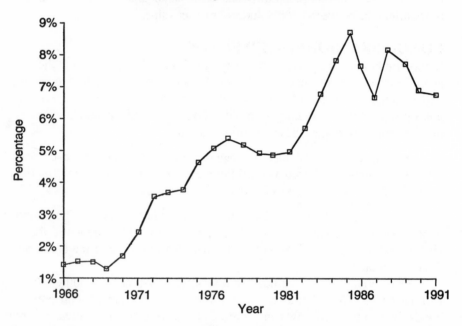

CORPORATE BONDS PAYABLE

CORPORATE BONDS (LIABS)
Share Issued by Commercial Banks

Source: Author's graphic based on data from Board of Governors of the Federal Reserve System, *Flow of Funds Accounts; Financial Assets and Liabilities*, various issues.

assets falls below that of depositors and subordinated debt holders, but above that of common shareholders. Most preferred stock is perpetual (no maturity date) and has no voting rights. Some preferred stock has a limited life, with a minimum stated maturity of 25 years.

Common stock is the residual claim on the bank with voting rights and a variable dividend, usually payable only after all current and past dividends to preferred shareholders have been paid. All claims on the firm have a higher priority than the claims of common stockholders. Frequently, the stock is recorded at par value, a relatively low dollar amount when compared to the price at which the stock sells in securities markets.

Capital surplus is an account linked to the common stock account. When stock is sold at a price that exceeds the par value, the excess is recorded in capital surplus. In nonfinancial corporations, this account is called *paid-in capital*.

Undivided profits is an accumulation of all past and current profits that have not been paid as preferred or common stock dividends. In nonfinancial corporations, this account is called *retained earnings*.

From a market value standpoint, equity is the difference between assets and liabilities. Therefore, the market value of equity is not estimated in the same way. It is the residual of the market value of assets less the market value of liabilities.

OFF-BALANCE-SHEET ITEMS

Off-balance-sheet items are financial assets and liabilities that are not reflected directly in the statement of financial condition, the balance sheet. These are to be distinguished from embedded optionlike instruments in securities, loans, and deposits. The four categories of off-balance-sheet items are:

➤ Interest rate swaps.
➤ Commitments to extend credit.
➤ Standby letters of credit.
➤ Financial guarantees written.

Interest Rate Swaps

An *interest rate swap* is an agreement between two parties (counterparties) to exchange cash flows for a specified period of time at predetermined intervals. No principal changes hands; instead a *notational principal* is agreed on for a given length of time. Interest rate swaps enable the participants to change the nature of cash flows on the notational principal. For this reason, they are useful in hedging interest rate risk.

In a *coupon swap*, one party agrees to pay a fixed rate of interest on the notional principal at specified intervals, perhaps monthly or quarterly. The counterparty agrees to pay a rate that floats with a published rate or *basis*, perhaps the Treasury bill rate, the commercial paper rate, or LIBOR.

In a *basis rate swap*, both interest rates float, but the bases are different. For example, six-month LIBOR may be swapped for one-month LIBOR; or LIBOR may be swapped for the commercial paper rate.

Swaps with timing mismatches involve counterparty payments according to different schedules. Perhaps one counterparty pays interest monthly while the other pays quarterly. A zero swap requires one party to pay at specified intervals throughout the term of the swap as described earlier. The other pays only at the end of the term, a zero coupon arrangement.

Swaps with optionlike payoffs are similar to coupon swaps within specified ranges of market interest rate changes. Beyond these ranges, the terms of the swap change. For example, one party may agree to receive fixed-rate interest and pay floating rate interest as long as the floating rate is within 2 percentage points of the current 10 percent. If the market rate exceeds 12 percent, the party's obligation is then to pay the fixed rate of 12 percent. Likewise, if the market rate falls below 8 percent, the party's obligation converts to a fixed rate of 8 percent. Alternatively, one party may agree to pay fixed-rate interest of 10 percent as long as the market rate remains within the plus-or-minus 2 percent range. Should the market rate go beyond this range (above 12 percent or below 8 percent), the party pays a floating rate.

Commitments to Extend Credit
A *loan commitment* is a bank's agreement to make a loan at a quoted rate during a specified future period. This agreement is evidenced in a *commitment letter* stating the bank's willingness to provide financing, the borrower's identity, the amount of the loan, and the terms of repayment. Often, loan commitments to finance real estate contain a *lock-in period* of 30 to 60 days, during which the mortgage rate and points (percentage points of the loan amount that will be paid in up-front fees) to be paid by the borrower are guaranteed not to change.

Standby Letters of Credit
A s*tandby letter of credit* is a contingent liability that is a form of guarantee to back up an obligation of a bank client. It may be used by a customer who issues commercial paper. The line of credit is an added assurance that the bank customer can redeem its commercial paper when it matures. Most standby letters are never funded or drawn against.

Financial Guarantees Written
Financial guarantees written are noncancellable indemnity bonds guaranteeing the timely payment of interest and principal due on securities issued by bank clients. They are similar to standby letters of credit except that they are written by insurance companies. The 1982 Garn-St Germain Act prohibited banks from operating in this industry. However, those banks already operating insurance facilities were permitted to continue through a grandfathering clause.

All of these off-balance-sheet items earn the bank fee income. The market value of each is based on the fee income associated with the item.

FACTORS BY ASSET AND LIABILITY CATEGORIES

Table 2–1 is a summary of the factors that affect the market value of assets and liabilities. This table is an overview of the discussion in this chapter and should be used as a quick reference in analyzing the market value of a particular asset or liability.

SELECTED REFERENCES

Chew, Donald, ed. New Developments in Commercial Banking. Cambridge, MA: Blackwell Publishers, 1991.

Fitch, Thomas. *Dictionary of Banking Terms*. Hauppauge, NY: Barron's Educational Series, 1990.

ENDNOTES

1 See U.S. Treasury securities and government agency securities in the following section.

2 Before the 1982 Garn-St Germain Act, savings and loan associations could pay a rate that was 25 basis points higher than the rate permitted for commercial banks.

Table 2-1.

FACTORS THAT AFFECT MARKET VALUE BY ASSET AND LIABILITY CATEGORIES

	Time to Maturity	Fixed Rate	Callable	Pre-Payments	Caps & Floors	Interest Penalty	Off-Balance-Sheet	None
ASSETS								
Cash								
Vault cash								X
Due from banks								X
Due from Fed								X
Cash items								X
Temp Investments								
Int-bearing time	X							
Federal funds sold	X							
Term Fed funds sold	X							
Sec purch U/A to resell	X							
Investment Sec								
U.S. Treasury	X	X						
U.S. government agency	X	X		X				
Tax-exempt	X	X	X					
Bond trading account	X	X						
Loans								
Commercial	X	X						
Real estate	X	X		X	X			
Consumer	X	X			X			
Securities					X			X
Overdrafts								X
Reserve for loan loss								X[1]
Other Assets								
Premises and equipment								X[2]
Other real estate								X[3]
Investments in subs								X[4]

Table 2–1. (Concluded)
FACTORS THAT AFFECT MARKET VALUE BY ASSET AND LIABILITY CATEGORIES

	Time to Maturity	Fixed Rate	Callable	Pre-Payments	Caps & Floors	Interest Penalty	Off-Balance-Sheet	None
LIABILITIES								
Deposits								
Noninterest-bearing								X
Interest-bearing								X
Savings accounts								X
Small time deposits	X	X				X		
IRA accounts	X	X				X		
Large time	X	X				X		
Borrowed Funds								
Short-term funds	X							
Long-term funds	X	X						
OFF-BALANCE-SHEET ITEMS								
Interest rate swaps							X	
Loan commitments							X	
Standby LCs							X	
Financial guarantees							X	

1 The market value of the reserve for loan loss is estimated as a percentage of the market value of gross loans.
2 The market value of premises and equipment is estimated based on appraisals.
3 Other real estate values are based on appraisals.
4 The market value of investments in subsidiaries is based on the bank's percentage ownership and the market value of subsidiary equity.

CHAPTER 3

TIME VALUE OF MONEY

INTRODUCTION

The time value of money is based on the premise that $1 received today is worth more than $1 received one year from today. The concepts of time value of money form the basis for:

➤ Interest income and expense calculations used in the day-to-day operations of a commercial bank.
➤ Models used for market valuation of bank assets and liabilities.

This chapter describes these concepts including:

➤ Present value.
➤ Future value.
➤ Expected rates of return.
➤ Single amount calculations.
➤ Intrayear compounding.
➤ Annuities.
➤ Perpetuities.
➤ Amortization schedules.
➤ Mixed cash flows.
➤ Bonds.

SINGLE AMOUNTS

The basic premise of the time value of money is that a single cash flow may be valued anywhere along the time line. A time line is a graphic description of time, with each point on the time line representing a point in time.

	Year	
0	1	2

Specifically, each point on the time line is the end of a period. In the preceding time line, year 0 is today, year 1 represents the moment in time exactly one year from now, and year 2 the moment in time exactly two years from now. The period of one year is represented by the distance between year 0 and year 1 or between year 1 and year 2.

Future Value
Suppose that $100,000 is invested in a two-year certificate of deposit paying 5 percent. Figure 3–1 illustrates how the value of the CD grows. Year 2 is designated with an asterisk because it is the *point of valuation* or *POV*. The point of valuation is the point on the time line at which a cash flow is valued. The POV is distinguished from the timing of the actual cash flow. In this example, the cash flow occurs at year 0—the date of the deposit—while the POV is year 2.

At the end of year 1, the CD is worth $105,000.

$$\$100,000(1.05) \ = \ \$105,000$$

During the second year, the entire $105,000 balance grows at the rate of 5 percent.

$$\$105,000(1.05) \ = \ \$110,250$$

In time-value-of-money terms, the $100,000 is the *present value* or *PV*. The $105,000 is the *future value at year 1* or FV_1. Likewise, the $110,250 is the *future value at year 2* or FV_2. Defining k as the interest rate which is 5 percent in this case

---

Figure 3–1.

FUTURE VALUE OF A SINGLE AMOUNT

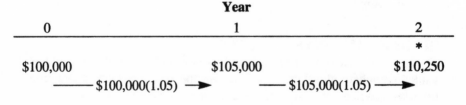

	Year	
0	1	2

Note: Exhibit represents the growth of $100,000 from year 0 to year 2 at 5 percent compounded annually.

$$FV_1 = PV(1 + k) \text{ and}$$

$$FV_2 = FV_1(1 + k)$$

Substituting the value of FV_1 (first equation) in the second equation

$$FV_2 = PV(1 + k)(1 + k) = PV(1 + k)^2$$

In general,

$$FV_n = PV(1 + k)^n$$

where

n = The number of years that elapses between the timing of the cash flow and the point of valuation.

Present Value
Since cash flows may be valued anywhere along the time line, the future value equation also can be used to find the present value of a cash flow. In this case, PV is the unknown and is isolated on one side of the equation.

$$FV_n = PV(1 + k)^n$$

$$PV = FV_n(1/(1 + k)^n)$$

Figure 3–2 illustrates this process. The CD is an investment that promises to pay $110,250 at the end of two years. Assume that the required return is 5

Figure 3–2.

PRESENT VALUE OF A SINGLE AMOUNT

Year

0	1	2
*		
$100,000	$105,000	$110,250

◄— $105,000(1/1.05) ——   ◄— $110,250(1/1.05) ——

Note: Exhibit represents the value at year 0 of $110,250 to be received at year 2 at a 5 percent discount rate.

---

percent and that the point of valuation is year 0. The calculation of *PV* answers the question, What is the maximum amount that an investor would pay for this CD today, that is, what is the market value of the CD? When the deposit rate paid by the bank is the same as the rate of return required by the investor, the market value is the same as the face value of the financial instrument. The $100,000 market value is equal to the $100,000 book value.

$$PV_0 = 110,250(1/(1.05)^2)$$
$$= 100,000^0$$

If the CD is negotiable, an investor may sell it in the secondary market before it matures. Assume that market interest rates increase after the CD is issued and that the CD is sold at year 1. Figure 3–3 shows the value of the CD if the required return is 6 percent at year 1.

$$PV_1 = 110,250(1/(1.06))$$
$$= 104,009.43$$

When the deposit rate is not equal to the market interest rates, the market value of the instrument ($104,009.43) does not equal its book value ($105,000).

Figure 3–3.

VALUE OF A SINGLE AMOUNT AT YEAR 1

Year		
0	1	2
	*	
	$104,009.43	$110,250
	◄— $110,250(1/1.06) ——	

Note: Exhibit represents the value of a year 2 cash flow of $110,250 as of year 1 at a 6 percent discount rate.

Expected Rate of Return
The future value formula for a single amount may also be used to determine the expected rate of return when a financial instrument:

➤ Promises a known future payoff.
➤ Is available currently for a known market price.

In this case, k is the unknown.

$$FV_n = PV(1 + k)^n$$

$$(1 + k)^n = FVn/PV$$

$$(1 + k) = (FVn/PV)^{1/n}$$

$$k = (FVn/PV)^{1/n} - 1$$

Suppose that the market value of a 12-month Treasury bill is selling for $9,650 and has a maturity value of $10,000 as shown in Figure 3–4. Applying the formula above, the expected rate of return to an investor purchasing this instrument is 3.627 percent.

$$k = (10,000/9,650)^1 - 1$$

$$= 0.03627$$

Thus, one may solve for FV_n, PV, or k using the future value formula for a single cash flow.

Rule of 72

The *Rule of 72* provides a method of estimating the length of time required to double the amount of an investment. The number of years that will be required is less than 72 divided by k.

Figure 3–4.

EXPECTED RATE OF RETURN

Year

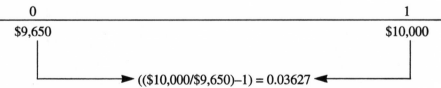

Note: Exhibit represents the expected rate of return on a $9,650 investment at year 0 that returns $10,000 at year 1.

$$N \; < \; 72/k$$

where

N = Number of years required to double the amount of an investment

k = Annual rate of return

Table 3–1 illustrates the rule of 72 when the annual rate of return is 7 percent. In less than 10.29 years (72/7 = 10.2857), an investment of $100,000 doubles.

Interest Factors
The future value formula and its present value derivative have components or *interest factors* that can be isolated—the *future value interest factor* (*FVIF*) and the *present value interest factor* (*PVIF*).

$$FV_n \; = \; PV(FVIF_{k,n})$$

Table 3–1.

RULE OF 72

Year	Value
0	$100,000.00
1	107,000.00
2	114,490.00
3	122,504.30
4	131,079.60
5	140,255.17
6	150,073.04
7	160,578.15
8	171,818.62
9	183,845.92
10	196,715.14
10.29	200,613.00

Note: Exhibit illustrates the Rule of 72 when $100,000 grows at an annual rate of 7 percent. It takes less than 10.29 years (72/7 = 10.2857) for the original amount to double in value.

---

where

$$FVIF_{k,n} = (1+k)^n$$
$$PV = FV_n(PVIF_{k,n})$$

where

$$PVIF_{k,n} = (1/(1+k)^n)$$

These factors have the parameters of k and n. Tables containing the factors for selected combinations of k and n are in Appendix A. The factors for those combinations not included in the tables may be calculated easily using the factor formulas. For example, if k is 6.5 percent and n is 2.5 years, the $FVIF$ and $PVIF$ are

$$FVIF_{.065,2.5} = (1.065)^{2.5}$$
$$= 1.170507$$
$$PVIF_{.065,2.5} = 1/(1.065)^{2.5}$$
$$= 0.854331$$

It is also possible to find the expected rate of return of a single amount using the interest factors in the tables. If an investment costs $1,000 today and promises to pay $1,538.60 in five years, the future value formula in this situation is as follows

$$FVn = PV(FVIF_{k,n})$$
$$1,538.60 = 1,000(FVIF_{k,5})$$
$$1,538.60/1,000 = (FVIF_{k,5})$$
$$1.5386 = (FVIF_{k,5})$$

Referring to the five-period row in the $FVIF$ table, the factor 1.5386 is in the 9 percent column, indicating that 9 percent is the expected rate of return.

The answer of 9 percent also is derived when the present value factor is used.

$$PV = FV_n(PVIF_{k,n})$$
$$1,000 = 1,538.60(PVIF_{k,5})$$
$$1,000/1,538.60 = (PVIF_{k,5})$$
$$0.6499 = (PVIF_{k,5})$$

Referring to the five-period row in the PVIF table, the factor 0.6499 is found in the 9 percent column, verifying the expected return of 9 percent.

Terminal Value

The future value calculations described above assume that k is constant from the timing of the cash flow to the point of valuation. The *terminal value* allows for changing interest rates.

$$TV_n = PV(1 + k_1)(1 + k_2) \ldots (1 + k_n)$$

where

$$TV_n = \text{Terminal value in year } n$$

$$k_i = \text{Interest rate for year } i$$

Table 3–2 provides an example of the difference between terminal value and future value. The proceeds of a $100,000, five-year bullet loan (no interest or principal payments until maturity) are analyzed first under the assumption of a 7.5 percent, fixed-rate loan, then under the assumption of variable rates that

---

Table 3–2.

TERMINAL VALUE: FIXED VERSUS VARIABLE RATES

Fixed Rate

			Year		
0	1	2	3	4	5
$100,000.00	$107,500.00	$115,562.50	$124,229.69	$133,546.91	$143,562.93

Variable Rate

			Year		
0	1	2	3	4	5
$100,000.00	$107,000.00	$115,025.00	$124,227.00	$134,040.93	$143,959.96

Note: Exhibit illustrates the way a $100,000 investment grows at a fixed rate of 7.5 percent and at variable rates of 7.0, 7.5, 8.0, 7.9, and 7.4 percent, with both compounding annually.

---

range from 7 to 8 percent over the life of the loan. The beginning and ending values of each loan determine the effective interest rates.

$$FV_n = PV(1 + k)^n$$

$$k = (FV_n /PV)^{1/n} - 1$$

Fixed rate: $\quad k = (143,562.93/100,000)1/5 - 1$

$$= 0.0750$$

Variable rate: $\quad k = (143,959.96/100,000)^{1/5} - 1$

$$= 0.075593932$$

Notice that for the fixed-rate loan, the effective rate equals the stated rate. For variable-rate loans (or deposits), the *effective rate of a variable-rate instrument* is an average rate that, if applied each year over the term of the instrument, yields the same terminal value as applying the variable rates.

$$FV_5 = 100,000(1.075593932)^5$$

$$= 143,959.96$$

The effective rate is also the geometric mean of the variable rates (or the variable rates anticipated).

$$(1 + k^*)^n = (1 + k_1)(1 + k_2)...(1 + k_n)$$

where

$$k^* = \text{Effective rate for a variable-rate instrument}$$

Substituting the variable rates in this example,

$$(1 + k^*)5 = (1.070)(1.075)(1.080)(1.079)(1.074)$$

$$= 1.43959962$$

$$k^* = (1.43959962)^{1/5} - 1$$

$$= 0.075593935$$

If over the five-year term, market interest rates change, the effective interest rate of the fixed-rate loan does not. In a changing interest rate market environment, this causes the market value of the fixed-rate loan to differ from its book value. On the other hand, the effective rate of the variable-rate loan depends more on market conditions and is closer to market interest rates. For the variable-rate loan, there is a smaller difference between book and market values.

Intrayear Compounding
Up to this point, all examples have been of financial instruments that compound or pay interest once per year. When there is more frequent compounding or *intrayear compounding,* effective rates of interest differ from stated rates.

Future value. Suppose that a $100,000 deposit earns 10 percent compounded semiannually. The deposit balance grows in the following way:

End of Month		Balance
0		$100,000.00
6	[(100,000)(1.05)]	105,000.00
12	[(105,000)(1.05)]	110,250.00

Notice that the future value is greater than the $110,000 obtained with annual compounding [(100,000)(1.10)]. The difference of $250 is directly attributable to *interest on interest,* that is, interest accruing during the second half of the year on the interest of $5,000 earned during the first half of the year [($5,000)(1.05) = $250]. In general, the more frequently interest is compounded the higher will be the future value.

Intrayear compounding requires new definitions of k and n. The interest rate, $k,$ is the *interest rate per period* and n is the *number of periods,* instead of the number of years. In the example above, k is 5 percent and n is 2. The conversion of these parameters depends on $m,$ the number of times per year that interest is compounded or paid. For intrayear compounding,

k/m = Annual interest rate divided by number of times per year interest is compounded or paid

   = Interest rate per period

$n^{*}m$ = Number of years in the term of the financial instrument multiplied by the number of periods per year

   = Total number of periods

Table 3–3 shows the effect of intrayear compounding on a $100,000 deposit at 10 percent. Both discrete and continuous compounding is illustrated.

Discrete compounding applies to those situations for which there are clearly defined, measurable periods of time during which the amount of interest earned does not change. The exhibit shows semiannual, quarterly, monthly, and daily compounding for a one-year deposit. Adjustments for rate per period and number of periods are based on $m.$

Compounding Method	m	k/m	n·m
Semiannual	2	0.0500000	2
Quarterly	4	0.0250000	4
Monthly	12	0.0083333	12
Daily	365	0.0002740	365

Table 3–3.

INTRAYEAR COMPOUNDING: DISCRETE AND CONTINUOUS

Discrete
Month

m	0	3	6	9	12
2	$100,000.00		$105,000.00		$110,250.00
4	$100,000.00	$102,500.00	$105,062.50	$107,689.06	$110,381.29
12	$100,000.00		. . .		$110,471.26
		⟶	$100,000(1.0083333)^{12}	⟶	
365	$100,000.00		. . .		$110,516.68
		⟶	$100,000(1.0002740)^{365}	⟶	

Continuous
Month

m	0	3	6	9	12
	$100,000.00				$110,517.09
		⟶	$100,000.00(e^{10})	⟶	

Note: Exhibit demonstrates how $100,000 grows at the rate of 10 percent when interest is compounded on an intrayear basis.

For the discrete calculations:
$$FV = 100,000(1 + .10/m)^m$$
where m = Number of times per year interest is compounded

For the continuous calculation:
$$FV = 100,000(e^k)$$

The future value of the deposit ranges from \$110,250 for semiannual compounding to \$110,516.68 for daily compounding. Thus, a future value that is higher by up to \$516.68 is possible because of more frequent compounding.

Continuous compounding is characterized by compounding periods that are infinitely small, so small that they cannot be measured. Contrasting this with semiannual compounding, note that in the semiannual case, the balance remains \$100,000 for each day of the first six months and then remains \$105,000 for the second six months. In the case of continuous compounding, the balance theoretically changes by a very small amount every second or fraction thereof. Under continuous compounding, the future value is computed as follows

$$FV_n = PV(e^{kt})$$

where

e = The number used as the base for natural logarithms, with an approximate value of 2.718281828

k = Annual rate of interest

t = Number of years

The calculation is performed either by using the e^x function that is available on many handheld calculators or by substituting the value of e in the formula.

Table 3–3 also shows the balance of the \$100,000 at the end of one year using continuous compounding.

$$FV^1 = 100,000(e^{10})$$

$$= 110,517.09$$

Thus, in this example, there is a difference of \$517.09 when annual compounding is compared to continuous compounding.

Present value. Just as the future value of an amount will be higher when intrayear compounding replaces annual compounding, the present value is smaller under intrayear compounding. Using an example of a \$10,000 payoff in one year and a stated interest rate of 10 percent, the amount that must be invested today depends on the compounding method. This exercise is equivalent to answering the question, What is the exact amount that must be invested today to realize \$10,000 one year from today?

$$0 \qquad\qquad 1$$

$$*$$

? 10,000

Using the same combinations of k/m and n^*m as in the future value case, the present values under discrete compounding for annual, semiannual, quarterly, monthly, and daily discrete compounding are

m	$FV(1 + k/m)^m$	PV
1	$10,000(1/(1.10)$	9,090.91
2	$10,000(1/1.05)^2$	9,070.29
4	$10,000(1/1.025)^4$	9,059.51
12	$10,000(1/1.0083333)^{12}$	9,052.13
365	$10,000(1/1.0002740)^{365}$	9,048.41

The calculation for continuous compounding also requires solving for PV

$$FV^n = PV(e^{kt})$$

$$PV = FV^n/(e^{kt})$$

$$PV = 10,000/(e^{10})$$

$$= 9,048.37$$

This example shows that using intrayear compounding results in a smaller present value than using annual compounding.

Effective interest rates. In both future value and present value calculations, using intrayear compounding is equivalent to using a rate that is higher than the stated rate. The *effective interest rate under intrayear compounding* is that rate which, if compounded annually, causes an investor to be indifferent between it and the stated rate compounded more frequently. The effective rate is computed as follows:

Discrete:

$$k' = (1 + k/m)^m - 1$$

Continuous:

$$k' = e^k - 1$$

where

$$k' = \text{Effective annual interest rate}$$

$$k = \text{Stated annual interest rate}$$

Table 3–4 gives the effective interest rates for stated rates that range from 1 to 20 percent using annual, quarterly, monthly, daily, and continuous compounding.

Just as it is possible to find expected rates of return implied by the present value and future value of an amount under annual compounding, it is also possible to find the implied stated rates under the assumption of intrayear compounding. The process is the same as before:

➤ Substitute the future and present values in the formulas.
➤ Solve for k.

Using the examples for monthly and continuous compounding above, recall that investments of \$9,052.13 and \$9,048.37, respectively, are required to realize \$10,000 at the end of one year.

Discrete:

$$FV_n = PV(1 + k/m)^m$$
$$10,000 = 9,052.13(1 + k/12)^{12}$$
$$10,000/9,052.13 = (1 + k/12)^{12}$$
$$1.104712372 = (1 + k/12)^{12}$$
$$(1.104712372)^{1/12} = 1 + k/12$$
$$(1.0083333 - 1)(12) = k$$
$$= 0.10$$

Continuous:

$$FV_n = PV(e^{kt})$$
$$10,000 = 9,048.37(e^k)$$
$$10,000/9,048.37 = e^k$$
$$1.105171429 = e^k$$

Finding the natural log (exponent of e) of 1.105171429,

$$k = 0.10$$

In both examples, the calculations verify that 10 percent is the stated rate. Notice that the discrete compounding computation always yields the annual

Table 3–4.

INTRAYEAR COMPOUNDING: EFFECTIVE INTEREST RATES

Stated Rate	EFFECTIVE RATE COMPOUNDING METHOD				
	Annual	**Quarterly**	**Monthly**	**Daily**	**Contin.**
1.000%	1.000%	1.004%	1.005%	1.005%	1.005%
2.000%	2.000%	2.015%	2.018%	2.020%	2.020%
3.000%	3.000%	3.034%	3.042%	3.045%	3.045%
4.000%	4.000%	4.060%	4.074%	4.081%	4.081%
5.000%	5.000%	5.095%	5.116%	5.127%	5.127%
6.000%	6.000%	6.136%	6.168%	6.183%	6.184%
7.000%	7.000%	7.186%	7.229%	7.250%	7.251%
8.000%	8.000%	8.243%	8.300%	8.328%	8.329%
9.000%	9.000%	9.308%	9.381%	9.416%	9.417%
10.000%	10.000%	10.381%	10.471%	10.516%	10.517%
11.000%	11.000%	11.462%	11.572%	11.626%	11.628%
12.000%	12.000%	12.551%	12.683%	12.747%	12.750%
13.000%	13.000%	13.648%	13.803%	13.880%	13.883%
14.000%	14.000%	14.752%	14.934%	15.024%	15.027%
15.000%	15.000%	15.865%	16.075%	16.180%	16.183%
16.000%	16.000%	16.986%	17.227%	17.347%	17.351%
17.000%	17.000%	18.115%	18.389%	18.526%	18.530%
18.000%	18.000%	19.252%	19.562%	19.716%	19.722%
19.000%	19.000%	20.397%	20.745%	20.919%	20.925%
20.000%	20.000%	21.551%	21.939%	22.134%	22.140%

Note: Effective rates for discrete compounding $= (1 + k/m)^m - 1$; for continuous compounding, effective rate $= e^k - 1$.

stated rate. On the other hand, the continuous compounding computation yields the annual stated rate multiplied by the number of years. It is, therefore, necessary to divide by the number of years to obtain the annual stated rate.

Suppose that, under continuous compounding, $8,187.31 must be invested to receive $10,000 in two years. The calculation for the implied stated rate changes in the following way:

$$FV_n = PV(e^{kt})$$
$$10,000 = 8,187.31(e^{2k})$$
$$10,000/8,187.31 = e^{2k}$$
$$1.22140239 = e^{2k}$$

Finding the natural log (exponent of e) of 1.22140239,

$$2k = 0.20$$
$$k = 0.10$$

Formulas for Annual and Intrayear Compounding
Table 3–5 summarizes the formulas just discussed for both annual and intrayear compounding. The table serves as a quick reference for both future value and present value formulas of single amounts. Of course, these are also the formulas that are used to find implied stated interest rates by substituting present value, future value, and the appropriate number of periods, and then solving for k.

Computing Interest on Interest
This section discusses calculations of the *interest on interest* contained in any future value or terminal value. Interest on interest is the residual after reducing the future value by principal and interest on principal.

Table 3–5.

ANNUAL AND INTRAYEAR COMPOUNDING: FUTURE VALUE AND PRESENT VALUE FORMULAS; SINGLE CASH FLOWS

Compounding Method	Future Value	Present Value
Annual	$FV_n = PV(1+k)^n$	$PV = FV_n(1/(1+k)^n)$
Intrayear		
Discrete	$FV_n = PV(1+k/m)^{nm}$	$PV = FV_n(1/(1+k/m)^{nm})$
Continuous	$FV_n = PV(e^{kt})$	$PV = FV_n(1/e^{kt})$

Note: FV =   Future value
      PV =   Present value
        n =   Number of years
     m =   Number of times per year interest is calculated
      k =   Annual stated interest rate

Assume that $100,000 is placed on deposit at the rate of 10 percent compounded daily. At the end of five years, the balance in the account is $164,860.96.

$$FV^n = PV(1 + k)^n$$
$$= 100,000(1 + .10/365)^{(365)(5)}$$
$$= 164,860.96$$

Deducting principal and interest on principal, interest on interest is $14,860.96.

FV_5	164,860.96
Principal	(100,000.00)
Interest on principal	
[(100,000)(.10)(5)]	(50,000.00)
Interest on interest	14,860.96

ANNUITIES

The principles that relate to the future and present value of a single cash flow also govern the valuation of annuities. An annuity is a series of cash flows that are defined by the following conditions:

➤ Stream of cash flows.
➤ Cash flows of equal amount.
➤ Equal time interval between the cash flows.
➤ Finite number of cash flows.

The annuity may begin in the near term or it may begin at some time in the future. As long as these criteria are satisfied, the cash flows constitute an annuity.

Future Value

Consider a $1,000 annuity that begins at year 1, ends at year 3, and earns an 8 percent rate of return. Figure 3–5 shows how to analyze the future value of such an annuity. The future value of the annuity is simply the future value of the individual cash flows. In this case, the point of valuation (*POV*) is year 3. The cash flow in year 1 (*CF*$_1$) is compounded for two years, that is, it grows for the number of periods between the cash flow and the *POV*. Likewise, *CF*$_2$ is compounded for one year and *CF*$_3$ for zero years.

$$FV = 1{,}000((1.08)^2) + 1{,}000((1.08)^1) + 1{,}000((1.08)^0)$$
$$= 1{,}000(1.1664) + 1{,}000(1.08) + 1{,}000(1)$$
$$= 1{,}000(1.1664 + 1.08 + 1)$$
$$= 1{,}000(3.2464)$$
$$= 3{,}246.40$$

At year 3, the value of this annuity is \$3,246.40. The future value of the annuity is the amount of the payment multiplied by the sum of the future value interest factors (FVIFs) for the individual amounts.

$$FV = \sum_{t=1}^{n} Pymt(1+k)^{n-t}$$

$$= Pymt\sum_{t=1}^{n} (1+k)^{n-t}$$

where

$$Pymt = \text{Amount of the periodic } CF$$

$$n = \text{Number of } CFs \text{ in the annuity}$$

The summation of the individual single amount factors is itself an interest factor—the future value interest factor of an annuity (FVIFA).

Figure 3–5.

FUTURE VALUE OF AN ANNUITY

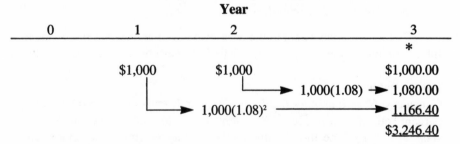

Note: Exhibit shows the value of a three-year annuity beginning at year 1 at 8 percent when the point of valuation is year 3.

$$FVIFA_{k,n} = \sum_{t=1}^{n}(1+k)^{n-t}$$

Figure 3–6 shows how the sum of these individual factors converges to a form that does not require n iterations of the calculation.

Figure 3–6.

DERIVATION OF THE FUTURE VALUE INTEREST FACTOR OF AN ANNUITY

$$FVIFA = \sum_{t=1}^{n}(1+k)^{n-t} = (1+k)^{n-1} + (1+k)^{n-2} + (1+k)^{n-3} + \ldots + (1+k)^{0}$$

Reversing the order to the terms on the right side,

$$FVIFA = (1+k)^{0} + (1+k)^{1} + (1+k)^{2} + \ldots + (1+k)^{n-1}$$
$$= 1 + (1+k)^{1} + (1+k)^{2} + \ldots + (1+k)^{n-1}$$

This is a geometric progression in which each successive term increases by the multiplicative factor of $(1+k)$ and the terms on the right side converge to:

$$(1-q^{n})/(1-q)$$

where $\quad q = \{1+k\}$

$\quad\quad n$ = The number of terms in the progression

Substituting $\{1+k\}$ for q,

$$FVIFA = (1 - \{1+k\}^{n})/(1 - \{1+k\})$$
$$= (1 - \{1+k\}^{n})/(-k)$$
$$= (-1/k) + (\{1+k\}^{n}/k)$$
$$= (\{1+k\}^{n}/k) - (1/k)$$
$$= (1/k)(\{1+k\}^{n} - 1)$$

$$FVIFA_{k,n} = (1/k)(\{1 + k\}^n - 1)$$

The combination of 8 percent and three payments yields an *FVIFA* of 3.2464, just as in the case of the sum of individual factors.

$$FVIFA_{.08,3} = (1/.08)(\{1.08\}^3 - 1)$$

$$= (12.5)(.259712)$$

$$= 3.2464$$

The valuation formula for the future value of an annuity can therefore be stated as:

$$FV = Pymt[(1/k)(\{1 + k\}^n - 1)]$$

$$= Pymt(FVIFA_{k,n})$$

The Appendix contains *FVIFA*s for specific combinations of k and n. For those combinations not shown, the factor may be computed using the formula.

Present Value
The present value of an annuity is the present value of the individual cash flows. The same $1,000 three-year annuity is shown in Figure 3–7. The difference is that the point of valuation is now year 0. Each cash flow is discounted for the number of periods between it and the point of valuation—year 0. CF_1 is discounted for one year, CF_2 for two years, and CF_3 for three years.

$$PV = 1,000((1/.08)^1) + 1,000((1/.08)^2) + 1,000((1/.08)^3)$$

$$= 1,000(.92593) + 1,000(.85734) + 1,000(.79383)$$

$$= 1,000(2.5771)$$

$$= 2,577.10$$

The present value of the annuity is the periodic payment multiplied by the sum of the individual present value interest factors (*PVIFs*).

$$PV = \sum_{t=1}^{n} Pymt\left(\frac{1}{(1+k)^t}\right)$$

$$= Pymt\sum_{t=1}^{n}\left(\frac{1}{(1+k)^t}\right)$$

Figure 3–7.

PRESENT VALUE OF AN ANNUITY

Year

0	1	2	3

*

| | $1,000 | $1,000 | $1,000 |

$ 925.93 ◄— −1,000(1/1.08) ──┘

857.34 ◄─────────── 1,000(1/1.08)² ──┘

793.83 ◄──────────────────── 1,000(1/1.08)³ ──┘

$2,577.10

Note: Figure shows the value of a three-year annuity beginning at year 1 at 8 percent when the point of valuation is year 0.

The sum of the relevant individual factors is the present value interest factor of an annuity (PVIFA).

$$PVIFA_{k,n} = \sum_{t=1}^{n}\left(\frac{1}{(1+k)^{t}}\right)$$

Figure 3–8 shows that this series of terms also converges to a closed form.

$$PVIFA_{k,n} = (1/k)(1 - \{1/(1+k)^{n}\})$$

Applying this formula to the combination of 8 percent and three periods, the *PVIFA* is the same as the sum of the individual present value factors.

$$PVIFA_{.08,3} = (1/.08)(1 - \{1/(1.08)^{3}\})$$

$$= (12.5)(.206167759)$$

$$= 2.5771$$

The valuation formula for the present value of an annuity is

$$PV = Pymt[(1/k)(1 - \{1/(1+k)^{n}\})]$$

$$= Pymt(PVIFA_{k,n})$$

Figure 3–8.

DERIVATION OF THE PRESENT VALUE INTEREST FACTOR OF AN ANNUITY

$$PVIFA = \sum_{t=1}^{n} 1/(1+k)^t = 1/(1+k)^1 + 1/(1+k)^2 + 1/(1+k)^3 + \ldots + 1/(1+k)^n$$

$$= (1/(1+k))\left[1 + 1/(1+k)^1 + 1/(1+k)^2 + \ldots + 1/(1+k)^{n-1}\right]$$

The terms in the brackets represent a geometric progression in which each successive term increases by the multiplicative factor of $1/(1+k)$. The terms within the brackets converge to:

$$(1-q^n)/(1-q)$$

where $q = \{1/(1+k)\}$

n = The number of terms in the progression

Substituting $\{1/(1+k)\}$ for q, the bracketed quantity

$$= \left(1 - \{1/(1+k)^n\}\right)/\left(1 - \{1/(1+k)\}\right)$$

$$= \left(1 - \{1/(1+k)^n\}\right)/\left((1+k-1)/(1+k)\right)$$

$$= \left(1 - \{1/(1+k)^n\}\right)/\left(k/(1+k)\right)$$

$$= (1+k)/k - (1+k)/\left(k(1+k)^n\right)$$

Substituting the bracketed quantity,

$$PVIFA = (1/(1+k))\left[(1+k)/ - (1+k)/\left(k(1+k)^n\right)\right]$$

$$= 1/k - 1/\left(k(1+k)^n\right)$$

$$= 1/k - (1/k)\{1/(1+k)^n\}$$

$$= (1/k)\left(1 - \{1/(1+k)^n\}\right)$$

The Appendix contains *PVIFA*s for selected combinations of k and n. The factors for those combinations not included in the Appendix may be calculated using the *PVIFA* formula.

Implied Point of Valuation

In the previous examples, results were obtained that coincided exactly with the *FVIFA* and *PVIFA* given in the tables. The results were exactly the same because the points of valuation for the examples coincided exactly with the implied points of valuation for the factors in the tables.

➤ The implied point of valuation for a future value interest factor of an annuity (FVIFA) coincides with the last cash flow in the annuity.

➤ The implied point of valuation for a present value interest factor of an annuity (PVIFA) is one period prior to the first cash flow in the annuity.

This is not to suggest that the factors cannot be used when the *POV* in the problem or situation is different. Instead, certain adjustments are necessary.

Figure 3–9 contains a time line with the same three-year annuity of $1,000 beginning in year 1. In this future value problem, the *POV* is now year 10, not year 3. Perhaps the three payments will be placed in an account but the funds will not be needed until year 10. The question is, What will be the balance in the account at year 10 if three payments are made beginning with year 1 and ending with year 3?

The value of the three payments is $3,246.40 as of year 3, the date of the last cash flow in the annuity. This amount then continues to grow at the rate of 8 percent for another seven years.

$$FV_{10} = FV_3(1 + k)^7$$

$$= 3,246.40(1.08)^7$$

$$= 3,246.40(1.713824)$$

$$= 5,563.76$$

In general,

$$FV_n = Pymt[(1/k)(\{1 + k\}^{n-1})]$$

$$FV_a = FV_n(1 + k)^{a-n}$$

where

$$a > n$$

The basic rule is (1) to find the future value of the annuity using the *FVIFA* and (2) then compound this amount to the desired point of valuation.

Figure 3–10 moves the three-year annuity out on the time line to begin at year 8 and end at year 10. The point of valuation of this present value problem

---

Figure 3–9.

IMPLIED POINT OF VALUATION OF FVIFA

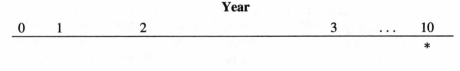

Year

| 0 | 1 | 2 | | 3 | . . . | 10 |

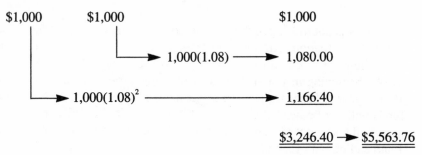

$$FV_3 = 1,000\left(FVIFA_{.08,\,3}\right) = 1,000\left[(1/.08)\left(\{1.08\}^3 - 1\right)\right]$$
$$= 1,000[3.2464]$$
$$= 3,246.40$$
$$FV_{10} = FV_3(1.08)^7 \qquad = 5,563.76$$

Note: Figure shows the value of a three-year annuity beginning at year 1 at 8 percent when the point of valuation is year 10. The implied point of valuation for the annuity factor is the time of the last payment of the annuity.

---

is year 0. A possible question may be, What is the most that an investor should pay today for an investment that promises to return three $1,000 payments beginning at year 8 and ending at year 10?

The present value of this annuity is $2,577.10 as of year 7, one period before the first cash flow in the annuity. This amount is then discounted back to year 0 using an 8 percent discount rate.

Figure 3–10.

IMPLIED POINT OF VALUATION OF PVIFA

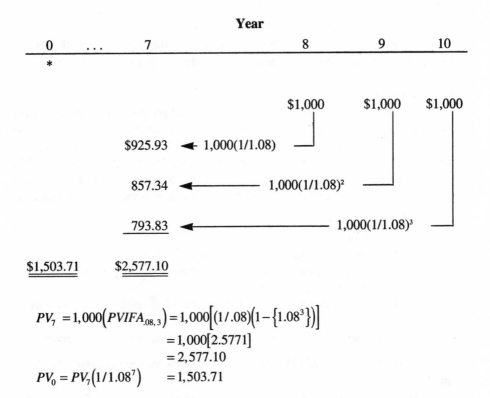

$$PV_7 = 1,000 \left(PVIFA_{.08,\, 3} \right) = 1,000 \left[(1/.08)\left(1 - \left\{ 1.08^3 \right\} \right) \right]$$
$$= 1,000[2.5771]$$
$$= 2,577.10$$
$$PV_0 = PV_7 \left(1/1.08^7 \right) \quad = 1,503.71$$

Note: Figure shows the value of a three-year annuity beginning at year 8 at 8 percent
            when the point of valuation is year 0. The implied point of valuation for the
            annuity factor is one period before the first cash flow of the annuity.

$$PV_0 = PV_7(1/(1 + k)^7)$$
$$PV_0 = 2,577.10(1/(1.08)^7)$$
$$= 2,577.10(.583490)$$
$$= 1,503.71$$

In general,

$$PV_n = Pymt[(1/k)(1 - \{1/(1 + k)^n\})]$$

$$PV_b = PV_n(1/(1 + k)^{n-b})$$

where

$$b < n$$

The process is to (1) find the present value of the annuity using the *PVIFA* factor and (2) then discount this amount to the desired point of valuation.

Expected Return

The expected rate of return that is implied when all parameters are given except the rate, theoretically is found by using the appropriate valuation formula and solving for k, as explained in the material on single cash flows. Finding the implied rate of return using annuity valuation formulas, however, is not feasible because the factors themselves are too involved to isolate k on one side of the equation. This means that finding the expected return is essentially a trial-and-error process:

➤ Select a rate.
➤ Find the present value or future value of the annuity.
➤ If the calculated result matches the future value or present value that is given, the rate is correct.
➤ If the calculated result does not match, select another rate and start the process again.
➤ Continue until the calculated value equals the value that is given.

By using a handheld calculator, you can perform the necessary iterations quickly.

Also, the annuity factors on the tables can be used to find or to approximate the expected rate of return. If the k which solves the equation is a whole percentage, the factor may appear on the table in the row for the appropriate number of periods. For example, consider a $5,000 annuity for six years that grows to $35,766.50 as of the time of the last payment. Solving for the *FVIFA* that is implied

$$FV = Pymt(FVIFA_{k,n})$$

$$35,766.50 = 5,000(FVIFA_{k,6})$$

$$35,766.50/5,000 = FVIFA_{k,6}$$

$$7.1533 = FVIFA_{k,6}$$

Referring to the six-period row of the *FVIFA* table, this factor is found in the 7 percent column; that is, the implied rate of return is 7 percent.

Now consider an 11-year, $4,000 annuity that begins one year from now and has a cost at year 0 (present value) of $23,750.80. Solving for the *PVIFA*

$$PV = Pymt(PVIFA_{k,n})$$

$$23,750.80 = 4,000(PVIFA_{k,11})$$

$$23,750.80/4,000 = PVIFA_{k,11}$$

$$5.9377 = PVIFA_{k,11}$$

Referring to the 11-period row of the *PVIFA* table, this factor is found in the 12 percent column. Thus, the implied return is 12 percent.

In those cases in which the factor is not found on the table, it is possible to use interpolation to estimate the rate. This involves finding the two factors in the correct row between which the derived factor lies. The implied rate of return is:

> ➤ The lower percentage represented by the two factors on the table.
> ➤ *Plus* an increment that equals the difference between the derived factor and the factor for the lower percentage.
> ➤ Divided by the difference between the factor for the higher percentage and the factor for the lower percentage.

Suppose that the future value of an eight-year $100 annuity is given as $1,007.69 (as of the time of the last cash flow). The implied *FVIFA* is 10.0769.

$$1,007.69/100 = FVIFA_{k,8}$$

$$10.0769 = FVIFA_{k,8}$$

On the eight-period row of the *FVIFA* table, this factor falls between 9.8975 (6 percent) and 10.260 (7 percent). The implied rate of return for this annuity is between 6 percent and 7 percent. The percentage is estimated as previously described.

> ➤ 6 percent *plus*
> ➤ $(10.0769 - 9.8975)/(10.260 - 9.8975) = 0.494897$

The implied return is approximately 6.494897 percent.

Now consider a five-year $100 annuity whose present value is given as $407.29 (as of one period prior to the first cash flow). The implied factor is 4.0729.

$$407.29/100 = PVIFA_{k,5}$$

$$4.0729 = PVIFA_{k,5}$$

On the five-period row of the *PVIFA* table, this factor falls between 4.1002 (7 percent) and 3.9927 (8 percent). The implied rate of return is estimated as follows:

➤ 7 percent *plus*
➤ $(4.0729 - 4.1002)(3.9927 - 4.1002) = .253953$

The implied rate of return is approximately 7.253953.

Amortization Schedule

An *amortization schedule* describes how the unpaid balance of an installment loan is reduced by each payment. Since the payments are all equal and at equal intervals, these payments constitute an annuity. Interest is assessed only on the unpaid balance; the remainder of the payment reduces the unpaid balance.

Assume that an automobile loan is used for the purchase of a $19,000 car with a $2,000 down payment. The interest rate is 11 percent, or .91667 percent per month, and the loan is for 24 months. The amount (present value) of the loan is $17,000. The monthly payment is $792.33.

$$PV = Pymt(PVIFA_{.0091667,24})$$

$$17,000 = Pymt[(1/.0091667)(1 - \{1/1.0091667)24\})]$$

$$17,000 = Pymt[21.45561003]$$

$$17,000/21.45561003 = Pymt$$

$$792.33 = Pymt$$

Table 3–6 provides the amortization schedule for this loan. Each month the amount of interest in the $792.33 payment depends on the unpaid balance. In the first payment, $155.83 is the interest amount ($17,000 × .0091667), leaving $636.50 ($792.33 − 155.83) to reduce the unpaid balance to $16,363.50 ($17,000 − 636.50). This process continues until the unpaid balance is reduced to zero.

PERPETUITIES

A perpetuity is a series of cash flows that does not end. The following conditions describe a perpetuity.

Table 3–6.

AMORTIZATION SCHEDULE

Payment Number	Interest	Principal Reduction	Unpaid Balance
			17,000.00
1	155.83	636.50	16,363.50
2	150.00	642.33	15,721.17
3	144.11	648.22	15,072.94
4	138.17	654.16	14,418.78
5	132.17	660.16	13,758.62
6	126.12	666.21	13,092.40
7	120.01	672.32	12,420.09
8	113.85	678.48	11,741.60
9	107.63	684.70	11,056.90
10	101.35	690.98	10,365.92
11	95.02	697.31	9,668.61
12	88.63	703.70	8,964.91
13	82.18	710.15	8,254.75
14	75.67	716.66	7,538.09
15	69.10	723.23	6,814.85
16	62.47	729.86	6,084.99
17	55.78	736.55	5,348.43
18	49.03	743.31	4,605.13
19	42.21	750.12	3,855.01
20	35.34	757.00	3,098.01
21	28.40	763.93	2,334.08
22	21.40	770.94	1,563.14
23	14.33	778.00	785.14
24	7.20	785.14	0.00

Notes: a. This schedule is for a $17,000 loan at 11 percent to be repaid in 24 monthly installments of $792.33.

b. The sum of principal reduction and new unpaid balance may differ from previous unpaid balance due to rounding.

➤ Stream of cash flows.
➤ Cash flows of equal amount.
➤ Equal time interval between the cash flows.
➤ Infinite number of cash flows.

The concept of a future value for an annuity has no meaning since the cash flows are infinite. The present value of a perpetuity is

$$PV = Pymt \sum_{t=1}^{\infty} \left(\frac{1}{(1+k)^t} \right)$$

The sum of the *PVIF*s from 1 to ∞ is a geometric progression that converges to $1/k$. Thus,

$$PV = Pymt(1/k)$$

The implied point of valuation for a perpetuity is one period before the first cash flow in the stream.

If a perpetuity promises to pay $100 per year beginning in year 1 and the investor believes that 7 percent is the appropriate required rate of return, the value of the perpetuity is $1,428.57.

$$PV = 100/.07$$

$$= 1,428.57$$

However, if the perpetuity does not begin until year 5, the $1,428.57 is the appropriate value as of year 4. The value of the perpetuity at year 0 is $1,089.85.

$$PV = 1,428.57/(1.07)^4$$

$$= 1,428.57/1.310796$$

$$= 1,089.85$$

Preferred stock is a good example of a perpetuity in the United States. The United Kingdom issues government *consuls* or perpetual bonds.

UNEQUAL CASH FLOWS

All streams of cash flows do not have equal payments. This is particularly true for nonfinancial capital assets. Table 3–7 is an example of an investment that costs $11,000 and returns five unequal future cash flows. The expected rate of return on this investment is 11.0455 percent, that is, when each cash flow is discounted at 11.0455 percent, the total is $11,000.

Table 3–7.

UNEQUAL CASH FLOWS AND EXPECTED RATE OF RETURN

			Year		
0	1	2	3	4	5
($11,000)	$2,000	$1,500	$3,500	$6,000	$2,500

The expected rate of return is that rate which causes the present value of the future cash flows to exactly equal the price. In this case, the expected rate of return is 11.0455 percent and the value of each year's cash flow at this rate is:

Year	PV
1	$1,801.06
2	1,216.43
3	2,556.02
4	3,945.90
5	1,480.59
	$11,000.00

In terms of financial instruments that involve unequal cash flows, an interest-bearing bond is a good example. Table 3–8 provides the cash flows of a five-year bond with an annual 8.5 percent coupon payment on the par value of $1,000. The bond is currently selling for $920. The expected rate of return implied for this bond is called the *yield to maturity* (*YTM*). The YTM is defined alternatively as:

> ➤ The average annual rate of return earned if an investor buys a bond today and holds it to maturity.
> ➤ The rate causing the present value of future cash flows (interest and maturity value) to exactly equal the market price.

Because the cash flows are mixed, the YTM can be found exactly by using the trial-and-error method. The *YTM approximation* also can be used.

$$YTM \cong [I + (M - P_0)/n]/[(M + 2(P_0))/3]$$

where

$$M = \text{Maturity or par value of the bond}$$

$$I = \text{Annual interest payment}$$

$$= (M)(\text{coupon rate})$$

$$P_0 = \text{Price or market value of the bond}$$

The numerator of the approximation is the sum of annual interest payments and the average annual capital gain (or loss) until the bond matures. The denominator is the average investment in the bond. The actual *YTM* of this bond is 10.645 percent. The formula provides a close approximation of 10.669 percent.

SUMMARY OF TIME VALUE OF MONEY CONCEPTS

Table 3–9 is a summary of the time value of money concepts discussed in this chapter. It should be used as a quick reference in terms of the appropriate formulas and their interpretations. These concepts form the basis for valuation models for the financial assets and liabilities of a commercial bank.

Table 3–8.

BOND YIELD TO MATURITY

			Year		
0	1	2	3	4	5
($920)	$85	$85	$85	$85	$85
					1,000

The yield to maturity (*YTM*) is the expected rate of return for a bond. This bond has a $1,000 par and an 8.5 percent coupon. It matures in five years and has a current market value of $920. The actual *YTM* is 10.645 percent and the approximate *YTM* is:

$$YTM \cong \left[I + \left(M - P_0\right)/n\right]/\left[\left(M + 2\left(P_0\right)\right)/3\right]$$

$$\cong \left[85 + \left(1000 - 920\right)/5\right]/\left[\left(1000 + 2\left(920\right)\right)/3\right]$$

$$\cong 101/946.67$$

$$\cong .10669$$

Table 3–9.

SUMMARY OF TIME VALUE OF MONEY CONCEPTS

Single Amount	Annuity	Perpetuity
When applicable: 2 *CFs*— *PV* and *FV*	Finite number of equal *CFs* at equal intervals	Infinite number of equal *CFs* at equal intervals
FUTURE VALUE		
Formula: $FV = PV(1+k)^n$	$Pymt[(1/k)(\{1+k\}^n-1)]$	n/a
Meaning of *n*: Number of periods after *CF*	Number of payments	n/a
Implied *POV*: *n* periods after *CF*	same point as last *CF*	n/a
PRESENT VALUE		
Formula: $PV = FV(1/(1+k)^n)$	$Pymt[(1/k)(1-\{1/(1+k)^n\})]$	$Pymt(1/k)$
Meaning of n: Number of periods before *CF*	Number of payments	n/a
Implied *POV*: *n* periods before *CF*	one period before first *CF*	one period before first *CF*

Legend:

PV	Present value	*Pymt*	Periodic payment
FV	Future value	*k*	Rate of return
CF	Cash flow	n/a	Not applicable
POV	Point of valuation		

CHAPTER 4

MARKET VALUATION MODELS FOR THE BALANCE SHEET

INTRODUCTION
All market valuation models for bank assets and liabilities are based on time value of money concepts. The exact specifications of a model, however, depend on the characteristics of the particular financial instrument. The market value of some instruments is reliably approximated by book value. For a few categories, professional appraisals are the best estimates. This chapter describes the valuation models in each asset and liability category.

THE BASIS FOR THE MODELS
In general, the major parameters of market valuation models are:

➤ Future cash flows.
➤ Time to maturity.
➤ Appropriate discount rate.

The basic model is

$$MV = \sum_{t=1}^{n} \frac{CF_t}{(1 = k)^t}$$

where

MV = Market value

CF_t = Cash flow in year t

n = Number of periods in the term of a fixed-income instrument

k = Appropriate discount rate

The market value of a bank's equity is the difference between the market value of assets and the market value of liabilities.

$$MV_E \; = \; MV_A - MV_L$$

where

$$MV_E \; = \; \text{Market value of equity}$$

$$MV_A \; = \; \text{Market value of assets}$$

$$MV_L \; = \; \text{Market value of liabilities}$$

Cash Flows
Future cash flows should be determined for major classifications of assets and liabilities. The group of U.S. Treasury bonds, for example, is a homogeneous group of assets, as is the classification of consumer automobile loans. These instruments should be grouped to determine the total balance, the coupon rate (whether that be the loan or deposit rate), and the average maturity.

For example, suppose that a portfolio of automobile loans has a total balance of $500 million, an average time to maturity of 25 months, and an average loan rate of 11 percent. This portfolio can be interpreted as providing 25 payments that will amortize the $500 million balance at the rate of 11 percent. This is an annuity and the amount of each payment should be estimated as follows

$$PV = Pymt\left(PVIFA_{\frac{k}{m},25} \right)$$

$$PVIFA_{\frac{k}{m},n} = \frac{1}{\left(\dfrac{k}{m}\right)}\left(1 - \frac{1}{1+\left(\dfrac{k}{m}\right)^{n}} \right)$$

$$PVIFA_{\frac{.11}{12},25} = \frac{1}{.00916667}\left(1 - \frac{1}{1.00916667^{25}} \right)$$

$$= 22.251644$$

$$\$50 \text{ million} = Pymt(22.251644)$$

$$\frac{\$50 \text{ million}}{22.251644} = Pymt$$

$$\$2.247025 \text{ million} = Pymt$$

The estimated cash flows of the portfolio are a $2.247 million annuity to be received over 25 months. The assumption of an amortizing annuity is reasonable for the automobile loan category. Other financial instrument categories should be analyzed based on the typical cash flow pattern for that group.

Interest Rates

The interest rate used for discounting the cash flow stream is not the coupon rate. It is a rate determined by current market conditions. The factors that are important in setting the rate are:

➤ The current level of widely quoted interest rates.
➤ The normal relationship of interest rates for the category to other widely quoted interest rates.
➤ The shape of the yield curve in terms of short- and long-term rate differentials.
➤ Default risk for securities and loans.

The current level of interest rates depends on conditions at the time of valuation. The sections that follow include discussions of the relationships between (1) interest rates for specific categories of assets and (2) interest rates on U.S. Treasury securities. The differential of short-term versus long-term rates is also addressed.

Figure 4–1 shows the historical effect of default risk on interest rates. In the top panel, the U.S. Treasury bond (T-bond) rate is plotted over the 30 years ended 1991. Also shown are the yields on corporate bonds rated Aaa, Aa, A, and Baa. When the average T-bond rate peaked at 12.87 percent in 1981, the yield on Baa bonds was 16.04 percent, for a 317-basis-point difference. These differentials, which are risk premiums on corporate bonds, are provided in the bottom panel of Figure 4–1. The Baa spread over the T-bond rate was even higher in 1982 at 388 basis points. During the same two years, the Aaa rate exceeded the T-bond rate by 130 and 156 basis points, respectively.

The late 1970s and early 1980s represent the highest level of interest rates in recent history. These years also are characterized by high differentials between Treasury and corporate rates. In general, risk premiums increase during periods of high interest rates. This occurred in 1970–1971 when risk premiums ranged from 145 to 282 basis points and again in 1975 when the range was from 185 to 363 basis points. On the other hand, when rates have been relatively low, risk premiums also have been reduced. For example, during the early 1960s, all spreads over the T-bond rate were generally under 100 basis points. After the level of interest rates moderated during the late 1980s, average 1990 risk premiums were in the range of 58 to 162 basis points.

Figure 4–1.

CORPORATE BOND RATES
1961–1991

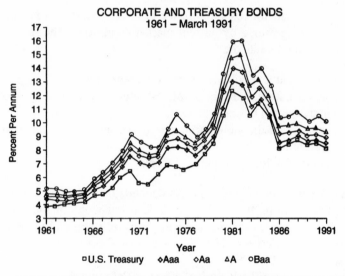

CORPORATE AND TREASURY BONDS
1961 – March 1991

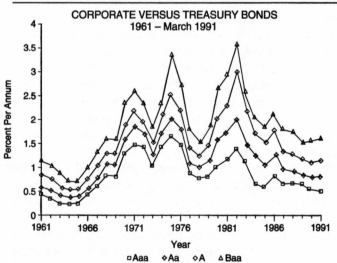

CORPORATE VERSUS TREASURY BONDS
1961 – March 1991

Source: Author's graphic based on data from U.S. Department of Commerce, Economics and Statistics Administration, *Business Statistics, 1961–1988* (1989) and *Survey of Current Business* (April 1991).

The default risk premiums associated with particular bank assets should be set with some sensitivity to the interest rate environment. Relatively high default risk premiums are reasonable only when the general level of interest rates is high.

CASH
Cash includes the categories of:

➤ Vault cash.
➤ Due from other banks.
➤ Due from the Federal Reserve.
➤ Cash items in collection.

The balances in these accounts are funds that are available on a same-day or next-day basis. There is no difference between book value and market value for these assets.

TEMPORARY INVESTMENTS
Temporary investments are:

➤ Interest-bearing time deposits in other banks.
➤ Federal funds sold.
➤ Term federal funds sold.
➤ Securities purchased under agreement to resell.

These are short-term instruments whose coupon (earning) rates and discount (market) rates are similar. Thus, market value is quite close to book value.

Interest-Bearing Time Deposits in Other Banks
The valuation model of these deposits is:

$$MV = \frac{D(1+k_C)^n}{(1+k)^n}$$

where

D = Deposit amount

k_c = Contractual (coupon) rate

k = Appropriate discount rate

n = Fraction of the year remaining before maturity

Consider the following example:

Given: D = \$100,000; k_c = .05; k = .05; n = .5.

MV = $100,000(1.05)^{.5}/(1.05)^{.5}$

= 100,000

The contractual rate equals the discount rate and this equality causes the market value to equal book value.

The next example shows the effect on market value if the discount rate exceeds the contractual rate.

Given: D = \$100,000; k_c = .05; k = .055; n = .5.

MV = $100,000(1.05)^{.5}/(1.055)^{.5}$

= $100,000(1.024695)/(1.027132)$

= 99,762.74

The market value is only slightly lower than book because the time to maturity is relatively short.

The third example shows the extremely close relationship between market value and book value when time to maturity is even shorter.

Given: D = \$100,000; k_c = .05; k = .055; n = 1/12
                                        (one month).

MV = $100,000(1.05)^{.5}/(1.055)^{1/12}$

= $100,000(1.004074)/(1.004472)$

= 99,960.38

Even with a 50-basis-point difference between contractual and discount rates, the remaining time to maturity results in only a \$40 difference between market and book values.

Federal Funds Sold
The valuation model for federal funds follows the same format as that for time deposits.

$$MV = \frac{FF(1+k_C)^n}{(1+k)^n}$$

where

FF = Amount of funds loaned

The most typical case is an overnight transaction for which there is no difference between contractual and market rates.

Given: FF $=$ $1,000,000; k_c = .04; k = .04;$
                                                              $n = 1/365.$

                                          MV $=$ $1,000,000(1.04)^{1/365}/(1.04)^{1/365}$

                                                $=$ $1,000,000$

Even if there is a significant difference in rates, the short duration of an overnight transaction forces the market value to be close to book value.

Given: FF $=$ $1,000,000; k_c = .04; k = .06; n = 1/365.$

                                          MV $=$ $1,000,000(1.04)^{1/365}/(1.06)^{1/365}$

                                                $=$ $1,000,000(1.000107)/(1.000160)$

                                                $=$ $999,947.01$

This is a contrived example with an unrealistic difference in rates. However, it illustrates the point—there is only a \$53 difference in book versus market value.

Term Federal Funds Sold

Term federal funds sold (and securities purchased under agreement to resell) are slightly longer-term investments. Thus, the rate used to discount the cash flows has a more significant impact on market value. Figure 4–2 is a comparison of the publicly quoted commercial paper rates. These rates and other money market rates are closely related to the T-bill rate. As shown in the exhibit, the commercial paper rate is within 100 basis points of the T-bill rate except for those periods when interest rates are generally elevated.

Term federal funds sold are valued by the same model used for overnight transactions. This example is for a one-month contract:

Given: FF $=$ $1,000,000; k_c = .04; k = .045;$
                                                              $n = 31/365.$

                                          MV $=$ $1,000,000(1.04)^{31/365}/(1.045)^{31/365}$

                                                $=$ $1,000,000(1.003337)/(1.003745)$

                                                $=$ $999,593.52$

As the results indicate, there is still little difference between book and market values because of the short-term nature of the transaction.

Figure 4–2.

COMMERCIAL PAPER RATES
1961–1991

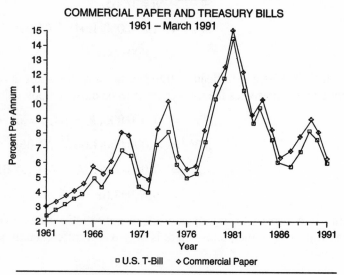

COMMERCIAL PAPER AND TREASURY BILLS
1961 – March 1991

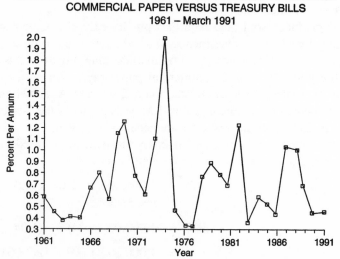

COMMERCIAL PAPER VERSUS TREASURY BILLS
1961 – March 1991

Source: Author's graphic based on data from U.S. Department of Commerce, Economics and Statistics Administration, *Business Statistics, 1961–1988* (1989) and *Survey of Current Business* (April 1991).

Securities Purchased under Agreement to Resell

The valuation model for these investments assumes that interest is earned on the securities while held by the bank.

$$MV = \sum_{t=1}^{n} \frac{CP_t}{\left(1+\dfrac{k}{m}\right)^t} + \frac{SP}{\left(1+\dfrac{k}{m}\right)^t}$$

where

CP_t	=	Coupon payment that the bank receives before resale
	=	$CR(M)/m$
CR	=	Coupon rate of securities purchased
M	=	Maturity value of securities purchased
SP	=	Selling price specified in resale agreement
n	=	Number of periods before resale
k	=	Appropriate discount rate

Consider the following example.

Given:		
SP	=	$1,050,000; $k = .045$; n = one six-month period; $m = 2$; $M = 1,000,000$; $CR = .05$.
CP_t	=	.05(1,000,000)/2
	=	25,000
MV	=	25,000/(1.0225) + 1,050,000/(1.0225)
	=	24,449.88 + 1,026,894.87
	=	1,051,344.75

In this case, the earned interest increases the market value of the investment.

INVESTMENT SECURITIES

Investment securities can have much longer maturities than temporary investments. Figure 4–3 compares short-term and long-term U.S. Treasury rates. The relationship between the rates cannot be predicted based on any consistent past

Figure 4–3.

SHORT- AND LONG-TERM U.S. TREASURY RATES
1961–1991

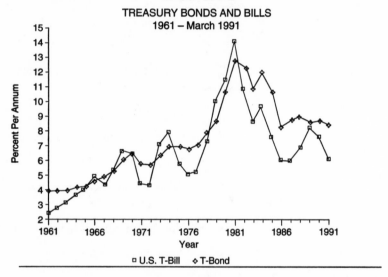

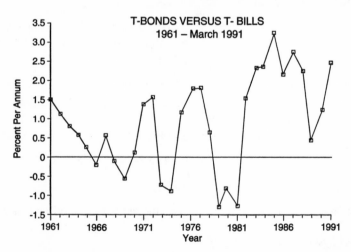

Source: Author's graphic based on data from U.S. Department of Commerce, Economics and Statistics Administration, *Business Statistics, 1961–1988* (1989) and *Survey of Current Business* (April 1991).

relationship. This is true because the yield curve is sometimes humped, that is, short-term rates are higher than long-term rates. The general rule is that the yield curve is upward sloping; that is, short-term rates are lower than long-term rates. The exception to this rule occurs when the rate of inflation is high. These situations are indicated in the exhibit in those years for which the difference between the T-bond rate and the T-bill rate is negative. Thus, unless there is unusually high inflation, the rates used to discount shorter-term instruments should be lower than the discount rates used for longer term instruments of the same type and/or risk class.

Treasury Bills

The market value of Treasury bills is easily obtained through market quotation because of the depth of the Treasury market. However, it is necessary to understand the basics of T-bill pricing.

$$MV = M - M(k)\left(\frac{N}{360}\right)$$
$$= M - D$$

where

M	=	Maturity or face value
k	=	Annual discount rate
N	=	Number of days until maturity
D	=	Discount from face value
	=	$M(k)(N/360)$

Because T-bills are issued on a discounted basis, the market value is always less than face value (minimum denomination $10,000). Original maturity never exceeds one year. Also, all other things being equal, the market value is necessarily greater than cost as time passes because the value increases as the maturity date approaches.

This example is a T-bill with an original maturity of six months purchased 82 days ago.

Given:	M	=	$10,000; k = .04; N = 100.$
	MV	=	$10,000 - 10,000(.04)(100/360)$
		=	$10,000 - 111.11$
		=	$9,888.89$

A second example is of a 12-month T-bill purchased 60 days ago.

Given: M = 10,000; k = .045; N = 300.

MV = 10,000 − 10,000(.0425)(300/360)

= 10,000 − 354.17

= 9,645.83

Treasury Notes

Like Treasury bills, Treasury notes are traded in a well-developed market. In contrast to Treasury bills, notes have original maturities for 2, 3, 5, 7, and 10 years. Another difference is that the vast majority of these securities pay interest on a semiannual basis. The model values both the annuity of interest payments and the maturity value (minimum denomination of $1,000).

$$MV = \sum_{t=1}^{n} \frac{\left(\dfrac{(M)(CR)}{m}\right)}{\left(1+\dfrac{k}{m}\right)^t} + \frac{M}{\left(1+\dfrac{k}{m}\right)^n}$$

where

M = Maturity or face value

CR = Coupon rate

m = Number of times per year interest is paid

= 2

$(M)(CR)/m$ = Periodic (semiannual) interest payments

n = Number of (semiannual) periods before maturity

k = Annual discount rate

Suppose that a bank holds Treasury notes with the following characteristics:

Given: M = 100,000; CR = .05; m = 2; k = .04; n = 6 (3 years).

The cash flows for these notes are shown in Figure 4–4. Notice that the maturity date of January 1, 1996, is exactly three years from the point of valuation, January 1, 1993.

$$MV = \left[\sum_{t=1}^{6}\frac{\frac{(100,000)(.05)}{2}}{(1.02)^t}\right] + \frac{100,000}{(1.02)^6}$$

$$= \left[\sum_{t=1}^{6}\frac{2,500}{(1.02)^t}\right] + \frac{100,000}{(1.02)^6}$$

$$= 2,500\left[\sum_{t=1}^{6}\frac{1}{(1.02)^t}\right] + \frac{100,000}{(1.02)^6}$$

$$= 2,500\left(PVIFA_{.02,6}\right) + \frac{100,000}{1.126162}$$

$$PVIFA_{.02,6} = \left(\frac{1}{.02}\right)\left(1 - \frac{1}{(1.02)^6}\right)$$

$$= 5.601431$$

$$MV = 2,500(5.601431) + 88,797.17$$

$$= 14,003.58 + 88,797.17$$

$$= 102,800.75$$

Figure 4–4.

THREE-YEAR U.S. TREASURY NOTES

			Date			
Jan. 1	July 1	Jan. 1	July 1	Jan. 1	July 1	Jan. 1
1993	1993	1994	1994	1995	1995	1996

			Time Line			
	$2,500	$2,500	$2,500	$2,500	$2,500	$2,500
						$100,000

Note: Time line describes $100,000 in 5 percent U.S. Treasury notes that pay interest semiannually and mature in exactly three years (six semiannual periods).

The market value of these notes is $102,800.75. The market quotation is not this exact amount because prices are stated as dollars and 32nds of a dollar per $100 of face value. Thus, the market quotation for these notes is between 102.25 or $102,781.25 (25/36 = .78125) and 102.26 or $102,812.50 (26/32 = .8125). Notice too that market value is higher than par value because the coupon rate exceeds the required return.

Now consider another example with the opposite relationship between coupon rate and required return.

Given: $M = 100,000; CR = .05; m = 2; k = .06;$
$n = 6.$

$$MV = \left[\sum_{t=1}^{6} \left(\frac{\frac{(100,000)(.05)}{2}}{(1.03)^t} \right) \right] + \frac{100,000}{(1.03)^6}$$

$$= 2,500\left(PVIFA_{.03,6} \right) + \frac{100,000}{1.194052}$$

$$PVIFA_{.03,6} = \left(\frac{1}{.03} \right)\left(1 - \frac{1}{(1.03)^6} \right)$$

$$= 5.417191$$

$$MV = 2,500(5.417191) + 83,748.45$$

$$= 13,542.98 + 83,748.45$$

$$= 97,291.43$$

The market value is $97,291.43. The market quotation is between 97.9 or $97,281.25 (9/32 = .28125) and 97.10 or $97,312.50 (10/32 = .3125). The market value of these notes is less than its par value because the required return exceeds the coupon rate.

In a third example, the two rates are equal.

Given: $M = 100,000; CR = .05; m = 2; k = .05; n = 6.$

$$MV = \left[\sum_{t=1}^{6} \frac{\frac{(100,000)(.05)}{2}}{(1.025)^t} \right] + \frac{100,000}{(1.025)^6}$$

$$= 2,500\left(PVIFA_{.025,6} \right) + \frac{100,000}{1.159634}$$

$$PVIFA_{.025, 6} = \left(\frac{1}{.025}\right)\left(1 - \frac{1}{(1.025)^6}\right)$$

$$= 5.508125$$

$$MV = 2,500(5.508125) + 86,229.69$$

$$= 13,770.31 + 86,229.69$$

$$= 100,000.00$$

These notes have a market value exactly equal to par value (price quotation 100 or $100,000) because of the equality between the coupon and required rates.

Bond Theorems: Coupon versus Discount Rate

These three examples illustrate basic principles with respect to bond pricing. Essentially, when the coupon rate equals the discount rate, a bond or note pays exactly the amount required by investors and its market value equals par. When the coupon rate is less than the discount rate, a bond pays less than the required amount and investors are not willing to pay the full face value for the bond. When the coupon rate is greater than the discount rate, a bond pays more than investors require and the market is willing to pay a premium for it. In other words, market forces adjust the price of a bond so that the bond yields exactly the required return.

These bond theorems are summarized as follows:

➤   If $CR = k$, then $MV = M$. When the coupon rate equals the required return, the bond sells at par value.

➤   If $CR < k$, then $MV < M$. When the coupon rate is less than the required return, the bond sells at a discount.

➤   If $CR > k$, then $MV > M$. When the coupon rate is greater than the required return, the bond sells at a premium.

Market Valuation between Coupon Dates

Figure 4–5 contains an example of Treasury notes being valued at a date that is not exactly one period before the next coupon payment. The point of valuation (POV) is January 1, 1993, while the next coupon payment will be made 45 days later on February 15. Because the maturity date is August 15, 1995, the time to maturity for these notes is two years and 7.5 months. The market valuation model is modified to account for this difference.

Figure 4–5.

TREASURY NOTES WITH THREE YEARS TO MATURITY VALUED BETWEEN COUPON DATES

			Date			
Jan. 1	Feb. 15	Aug. 15	Feb. 15	Aug. 15	Feb. 15	Aug. 15
1996	1996	1996	1997	1997	1998	1998

			Time Line			
0	.25	1.25	2.25	3.25	4.25	5.25
	$2,500	$2,500	$2,500	$2,500	$2,500	$2,500
						$100,000

Note: Time line describes $100,000 in 5 percent U.S. Treasury notes that pay interest semiannually and mature in two years, 7.5 months (5.25 semiannual periods).

$$MV = \left(\sum_{t=1}^{n+(1-p)} \frac{\left(\frac{(M)(CR)}{m} \right)}{\left(1+\frac{k}{m}\right)^{t}} \right) \left(1+\frac{k}{m}\right)^{(1-p)} + \frac{M}{\left(1+\frac{k}{m}\right)^{n}} + \frac{(M)(CR)}{m}(1-p)$$

where

p = Partial period until next interest payment

= (Number of days before next interest payment)/(total number of days per period)

n = Total number of periods before maturity, including full periods and partial period

$(1-p)$ = Partial period that has elapsed since last interest payment

$[(M)(CR)/m](1-p)$ = Interest accrued since last interest payment

Notice that the present value of the interest payments is computed for a whole number of periods—$(n + (1-p))$. That is, the present value of the interest payments is computed using a point of valuation that is immediately following the last interest payment, or $(1 - p)$ periods ago. Using this point of valuation makes it possible to use *PVIFA* factors for an integer (not fractional) number of periods and to correctly value all of the remaining interest payments. However, this valuation is valid only for $(1 - p)$ periods ago. To value these cash flows on the current date (time zero), it is necessary to compound the annuity results for $(1 - p)$ periods.

Figure 4–5 illustrates an example of a security being valued between coupon dates. The point of valuation (*POV*) is January 1, 1996, while the next coupon payment will be made 45 days later on February 15. Because the maturity date is August 15, 1998, the time to maturity for these notes is two years and 7.5 months.

Given: $M = 100,000;\ CR = .05;\ m = 2;\ k = .04;\ n = 5.25;$
$p = 45/182 = .24725 \cong .25;\ (1 - p) = (1 - .25) = .75.$

$$MV = \left[\sum_{t=1}^{(5.25+.75)} \frac{2,500}{(1.02)^t} \right]\left[(1.02)^{.75}\right] + \left[\frac{100,000}{(1.02)^{5.25}}\right] + \left[\frac{(100,000)(.05)}{2}\right](.75)$$

$$= 2,500\left(PVIFA_{.02,6}\right)(1.0149628) + \frac{100,000}{1.1095603} + 2,500(.75)$$

$$PVIFA_{.02,6} = \left(\frac{1}{.02}\right)\left(1 - \left\{\frac{1}{(1.02)^6}\right\}\right)$$

$$= 5.6014309$$

$$\therefore MV = 2,500(5.6014309)(1.049628) + 90,125.79 + 1,875$$

$$= 14,213.11 + 90,125.79 + 1,875$$

$$= 106,213.90$$

When the *POV* occurs between coupon payments, the market value includes the present value of future cash flows—adjusted for the partial period— and the interest already accrued.

Treasury Bonds

Treasury bonds have an original maturity of 10 to 30 years, typically pay interest semiannually, and have a minimum denomination of $1,000. Because of the similarities to Treasury notes, the market valuation model is the same as that described earlier. The differences involve the time to maturity and the required rate of return.

Given: $M = 100,000;\ CR = .085;\ m = 2;\ k = .075;$
$n = 56\ (28\ \text{years}).$

$$MV = \left[\sum_{t=1}^{56} \frac{\frac{(100,000)(.085)}{2}}{(1.0375)^t} \right] + \left[\frac{100,000}{(1.0375)^{56}} \right]$$

$$= 4,250 \left(PVIFA_{.0375,56} \right) + \frac{100,000}{7.858396}$$

$$PVIFA_{.0375,56} = \left(\frac{1}{.0375} \right) \left(1 - \left\{ \frac{1}{(1.0375)^{56}} \right\} \right)$$

$$= 23.273268$$

$$MV = 4,250(23.273268) + 12,725.24$$

$$= 98,911.39 + 12,725.24$$

$$= 111,636.63$$

These bonds sell at a premium as predicted by the bond theorems just discussed. The coupon rate is 100 basis points above the required return. However, the amount of the premium is greater than for the Treasury notes. In the case of the 5 percent notes discounted at 4 percent, the market values were $102,800.75 (notes with exactly six periods to maturity) and $104,343.55 (notes with 5.25 periods to maturity). The Treasury bonds have a higher premium because their time to maturity is longer.

Bond Theorem: Price Behavior over Time

Figure 4–6 shows the price behavior of a 5 percent bond that pays interest quarterly and matures in five years at various discount rates. When the discount rate is 6 percent and 20 quarters remain before maturity, the bond sells at $957.08, that is, at a discount as predicted by the bond theorems discussed previously. Assuming no change in the discount rate, as time passes the market value of the bond increases until it reaches $1,000. When the discount rate is 4 percent and 20 quarters remain before maturity, the market value of the bond is $1,045.11; that is, the bond sells at a premium. Over time, the market value declines until it reaches $1,000 at maturity. When the discount rate is 5 percent and equals the coupon rate, the bond sells at par throughout its life.

These observations can be summarized in the following bond theorem:

All other things being equal, the market value of a bond that is selling at a premium (discount) will decrease (increase) over time until market value equals par value at the time of maturity.

Figure 4–6.

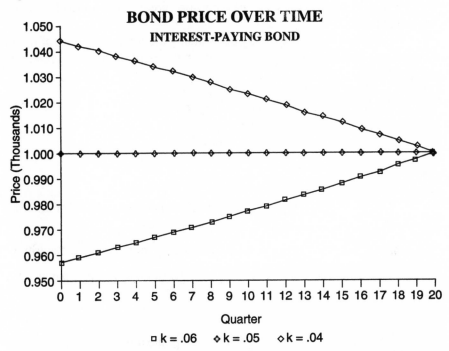

BOND PRICE OVER TIME
INTEREST-PAYING BOND

Price (Thousands) / Quarter

□ k = .06   ◇ k = .05   ◇ k = .04

Note: Exhibit shows the change in price over time of a 5 percent bond that pays interest
quarterly and has an original maturity of five years.

Government Agency Securities

The two primary classifications of government agency securities are pass-through certificates and mortgage-backed bonds. Generally, market quotations for government agency securities are readily available. Both types are mortgage related. However, their valuation is based on different patterns of cash flow.

Holders of pass-through securities receive a proportional share of the principal and interest payments from the underlying mortgages. Conceptually, this is equivalent to receiving an annuity. The actual term over which payments are received will not be the remaining time to maturity of the underlying mortgages, however. Mortgages are refinanced when market interest rates decline significantly and when the existing homes are sold to purchase new homes. As a result, the average term of a government agency security is typically less than 15 years.

The risk of prepayment is an important element in the market valuation of these securities. One approach to compensate for this risk is to increase the discount rate used, effectively reducing the market value. This is the approach used in this chapter. Another adjustment for prepayment, which is covered in Chapter 5, is to place a value on the embedded prepayment option by estimating prepayments.

Valuation is accomplished by determining the implied amount of monthly payments and discounting the value of this annuity at the appropriate discount rate.

$$MV = \frac{\sum_{t=1}^{n} CF_t}{\left(1 + \frac{k}{m}\right)^t}$$

where

CF_t = Implied monthly payment of interest and principal

n = Number of months before maturity

m = Number of times per year payments are made

  = 12

k = Appropriate discount rate

The appropriate discount rate should be related to other long-term yields, that is, bond yields. There is a difference in the frequency of payments between these two instruments, however. Bonds generally pay semiannual interest while mortgage pass-throughs pay monthly. As a result, a lower required rate on the mortgage provides the same effective return as the bond.

$$k_{EPT} = \left(1 + \frac{k_{PC}}{12}\right)^{12} - 1$$

where

k_{EPT} = Effective pass-through yield

k_{PT} = Stated pass-through yield

The first step is to establish the appropriate bond yield. The bond yield then is set equal to the effective pass-through yield and the equation is solved for the stated pass-through return. For example, suppose that an investor seeks the equivalent of a bond yield of 10.47 percent. Substituting this into the equation for effective pass-through yield,

$$.1047 = (1 + k_{PT}/12)^{12} - 1$$

$$1.1047 = (1 + k_{PT}/12)^{12}$$

$$1.1047^{1/12} = (1 + k_{PT}/12)$$

$$12(1.1047^{1/12} - 1) = k_{PT}$$

$$= .10$$

In the following example, the required return has been adjusted in this way.

Assume that a bank holds a portfolio of government agency pass-through securities with a face value of $1,000,000.

Given: $M = 1,000,000; CR = .08; m = 12; k = .10;$
                                $n = 360 = 12$ payments per year for
                                30 years.

(Notice that the 10 percent discount rate is substantially higher than the coupon rate to compensate for prepayment risk.)

The first step is to determine the implied monthly payment which will cause the present value of future cash flows to exactly equal $1,000,000 when using the 8 percent coupon rate.[1]

$$1,000,000 = CF_t(PVIFA_{.08/12,360})$$

$$CF_t = 1,000,000/(PVIFA_{.08/12,360})$$

$$PVIFA_{.08/12,360} = (1/(.08/12))(1 - \{1/(1 + .08/12)^{360}\})$$

$$= (1/.006667)(1 - \{1/(1.006667)^{360}\})$$

$$= 136.2783152$$

$$CF_t = 1,000,000/136.2783152$$

$$= 7,337.92$$

The market value of the securities is the present value of these implied monthly payments at the discount rate of 10 percent.

$$MV = \sum_{t=1}^{360} \frac{7,337.92}{\left(1 + \dfrac{.10}{12}\right)^t}$$

$$= (7{,}337.92)\sum_{t=1}^{360}\frac{1}{(1.008333)^t}$$

$$= (7{,}337.92)\left(PVIFA_{.008333,360}\right)$$

$$PVIFA_{.008333,360} = \left(\frac{1}{.0083333}\right)\left(1-\left\{\frac{1}{(1.0083333)^{360}}\right\}\right)$$

$$= 113.9512038$$

$$MV = 7{,}337.92(113.9512038)$$

$$= 836{,}164.82$$

Mortgage-backed bonds do not pay the principal and interest from the underlying mortgages. Instead, the bonds are collateralized by the mortgages, while paying interest and maturity value much like a Treasury or corporate bond. Because of this, the model for market valuation is the same as the model for Treasury bonds.

Municipal Bonds
Municipal bonds also are valued in the same manner as Treasury bonds. One important difference, however, is the required rate of return. Because the interest income from municipal bonds is exempt from federal taxation, the required return is lower than for Treasury bonds. Figure 4–7 compares the two rates and shows that in recent years, Treasury bond rates have exceeded municipal rates by at least 100 basis points.

Another important feature is that some municipal bonds are callable; that is, they can be redeemed by the issuer prior to the original maturity date. The call feature is essentially an option owned by the bond issuer. The value of this embedded option is discussed in the following chapter. This chapter describes the valuation of (1) noncallable bonds and (2) bonds for which there has already been an advance refunding.

The model for a noncallable bond is the same as for Treasury notes and bonds.

$$MV = \sum_{t=1}^{n}\frac{\left(\dfrac{(M)(CR)}{m}\right)}{\left(1+\dfrac{k}{m}\right)^t} + \frac{M}{\left(1+\dfrac{k}{m}\right)^n}$$

Figure 4–7.

MUNICIPAL BOND RATES
1961–1991

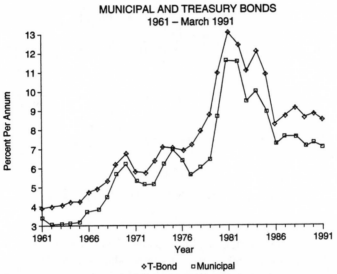

MUNICIPAL AND TREASURY BONDS
1961 – March 1991

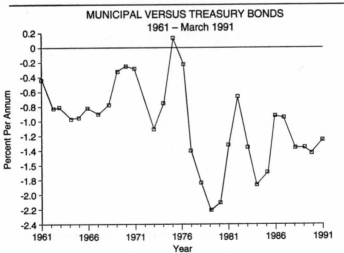

MUNICIPAL VERSUS TREASURY BONDS
1961 – March 1991

Source: Author's graphic based on data from U.S. Department of Commerce, Economics
and Statistics Administration, *Business Statistics, 1961–1988* (1989) and *Survey of
Current Business* (April 1991).

Assume that municipal bonds issued 5 years ago have 15 years remaining to maturity.

Given: M = 50,000; $CR = .07$; $m = 4$; $k = .05$;
                                        $n = 60$.

$$MV = \sum_{t=1}^{60} \left\{ \frac{\frac{(50,000)(.07)}{4}}{(1.0125)^t} \right\} + \left[\frac{50,000}{(1.0125)^{60}} \right]$$

$$= 875\left(PVIFA_{.0125,60} \right) + \frac{50,000}{2.107181}$$

$$PVIFA_{.0125,60} = \left(\frac{1}{.025} \right)\left(1 - \left\{ \frac{1}{(1.025)^{60}} \right\} \right)$$

$$= 42.03459179$$

$$MV = 875(42.03459179) + 23,728.38$$

$$= 60,508.65$$

Now assume the municipal bonds issued 5 years ago are callable and have call protection for a total of 10 years or another 5 years from now—year 0. If called in year 6, the bonds will be redeemed at 103, that is, for par value plus a call premium of 3. Because market interest rates are low, the bond issuers have structured an advance refunding, whereby new bonds have already been issued and the proceeds placed in trust until the first call date five years from now. The valuation model reflects these circumstances.

where

                    c = Number of periods before the first call
                             date.

$$MV = \sum_{t=1}^{c} \frac{\left(\frac{(M)(CR)}{m} \right)}{\left(1 + \frac{k}{m} \right)^t} + \frac{CP}{\left(1 + \frac{k}{m} \right)^c}$$

                    CP = Call price on first call date.

Given: M = 50,000; $CR = .07$; $m = 4$; $k = .05$;
                             $n = 60$; $c = 20$; $CP = 51,500$ (103% of
                             face value).

$$MV = \sum_{t=1}^{20} \left\{ \frac{\dfrac{(50,000)(.07)}{4}}{(1.0125)^t} \right\} + \left[\frac{51,500}{(1.0125)^{20}} \right]$$

$$= 875 \left(PVIFA_{.0125,20} \right) + \frac{51,500}{1.282037}$$

$$PVIFA_{.0125,40} = \left(\frac{1}{.0125} \right) \left(1 - \left\{ \frac{1}{(1.0125)^{20}} \right\} \right)$$

$$= 17.599316$$

$$MV = 875(17.599316) + 40,170.45$$

$$= 55,569.85$$

Under an advance refunding, the market value of municipal bonds is generally lower than it would be otherwise. As shown in this example, this is true even when the bonds will be called at a premium.

Zero-Coupon Bonds

Any entity can elect to issue a zero-coupon bond; that is, one which does not pay interim interest payments before maturity. The valuation model considers only the final principal payoff.

$$MV = \frac{M}{(1+k)^n}$$

where

M = Maturity value

n = Number of years until maturity

Consider two examples.

Given: M = 100,000; $k = .05$; $n = 10$.

MV = $100,000(1/(1.05)^{10})$

= $100,000(.613913)$

= $61,391.33$

Given: M = 100,000; $k = .05$; $n = 30$.

MV = $100,000(1/(1.05)^{30})$

$$= \ 100{,}000(.2313775)$$

$$= \ 23{,}137.75$$

These market values are substantially less than face value because there are no interest payments. The longer the time to maturity, the lower the market value. Unlike interest-paying bonds, zero-coupon bonds always sell below par. Figure 4–8 illustrates the way the price of a zero-coupon bond increases as its maturity date approaches. A bond with five years to maturity with a required return of 4 percent has a market value of $819.54. For the higher rates of 5 percent and 6 percent, the market values are lower.

Bond Theorem: Discount Rate and Price
The price behavior of the bonds in Figure 4–8 is not restricted to zero-coupon

Figure 4–8.

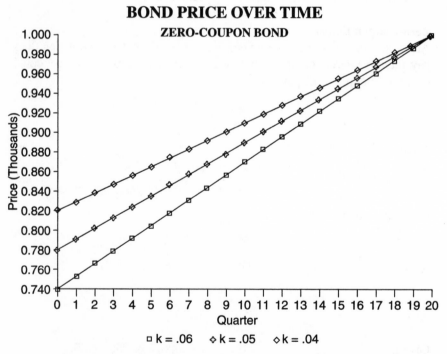

Note: Exhibit shows the change in price over time of a zero-coupon bond that has an original maturity of five years.

bonds. In general, the higher the discount rate used, the lower the price. The lower the discount rate used, the higher the price. The following is the basic principle:

> There is an inverse relationship between changes in the discount rate used and changes in the price of a bond.

This and the other theorems with respect to bond pricing apply to the pricing of loans as well.

LOANS

The investment securities portfolio contains financial instruments that have readily accessible market quotations. The loan portfolio is even more significant in terms of bank investment, but has much less readily available market information. The categories for which market models have been developed are:

➤ Commercial loans.
➤ Mortgage loans.
➤ Consumer installment loans.
➤ Lease financing.
➤ Nonaccrual loans.

Commercial Loans

Anticipated cash flows for commercial loans are contractually set and these form the basis for market valuation. The discount rate should be based on current interest rates, the time to maturity, and the risk characteristics of the borrowers in the pool of loans being valued. Figure 4–9 compares the short-term prime interest rate to the T-bill rate. The prime rate is the rate that banks charge their best, most creditworthy commercial customers, although loans are sometimes made at rates below prime. Prime also acts as the basis for pricing other commercial loans to smaller businesses. During the inflationary period of the early 1980s, the prime rate was almost 500 basis points above the T-bill rate. In recent years, however, prime has been within 200 to 300 basis points of the T-bill rate. Of course, if a pool of commercial clients has a higher risk profile, a larger differential is justified.

The terms of commercial loans can vary significantly but most fall into one of the following general classifications:

➤ Bullet loans.
➤ Working capital lines of credit.
➤ Term loans.

Figure 4–9.

COMMERCIAL LOAN RATES
1961–1991

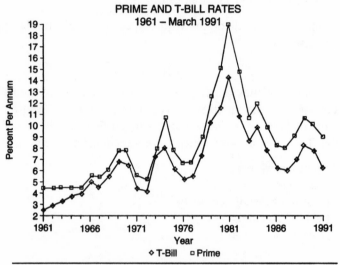

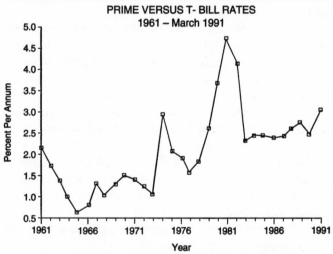

Source: Author's graphic based on data from U.S. Department of Commerce, Economics and Statistics Administration, *Business Statistics, 1961–1988* (1989) and *Survey of Current Business* (April 1991).

Bullet loans. Bullet loans require no payment of interest or principal until the loan matures. The market value of these loans is the present value of the future payoff of interest and principal.

$$MV = \frac{L\left(1+\dfrac{k_L}{m}\right)^n}{\left(1+\dfrac{k}{m}\right)^n}$$

where

L = Loan amount

k_L = Loan rate

n = Number of periods before loan matures

m = Number of times per year interest is compounded

The first example illustrates annual compounding.

Given: L = 250,000; k_L = .09; m = 1; k = .08; n = 5.

MV = $250{,}000(1.09)^5/(1.08)^5$

= $250{,}000(1.538624)/(1.469328)$

= 261,790.42

The second example compounds interest quarterly.

Given: L = 250,000; k_L = .075; m = 4; k = .08; n = 20 (five years).

MV = $250{,}000(1+.075/4)^{20}/(1+.08/4)^{20}$

= $250{,}000(1.449948)/(1.485947)$

= 243,943.42

Working capital lines of credit. These short-term lending arrangements involve a loan amount that will change. At any given point in time, however, the value of the portfolio of lines of credit must be based on actual borrowings outstanding and an estimate of when these balances will be repaid. These estimates are most appropriately based on past experience with these loans. In addition to normal interest payments, commitment fees are assessed on unused portions of the lines. These fees usually are stated in terms of percent per annum as are interest rates. The valuation model considers both the borrowings and the unused portion of the line.

$$MV = \frac{A(1+k_{LC})^n + (MX-A)\left((1+k_{CF})^n - 1\right)}{(1+k)^n}$$

where

$$A \;=\; \text{Actual borrowings to date}$$

$$MX \;=\; \text{Maximum credit available}$$

$$k_{LC} \;=\; \text{Interest rate on borrowings}$$

$$k_{CF} \;=\; \text{Commitment fee}$$

$$n \;=\; \text{Average maturity of lines of credit or average time before they are paid off}$$

Consider a portfolio of credit lines that have an average maturity of nine months.

Given: $A \;=\; 2{,}000{,}000; MX = 5{,}000{,}000;$
                $k_{LC} = .10; k_{CF} = .01; k = .105; n = .75$

$MV \;=\; [2{,}000{,}000(1.10)^{.75}$
$+ (5{,}000{,}000 - 2{,}000{,}000)$
$((1.01)^{.75} - 1)]/(1.105)^{.75}$

$\;=\; [(2{,}000{,}000)(1.0740995)$

$+ (3{,}000{,}000)(.0074907)]/(1.0777591)$

$\;=\; 2{,}014{,}059.64$

Term loans. Term loans are extended for periods of time in excess of one year. They are generally structured in one of two formats, as installment loans or as interest-only loans.

The market value of an installment loan is the present value of the payment annuity. The amount of the payment for a given loan is determined by the contractual loan rate and time to maturity.

$$MV = \left(\frac{L}{PVIFA_{\left(\frac{k_L}{m}, n\right)}} \right)\left(PVIFA_{\left(\frac{k}{m}, n\right)} \right)$$

where

L = Loan amount

m = Number of times per year that payments are made

n = Number of periods before maturity

$L/PVIFA_{k/m,n}$ = Periodic loan payment

Consider a three-year loan with quarterly payments.

Given:
L = 1,000,000; $k_L = .11$; $k = .105$; $m = 4$; $n = 12$.

MV = $[1,000,000/PVIFA_{.11/4,12}]$

$[PVIFA_{.105/4,12}]$

$PVIFA_{.11/4,12}$ = $(1/(.11/4))(1 - \{1/(1 + .11/4)^{12}\})$

= $(36.363636)(1 - .7221344)$

= 10.10420354

$PVIFA_{.105/4,12}$ = $(1/(.105/4))(1 - \{1/(1 + .105/4)^{12}\})$

= $(38.0952381)(1 - .732760345)$

= 10.18055829

MV = $[1,000,000/10.10420354]$

$[10.18055829]$

= $1,007,556.73$

The market value of an interest-only loan is the value of the interest payments and the payoff at the end of the term. In this sense, this type of loan is valued in the same way as an interest-paying bond.

$$MV = L\left(\frac{k_L}{m}\right)\left(PVIFA_{\left(\frac{k}{m},n\right)}\right) + \frac{L}{\left(1+\dfrac{k}{m}\right)^n}$$

where

$$L(k_L/m) \quad = \quad \text{Periodic interest payment}$$

Consider a three-year loan that compounds interest semiannually.

Given: $\qquad\qquad\quad L \;=\; 1,000,000; k_L = .11; k = .105; m = 2;$
$\qquad\qquad\qquad\qquad\quad n = 6.$

$$MV \;=\; [1,000,000(.11/2)(PVIFA_{.105/2,6})]$$
$$\qquad\qquad + [1,000,000/(1+.105/2)^6]$$

$$PVIFA_{.105/2,6} \;=\; (1/(.105/2))$$
$$\qquad\qquad (1-\{1/(1+.105/2)^6\})$$
$$\;=\; (19.047619)(1-.73564345)$$
$$\;=\; 5.0353628$$
$$MV \;=\; [(55,000)(5.0353628)]$$
$$\qquad\qquad + 735,643.45$$
$$\;=\; 1,012,588.40$$

A portfolio of term loans should be separated into the two classifications of installment and interest-only loans. In this way, each classification can be analyzed in terms of total balance, average loan rate, and average time to maturity.

Mortgage Loans
Mortgage loans are long-term loans secured by real estate. Until recently, the pricing of these loans had involved fairly stable interest rates especially when compared to long-term U.S. Treasury securities. Figure 4–10 shows the trend of new home mortgage rates over time and their spread over T-bond rates. Until the early 1980s, mortgage rates were consistently 150 to 200 basis points above T-bond rates. The 1980s first brought extremely high mortgage rates. For example, the average new home mortgage rate reached 14.5 percent with a 226 basis point spread over T-bonds. Then mortgage rates fell, at times falling

Figure 4–10.

HOME MORTGAGE RATES
1961–1991

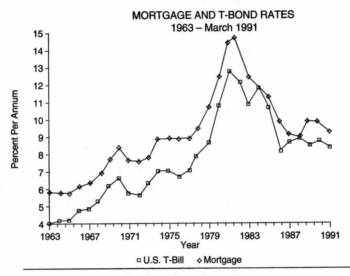

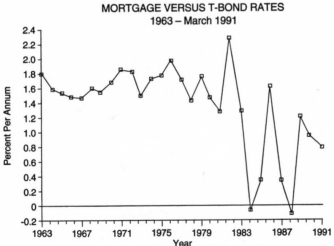

Source: Author's graphic based on data from U.S. Department of Commerce, Economics and Statistics Administration, *Business Statistics, 1961–1988* (1989) and *Survey of Current Business* (April 1991).

below Treasury bond rates. Given recent rate trends, a reasonable approach to pricing mortgage loans should include discount rates that do not exceed long-term Treasury bond rates by more than 100 basis points.

Both residential and commercial mortgage loans are governed by the same principles of market valuation. However, the two types of mortgages should be kept separate because they have significantly different risk profiles that affect discount rate selection. Within each of the two categories, subgrouping should include loans with common characteristics. The four subgroups are:

➤ Fixed-rate mortgages.
➤ Adjustable-rate mortgages (ARMs).
➤ Graduated payment mortgages (GPMs).
➤ Balloon mortgages.

Fixed-Rate Mortgages. The traditional home mortgage is a fixed-rate instrument with an original maturity of 25 to 30 years. The market value of a portfolio of such loans depends on the implied periodic (usually monthly) payment and the average time to maturity.

$$MV = \left(\frac{L}{PVIFA_{\left(\frac{k_L}{m},n\right)}} \right) \left(PVIFA_{\left(\frac{k}{m},n\right)} \right)$$

where

$L/PVIFA_{k/m,n}$ = Implied periodic payment based on the loan amount (L) and the contractual mortgage rate

The following is an example of a 25-year mortgage to be repaid in monthly installments.

Given:

$$L = 150{,}000; k_m = .10; k = .08; n = 300.$$

$$MV = (150{,}000/PVIFA_{.10/12,300})$$

$$(PVIFA_{.08/12,300})$$

$$PVIFA_{.10/12,300} = (1/.0083333)$$

$$(1 - \{1/(1.0083333)^{300}\})$$

$$= (120)(1 - .0829406)$$

$$= 110.047128$$

$$PVIFA_{.08/12,300} = (1/.0066667)$$
$$(1 - \{1/(1.0066667)^{300}\})$$
$$= (149.999)(1 - .1362352)$$
$$= 129.5638562$$
$$MV = (150,000/110.047128)(129.5638562)$$
$$= 176,602.32$$

If the borrower decides to prepay this mortgage, however, its true market value will not be $176,602.32. The same principle applies as with the advance refunding of a municipal bond. If it is repaid prior to the original maturity date, its market value declines. Unlike advance refunding, the bank does not know whether this particular loan will be prepaid. The borrower owns an option to prepay but is not obligated to do so. The value of this embedded option is described in Chapter 5.

Adjustable-rate mortgages. The loan rates for adjustable-rate mortgages (ARMs) vary with market interest rates. The rate adjustments are often made twice a year. As a result, the market value of a portfolio of ARMs is close to book value because the loan (coupon) rate is close to the market (required) rate.

These rate adjustments cause ARMs to be less subject to prepayments that are motivated by interest rate changes. However, if the loan contract includes interest rate caps (ceiling—maximum rate, floor—minimum rate, or collar—cap and floor), these provisions constitute options owned either by the borrower or the bank. These embedded options also are evaluated in Chapter 5.

Graduated payment mortgages. These mortgages are primarily fixed-rate instruments. Graduated payment mortgages (GPMs) allow the borrower to make smaller payments in the early years of the loan. Typically, payments increase over the first 5 to 10 years and then level off to a constant payment thereafter. During the early years, the payment reductions are added to the unpaid balance. The market valuation of GPMs depends on the precise cash flow stream to the bank. Thus, the actual payments must be analyzed.

$$MV = \sum_{t=1}^{g} \frac{\left(\dfrac{L}{PVIFA_{\left(\frac{k_L}{m},n\right)}} - PR_t \right)}{\left(1+\dfrac{k}{m}\right)^t} + \frac{\left(\left(\dfrac{L}{PVIFA_{\left(\frac{k}{m},n\right)}} \right)\left(PVIFA_{\left(\frac{k}{m},n-g\right)} \right) + \sum_{t=1}^{g} PR_t \right)}{PVIFA_{\left(\frac{k}{m},n-g\right)}}$$

$$* \left(PVIFA_{\left(\frac{k}{m}, n-g\right)} \right) * \left(\frac{1}{\left(1+\frac{k}{m}\right)^g} \right)$$

where

n	$=$	Total number of payments
m	$=$	Number of payments per year
g	$=$	Periods with graduated payments
PR_t	$=$	Payment reduction in period t
$L/PVIFA_{k/m,n}$	$=$	Normal monthly payment
$(L/PVIFA_{k/m,n})(PVIFA_{k/m,n-g})$	$=$	Unpaid loan balance after g periods under the normal amortization schedule
$\sum_{t=1}^{g} PR_t$	$=$	Total amount of payment reductions to be added to unpaid balance at period g

The following example illustrates the stages of this valuation process by analyzing:

➤ Normal amortization schedule.
➤ Amount of negative amortization during the early years.
➤ Necessary payment during the later years.
➤ Present value of all payments.

Given: L = $150,000; k_m = .10; k = .08; m = 12; n = 300; monthly PR = $250 in year 1, $200 in year 2, $150 in year 3, $100 in year 4, and $50 in year 5.[2]

The normal monthly payment for this loan is $1,363.05.

$$L = Pymt \left[(1/(k_m/m)) \right.$$
$$\left. (1-\{1/(1 + k_m/m)^n\}) \right]$$
$$150,000 = Pymt \left[110.047128 \right]$$
$$1,363.05 = Pymt$$

Table 4–1 shows the loan balance at the end of each year under the normal amortization schedule. These balances are computed as the present value of the remaining payments at the end of each year. Under the normal amortization schedule, the unpaid balance declines from $150,000 at time 0 to $141,245.54 by the end of year 5.

The graduated payments are lower than $1,363.05, however. Each of the first year's payments is $1,113.05 ($1,363.05 – $250) and each payment in the second year is $1,163.05 ($1,363.05 – $200). The payments increase by $50 each

Table 4–1.

GRADUATED PAYMENT MORTGAGE:
NORMAL AMORTIZATION FIRST 60 PAYMENTS

End of Year	Present Value of Remaining Payments	Unpaid Balance
0		$150,000.00
1	$1363.05(PVIFA_{.10/12,288})$ $= 1363.05(109.005045)$	148,579.33
2	$1363.05(PVIFA_{.10/12,276})$ $= 1363.05(107.85337295)$	147,010.03
3	$1363.05(PVIFA_{.10/12,264})$ $= 1363.05(106.5818563)$	145,276.40
4	$1363.05(PVIFA_{.10/12,252})$ $= 1363.05(105.1768013)$	143,361.24
5	$1363.05(PVIFA_{.10/12,240})$ $= 1363.05(103.6246187)$	141,245.54

Note: Exhibit represents the normal amortization of a 25-year, $150,000 mortgage during the first five years. Monthly payments are based on a mortgage loan rate of 10 percent:

$$PV = (1/(k_m/m))(1-\{1/(1 + k_m/m)^n\})$$

where k_m = Mortgage loan rate = .10
            m = Payments per year = 12
   150,000 = *Pymt* [110.047128]
   1363.05 = *Pymt*

year so that the monthly payment in year 5 is \$1,313.05. This is a total of \$9,000 in payment reductions, or negative amortization, over the five-year period.

Table 4–2 shows how the loan balance increases to \$150,245.54 by the end of year 5. This amount must be amortized over the remaining 240 months.

$$PV = Pymt(PVIFA_{k/m,n})$$

$$Pymt = PV/(PVIFA_{k/m,n})$$

$$= 150,245.54/PVIFA_{.10/12,240}$$

Table 4–2.

GRADUATED PAYMENT MORTGAGE:
NEGATIVE AMORTIZATION FIRST 60 PAYMENTS

Year	Balance under Normal Amortization		Negative Amortization	
	Beginning	Ending	During Year[1]	New Balance[2]
0		\$150,000.00		
1	\$150,000.00	148,579.33	\$3,000	\$151,579.33
2	148,579.33	147,010.03	2,400	152,410.03
3	147,010.03	145,276.40	1,800	152,476.40
4	145,276.40	143,361.24	1,200	151,761.24
5	143,361.24	141,245.54	600	150,245.54
			\$9,000	

[1]
The normal payment is reduced by a flat amount each month during the first 60 months:

Year	Monthly Reduction
1	\$250
2	200
3	150
4	100
5	50

[2]
The new balance under negative amortization equals the ending balance under normal amortization plus the cumulative payment reductions.

$$= \ 150,245.54/103.624619$$

$$= \ 1,449.90$$

The market value of this loan is the present value of the first 60 payments plus the present value of the 240 at $1,449.90 each.

$$PV_{240 \ payments} \ = \ 1,449.90(PVIFA_{.08/12,240})$$

$$= \ 1,449.90(119.554292)$$

$$= \ 173,341.77$$

Because the first payment in this annuity occurs in period 61, the point of valuation is period 60. Thus, the $173,341.77 must be discounted for 60 periods to time 0.

$$PV \ = \ 173,341.77(1/(1 + .08/12)^{60})$$

$$= \ 173,341.77(.67121043)$$

$$= \ 116,348.80$$

To this balance must be added the present value of the first 60 payments. Table 4–3 shows that the value of these payments at time 0 is $59,433.57. The value of this loan is, therefore, $175,782.37.

$$MV \ = \ 59,433.57 + 116,348.80$$

$$= \ 175,782.37$$

Valuing a portfolio of these loans requires an assessment of the payments to be received during the negative amortization period and the payments to be made thereafter. This is best accomplished by separating the loans that are still in the negative amortization phase from those that have reached the stable payment phase.

Balloon mortgages. Balloon mortgages are shorter-term loans that require a large payment at the end of the term of the loan. They are generally of two types; interest-only loans and amortized loans

Interest-only loans are similar to bonds that pay interest during the life of the loan and the entire principal at the end of the term.

$$MV = \frac{(L)\left(\dfrac{k_m}{m}\right)}{PVIFA_{\left(\frac{k_L}{m},n\right)}} + \frac{L}{\left(1+\dfrac{k}{m}\right)^n}$$

where

$$L = \text{Loan amount}$$

$$(L)(k_m/m) = \text{Periodic interest payment}$$

An example of annual interest payments illustrates this application.

Given:

$$L = 100,000; k_m = .09; k = .095; m = 1; n = 5.$$

$$MV = 100,000(.09)(PVIFA_{.095,5})$$

$$+ 100,000(1/(1.095)^5)$$

$$= 9,000(3.839709)$$

$$+ 100,000(.6352277)$$

$$= 34,557.38 + 63,522.77$$

$$= 98,080.15$$

Table 4–3.

GRADUATED PAYMENT MORTGAGE: PRESENT VALUE OF FIRST 60 PAYMENTS

Year	Monthly Payment	Pymt(PVIFA)[1]	POV[2]	PVIF[3]	Present Value of Payments[4]
1	$1,113.05	$12,795.38	0	1.0000000	$12,795.38
2	1,163.05	13,370.17	12	.9233615	12,345.50
3	1,213.05	13,944.96	24	.8525964	11,889.42
4	1,263.05	14,519.75	36	.7872546	11,430.74
5	1,313.05	15,094.54	48	.7269206	10,972.53
					$59,433.57

[1]   Factor is computed for the combination of 8 percent and 12 periods.

[2]   Point of valuation (*POV*) for a present value annuity factor is one period before the first cash flow in the annuity.

[3]   Factor is computed for the combination of 8 percent and the number of periods between the *POV* and time 0.

[4]   Value of the payments at time 0 is the product of the present value of the annuity (*Pymt(PVIFA)*) and the present value interest factor of a single amount (*PVIF*).

On the other hand, the payments for an amortizing balloon mortgage are established as if the loan will be repaid over a longer period of time, perhaps 30 years, while the balance is due after a shorter period of time.

$$MV = \left(\frac{L}{PVFA\left(\frac{k_L}{m}, n\right)} \right)\left(PVFA\left(\frac{k}{m}, b\right) \right) + \frac{B}{\left(1 + \frac{k}{m}\right)^b}$$

where

n = Number of periods over which the interim payments are set up

$(L/PVIFA_{k/m,n})$ = Periodic payment of interest and principal

b = Number of periods that will elapse before the date of the balloon payment

B = Amount of the balloon payment

= $(L/PVIFA_{k/m,n})(PVIFA_{k/m,n-b})$

= Value of the remaining payments

Some loan rates may be set below market for this type of loan because of the early payoff. The market value of the loan is the present value of the periodic payments and the balloon payment.

Consider a loan that is to be amortized over 30 years with a balloon payment after year 5.

Given: $L = 100,000$; $k_m = .07$; $k = .095$; $n = 360$; $b = 60$.

Monthly payment = $100,000/PVIFA_{.07/12,360}$

= $100,000/150.307568$

= 665.30

PV of payments = $665.30(PVIFA_{.095/12,60})$

= $665.30(47.614827)$

= $31,678.14$

B = $665.30(PVIFA_{.07/12,300})$

= $665.30(141.486903)$

= $94,131.24$

PV of B = $94,131.24/(1/(1 + .095/12)^{60})$

$$= \quad 94{,}131.24(.6230493)$$

$$= \quad 58{,}648.40$$

$$MV \quad = \quad 31{,}678.14 + 58{,}648.40$$

$$= \quad 90{,}326.54$$

When valuing a portfolio of balloon mortgages, it is necessary to determine the total loan amount, the average loan (coupon) rate, and the average loan term over which the payments have been set up. This information forms the basis of the estimate of the periodic payment. These implied payments are received until the average date of the balloon payment. The implied payments should then be discounted at the market rate. The average balloon payment is the value of the remaining payments as of the balloon payment date. This average must be discounted to time 0.

These valuation approaches for mortgage loans are cost effective and theoretically sound. The loans in each category have similar characteristics with respect to cash flow pattern and as long as the residential mortgages are separated from the commercial portfolio, differences in risk are minimized.

Consumer Installment Loans

The most common consumer installment loan is an automobile loan. These loans are valued as annuities in the same way as fixed-rate mortgage loans. The valuation model is as follows:

$$MV = \left(\frac{L}{PVIFA_{\left(\frac{k_L}{m}, n \right)}} \right) \left(PVIFA_{\left(\frac{k}{m}, n \right)} \right)$$

The following is an example of a four-year loan with monthly payments.

Given: $L \quad = \quad 20{,}000; \ k_L = .15; \ k = .13; \ n = 48.$

$$MV \quad = \quad (20{,}000/PVIFA_{.15/12,48})$$

$$(PVIFA_{.13/12,48})$$

$$= \quad (20{,}000/35.9314809)(37.2751898)$$

$$= \quad (556.61)(37.2751898)$$

$$= \quad 20{,}747.74$$

Consumer loans are subject to prepayment risk but not to the same extent as mortgage loans because consumer installment borrowers are less interest rate sensitive than mortgage borrowers.

Lease Financing

Lease financing is similar to purchase financing with the exception that the borrower must pay a residual value at the end of the term of the lease to obtain ownership of the asset. Commercial leases should be separated from consumer leases for purposes of market valuation because the collateral and risk profiles of portfolios may be quite different. Once separated, however, the principles of market valuation are the same.

The residual value is similar to a balloon payment in a mortgage. The difference is that the residual is not a legal obligation of the borrower. At the end of the lease, the borrower may elect to not pay the residual and relinquish possession of the asset. Because the bank would then sell the asset, it is vital that the residual used for valuation purposes be a realistic estimate of the fair market value at the end of the lease term.

The market value of a lease is the present value of lease payments plus the present value of the residual.

$$MV = \left(\frac{L}{PVIFA_{\left(\frac{k_L}{m},n\right)}}\right)\left(PVIFA_{\left(\frac{k}{m},n\right)}\right) + \frac{R}{\left(\frac{k}{m}\right)^n}$$

where

$$L \;=\; \text{Loan amount}$$

$$=\; \text{Amount to be amortized}$$

$$(L/PVIFA_{k/m,n}) \;=\; \text{Periodic payment of interest and principal}$$

$$R \;=\; \text{Residual value}$$

Consider the lease for a major piece of equipment to be leased over five years.

Given:

$$L \;=\; 1,000,000; R = 500,000; k_L = .12;$$
$$k = .10; n = 60.$$

$$MV \;=\; (1,000,000/PVIFA_{.12/12,60})$$

$$(PVIFA_{.10/12,60})$$

$$+ 500{,}000(1/(1 + .10/12)^{60})$$
$$= (1{,}000{,}000/44.955038)(47.065369)$$
$$+ 500{,}000(.6077886)$$
$$= 1{,}046{,}943.15 + 303{,}894.30$$
$$= 1{,}350{,}837.45$$

This example is for a commercial lease. Most consumer leases are for automobiles and their terms can vary with respect to the amount to be amortized relative to the original value of the asset. The key to appropriate market valuation of leases is the estimate of average residual value.

Nonaccrual or Impaired Loans
Because of their nature, the market valuation of nonaccrual or impaired loans must be accomplished through close examination of the portfolio. It may be necessary to adjust the contractual cash flows downward to a more reasonable estimate of actual anticipated receipts. It may necessary to increase the discount rate by some risk premium that is higher than normal. Once these issues have been addressed, the market value of nonaccrual loans is the present value of the adjusted cash flows.

$$MV = \sum_{t=1}^{n} \frac{CF_t}{(1+k)^t}$$

where

CF_t = Adjusted anticipated cash flow in year t

k = Normal discount rate plus an additional risk premium

Reserve for Loan Loss
The market value of the reserve for loan loss is directly linked to the market value of loans. If credit risk has been incorporated into the discount rate for loan valuation, then the reserve for loan loss is not necessary for valuation purposes.

On the other hand, if credit risk has not been explicitly considered in the discount rate, an estimate of the reserve for loan loss is required. An objective approach to valuing the reserve is to set it equal to the same percentage of the market value of loans as the book reserve is to the book value of loans. In any event, as long as the assumptions used in valuing the reserve are consistent with assumptions used for valuing the loans themselves, the estimate is reasonable.

OTHER ASSETS

Bank premises and equipment do not lend themselves to a present value analysis because they are not financial assets that yield measurable cash flows. Their market valuation is best estimated by professional appraisals. *Other real estate owned* is another category of assets that should be valued via up-to-date appraisal.

Investments in subsidiaries can be evaluated using present value analysis. It is necessary to first value the assets and liabilities of the subsidiary at market. In this way, an implied (market value) equity of the subsidiary may be established. The parent bank's asset is then the proportional share of the implied equity of the subsidiary.

All of the models discussed in the previous sections for the market valuation of commercial bank assets yield close approximations. They are especially useful for assets with little secondary market price information. In the cases for which there is ample market data, the models are useful in predicting changes in the market value of assets when interest rates change—the subject of Chapter 7.

LIABILITIES

The market value of bank liabilities is closer to the book value because most are relatively short-term and some are due on demand. The largest divergence of market value from book value is in long-term borrowings. The major categories of liabilities are:

➤ Deposits due on demand, including transactions and savings accounts.
➤ Time deposits.
➤ Short-term borrowings.
➤ Long-term borrowings.

Transactions and Savings Accounts

Transactions accounts are legally due on demand at book value; savings accounts are effectively due on demand at book value because the notification requirement is generally waived. Market value of these liabilities is equivalent to book value.

Time Deposits

Time deposits include both small and large time deposits with maturities from seven days to seven years or more. The market value depends on the face amount of the deposit, the deposit rate, the time to maturity, and the appropriate discount rate.

$$MV = \frac{D\left(1+\dfrac{k_D}{m}\right)^n}{\left(1+\dfrac{k}{m}\right)^n}$$

where

D = Deposit amount

k_D = Deposit rate

m = Number of times per year interest is paid or compounded

Consider the example of a large two-year CD.

Given: D = 1,000,000; k_D = .06; k = .065; m = 4; n = 8.

MV = 1,000,000$(1.015)^8(1/(1.01625)^8)$

= 1,000,000(1.12649259)

(.87901347)

= 990,202.16

Notice that even with a 50-basis-point difference between the deposit rate and the discount rate, the market value of this CD is 99.02 percent of the book value. This example illustrates the effect of short-term liabilities.

Short-Term Borrowings

Short-term borrowings include *federal funds purchased* (overnight), term *federal funds purchased*, and *securities sold under agreement to repurchase*. These are liabilities with a maturity of well under one year. As a result, the difference between book value and market value is small. The actual models for valuation are the same as for the corresponding asset categories.

Commercial paper is a short-term liability of a bank-holding company that is usually sold on a discount basis. The original maturity is no more than 270 days and the market valuation model is similar to that for Treasury bills.

$$MV = M - M(k)\left(\frac{N}{360}\right)$$

where

M = Maturity value

N = Number of days before maturity

This example is a new 270-day issue.

Given: M = 1,000,000; k = .045; N = 270.

MV = 1,000,000

   − 1,000,000(.045)(270/360)

   = 1,000,000 − 33,750

   = 966,250

Note that the market rate for the commercial paper can change over the life of the issue. The original discount rate plays no role in market valuation. The value depends on the maturity value, the time to maturity, and the market interest rate only.

Long-Term Borrowings

Long-term borrowings usually take the form of subordinated notes and debentures. To qualify as regulatory capital, these instruments must be long term and subordinated to deposits. These liabilities are valued using the same models developed for debt securities held as assets. The exact model depends on whether they are interest-paying or zero-coupon bonds.

SUMMARY OF VALUATION CONCEPTS

Table 4–4 is a summary of the valuation models discussed in this chapter. It serves as a quick reference and also can be used for comparative purposes when deciding which model is appropriate for a particular category of financial instruments.

Table 4–4.

SUMMARY OF VALUATION CONCEPTS

Category	Market Valuation Model
Interest-bearing time deposits in other banks	$D(1+k_c)^n/(1+k)^n$
Federal funds sold	$FF(1+k_c)^n/(1+k)^n$
Securities Purchased Under agreement to resell	$\left[\sum_{t=1}^{n} CP_t/\left((1+k/m)^t\right)\right] + SP/(1+k/m)^n$
Treasury bills	$M - M(k)(N/360)$
Treasury notes and bonds	$\left[\sum_{t=1}^{n}\{(M)(CR)/m\}/\left((1+k/m)^t\right)\right] + \left[M/(1+k/m)^n\right]$
Government Agency Pass-throughs	$\sum_{t=1}^{n} CF_t/\left((1+k/m)^t\right)$
Mortgage-backed	$\left[\sum_{t=1}^{n}\{(M)(CR)/m\}/\left((1+k/m)^t\right)\right] + \left[M/(1+k/m)^n\right]$
Municipal Noncallable	$\left[\sum_{t=1}^{n}\{(M)(CR)/m\}/\left((1+k/m)^t\right)\right] + \left[M/(1+k/m)^n\right]$
Advance refunding	$\left[\sum_{t=1}^{c}\{(M)(CR)/m\}/\left((1+k/m)^t\right)\right] + \left[CP/(1+k/m)^c\right]$
Zero-coupon bonds *Commercial Loans* Bullet	$M/\left((1+k)^n\right)$ $L\left((1+k_L/m)^n\right)/\left((1+k/m)^n\right)$

Table 4–4.

SUMMARY OF VALUATION CONCEPTS (Continued)

Category	Market Valuation Model
Line of credit	$\left[A\left((1+k_{LC})^{n}\right)+(MX-A)\left((1+k_{CF})^{n}-1\right)\right]/(1+k)^{n}$
Term	
Installment	$\left[L/PVIFA_{k/m,n}\right]\left[PVIFA_{k/m,n}\right]$
Interest only	$\left[L(k_{L}/m)\left(PVIFA_{k/m,n}\right)\right]+\left[L/\left((1+k/m)^{n}\right)\right]$
Mortgage Loans	
Fixed-rate	$\left(L/PVIFA_{k/m,n}\right)\left(PVIFA_{k/m,n}\right)$
Graduated pymt (GPM)	$\left[\displaystyle\sum_{t=1}^{g}\left\{\left(L/PVIFA_{k/m,n}\right)-PR_{t}\right\}/(1+k/m)^{t}\right]$ $+\left\{\left[\left(L/PVIFA_{k/m,n}\right)\left(PVIFA_{k/m,n-g}\right)+\displaystyle\sum_{t=1}^{g}PR_{t}\right]\right.$ $\left./\,PVIFA_{k/m,n-g}\right\}\left(PVIFA_{k/m,n-g}\right)\left(1/(1+k/m)^{g}\right)$
Balloon	
Interest only	$\left[\displaystyle\sum_{t=1}^{n}(L)(k_{m}/m)/\left((1+k)^{t}\right)\right]+L/\left((1+k/m)^{t}\right)$
Amortizing	$\left(L/PVIFA_{k/m,n}\right)\left(PVIFA_{k/m,n}\right)+B/\left((1+k/m)^{b}\right)$
Consumer installment loans	$\left(L/PVIFA_{k/m,n}\right)\left(PVIFA_{k/m,n}\right)$
Lease financing	$\left(L/PVIFA_{k/m,n}\right)\left(PVIFA_{k/m,n}\right)+R\left(1/(1+k/m)^{n}\right)$
Nonaccrual loans	$\left[\displaystyle\sum_{t=1}^{n}CF_{t}/\left((1+k)^{t}\right)\right]$

Table 4–4.

SUMMARY OF VALUATION CONCEPTS (Continued)

Category	Market Valuation Model
Time deposits	$D(1+k_D)^n /\left((1+k)^n\right)$
Short-Term Borrowings Fed funds purchased	$FF(1+k_c)^n /(1+k)^n$
Securities sold under agreement to repurchase	$\left[\sum_{t=1}^{n} CP_t /\left((1+k/m)^t\right)\right] + SP/(1+k/m)^n$
Commercial paper	$M - M(k)(N/360)$
Long-Term Borrowings	$\left[\sum_{t=1}^{n}\{(M)(CR)/m\}/\left((1+k/m)^t\right)\right] + \left[M/(1+k/m)^n\right]$

Note: For the following loan categories, the loan amount (*L*) is divided by *PVIFA* computed with the loan (contractual) interest rate and then multiplied by *PVIFA* computed with the required rate of return:

➤ commercial—term installment
➤ mortgages—fixed rate, graduated payment, and amortizing balloon
➤ consumer installment
➤ lease financing

Legend:

 A   actual borrowings for line of credit
 b   number of periods before balloon payment
 B   amount of balloon payment
 c   number of periods before first call date of a bond
CF$_t$ cash flow in period *t*
CP   call price
CP$_t$ coupon payment in period *t*
CR   coupon rate

Table 4–4.

SUMMARY OF VALUATION CONCEPTS (Concluded)

Legend:

D deposit

FF federal funds

g number of periods with graduated payments (GPM)

k discount rate

k_c contractual (coupon) rate

k_{CF} commitment fee for line of credit

k_D deposit rate

k_L loan rate

k_{LC} interest rate for line of credit

k_m mortgage rate

L loan amount

m number of times per year interest is either paid or compounded

M maturity value

MX maximum credit available for line of credit

n number of periods before maturity

N number of days before maturity

PR_t payment reduction in period t

R residual value in lease financing

ENDNOTES

1   Mortgage pass-through securities are subject to a *servicing fee* charged by a third party to cover the cost of collecting monthly payments, record-keeping, and sending periodic statements to mortgage borrowers. The coupon rate on the mortgage does not change. Instead, the owner of the pass-through receives less interest. For example, if a mortgage pool pays 8 percent and the servicing fee is .5 percent, the pass-through investor receives interest of 7.5 percent. As the balance declines, the net interest to investor and the servicing fee also declines. This process is illustrated in Chapter 5.

2   Alternatively, the payments in the early years may be computed based on lower interest rates. In such a case, PR_t is the difference between the normal payment and the computed lower payment.

CHAPTER 5

EMBEDDED OPTIONS

INTRODUCTION

Embedded options are rights to cash flows that are not recorded on a bank's balance sheet. They are essentially contingencies that can change the projected cash flow stream of a bank. In each case, they are connected with an asset or liability recorded on the balance sheet. Specifically, the categories that may include embedded options are:

➤ U.S. government agency securities.
➤ Callable bonds.
➤ Mortgage loans.
➤ Variable-rate loans.
➤ Deposits with interest penalties for early withdrawal.

To estimate the market value of embedded options, it is necessary to understand:

➤ The nature of options that are traded in organized exchange markets.
➤ The characteristics of embedded options.
➤ The valuation of exchange-traded options.

TYPES OF OPTIONS

An *option* is an agreement that confers the right to buy or sell an asset or stream of cash flows at a set price through some future date. To obtain this right, an investor must pay an *option premium*. The right itself is exercisable at the discretion of the option owner. The asset that may be bought or sold is the *underlying asset*. Should the option owner elect to exercise the option, the price at which the transaction occurs is the *exercise or strike price*. The owner of the option has the right to exercise at the strike price until the option's *expiration date*. If the option can be exercised only at the expiration date, it is a *European option*. If it can be exercised at any time during the life of the option, it is an *American option*.

If exercising the option results in profit for the option owner, the option is *in-the-money*. If exercising the option results in a financial loss for the owner, the option is *out-of-the-money*. If exercising the option causes the owner to break even, the option is *at-the-money*.

In general, the two basic types of options are call options and put options.

Call Options
A *call option* confers the right to acquire an asset or cash flow stream at the exercise price through the expiration date. Whether an option should be exercised depends on the market value of the underlying asset, the exercise price, and the option premium. The owner of a call option should exercise if the market price is sufficiently above the exercise price. Exercising the option enables the investor to purchase the asset at the exercise price (below its current market value) and resell at the higher market price.

Put Options
A *put option* confers the right to dispose of an asset or cash flow stream at the exercise price through the expiration date. The wisdom of exercising a put depends on the same factors that are relevant for a call—market value of underlying asset, exercise price, and option premium. The logic is reversed, however. The owner of a put option exercises if the market price is below the exercise price, because the asset can be bought at the lower market price and immediately sold for the higher exercise price.

Underlying Assets of Traded Options
The underlying assets of traded options include common stock, stock indexes, foreign currency, and futures contracts. Domestically, these options are traded on the:

➤ Chicago Board of Trade (CBOT).
➤ Chicago Board Options Exchange (CBOE).
➤ International Monetary Market (IMM) at the Chicago Mercantile Exchange (CME).
➤ New York Stock Exchange (NYSE).
➤ American Stock Exchange (AMEX).
➤ New York Futures Exchange (NYFE).
➤ Philadelphia Stock Exchange (PHLX).

Major exchanges abroad include:

> ➤ London International Financial Futures Exchange (LIFFE).
> ➤ Singapore International Monetary Exchange (SIMEX).

Expiration dates for these contracts are generally the third Friday of the month of expiration.

Stock and stock indexes. Stock options contracts are usually for the right to buy or sell 100 shares of the underlying asset. These options are readily available for firms whose stock is widely traded. A stock index option does not have a physical underlying asset. Instead, the contract is for some multiple of the underlying index.

For example, the Standard & Poor's 500 index option contract is valued in terms of 100 times the index level. The owner of the option receives the difference between the exercise price and market value without physically delivering anything. If an investor buys a call option with a strike price of 400 and the index is at 425 on the exercise date, the investor receives $2,500—the difference between the market value of the index and the exercise price multiplied by 100. Likewise, an investor who exercises an S&P 500 index put option with a strike price of 460 when the index is 425 receives the difference between the exercise price and the market value multiplied by 100—$3,500.

In addition to the S&P 500, stock index options are available on the:

> ➤ S&P 100.
> ➤ NYSE composite index.
> ➤ AMEX major market index.
> ➤ AMEX institutional index.
> ➤ AMEX computer technology index.
> ➤ AMEX oil index.
> ➤ PHLX value line index.
> ➤ PHLX national OTC index.

Foreign currency options. Currency option contracts (in which physical delivery does take place) are available in all major currencies. Contract specifics are:

Currency	Denomination	Exchange
Australian dollar	A$50,000	PHLX
Canadian dollar	C$50,000	PHLX
Deutsche mark	DM 62,500	PHLX
Deutsche mark	DM 125,000	SIMEX

Currency	Denomination	Exchange
European currency unit (ECU)	ECU 62,500	PHLX
Eurodollar	$1,000,000	SIMEX
French franc	FFr 250,000	PHLX
Japanese yen	¥6,250,000	PHLX
Japanese yen	¥12,500,000	PHLX
British pound	£31,250	PHLX
Swiss franc	SFr 62,500	PHLX

Futures contracts. A futures contract is an agreement to exchange a standard quantity of an asset at a specified date in the future at a predetermined price. A futures contract buyer agrees to purchase the asset; the seller agrees to sell. Futures contracts also are traded on organized exchanges. Unlike the buyer of an option, the buyer of a futures contract is obligated to close the contract either by taking delivery of the asset or by selling an offsetting futures contract. Examples of interest rate futures contracts include:

Instruments	Denomination	Exchange(s)
Treasury bonds	$100,000	CBOT, LIFFE
Treasury bonds	$50,000	CBOT, MCE[1]
5-yr. Treasury notes	$100,000	CBOT,FINEX[2]
2-yr. Treasury notes	$200,000	FINEX
Treasury bills	$1 million	IMM
Municipal bond index	1,000 times Bond Buyer MBI	CBOT
30-day interest rate	$5,000,000	CBOT
U.K. gilt (government bond)	£50,000	LIFFE
German government bond	DM 250,000	LIFFE
Yen bond	¥100,000,000	TSE,[3] LIFFE

[1] Midamerica Commodity Exchange.
[2] Financial Instrument Exchange, a division of the New York Cotton Exchange.
[3] Tokyo Stock Exchange.

Options on interest rate futures contracts include:

Instruments	Denomination	Exchange(s)
Treasury bonds	$100,000	CBOT, LIFFE
Treasury notes	$100,000	CBOT
Treasury bills	$1,000,000	IMM

Instruments	Denomination	Exchange(s)
Municipal bond index	$100,000 times index	CBOT
U.K. gilt (government bond)	£50,000	LIFFE
German government bond	DM 250,000	LIFFE

In general, options on foreign currency futures are also available primarily through IMM and LIFFE.

Options are well developed in stock, bond, and foreign currency markets. The notion of options within a bank's portfolio is less well developed. Thus, concepts must be borrowed from the active markets to accomplish a meaningful valuation of embedded options. One of the most important concepts is risk exposure.

RISK AND RETURN

There are four primary roles that an individual can play in an options transaction:

➤ Buy a call option.
➤ Write a call option.
➤ Buy a put option.
➤ Write a put option.

Buying a Call Option

When an investor buys a call option, the maximum loss exposure is the option premium. Figure 5–1 illustrates this point. In this case, the underlying instrument is a bond. The market price, exercise price, and call premium are expressed in terms of $100 of face value. The exercise price is $95, and the option premium $4. The maximum loss for a call option investor is the $4 premium. The option will not be exercised until the market price exceeds the exercise price. In fact, exercising the option will not be profitable until the market price exceeds the sum of the exercise price and the premium.

$$\text{Profit} = MV - X - C$$

where

$$MV = \text{Market value of the underlying bond}$$

$$X = \text{Exercise price}$$

$$C = \text{The value of the call option}$$

$$= \text{The call premium}$$

Substituting the values in this example:

$$\text{Profit} = MV - 95 - 4$$

Figure 5–1.

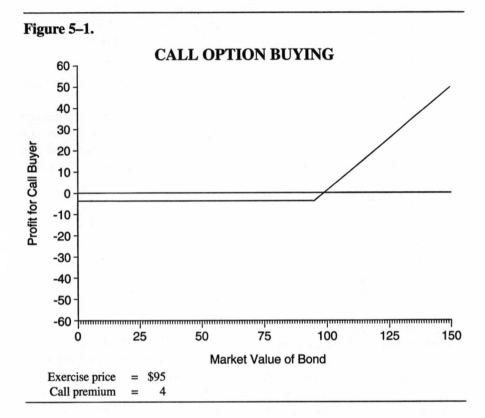

CALL OPTION BUYING

Exercise price = $95
Call premium = 4

Notice that for any market value less than $99, profit will be negative, that is, a loss will be sustained. At $99, the exercise price and option premium will be exactly offset. It will be profitable to exercise the option only when the market value exceeds $99.

Theoretically, the amount of profit is not bounded. All market value over $99 is profit for the option owner. In the case of stock options, there is no theoretical limit to the stock price and, hence, no limit to potential profits. The theoretical limit for the price of a bond is the present value of the promised future cash flows. Assuming a zero discount rate (the presumed lower limit for interest rates), the market value becomes the simple sum of the future cash flows. Consider a 20-year bond that pays an 8 percent coupon semiannually.

$$MV = 40(PVIFA_{k,40}) + 1000(PVIF_{k,40})$$
$$= 40\sum_{t=1}^{40}\left(1/(1+k)^t\right) + 1,000\left(1/(1+k)^{40}\right)$$

When k equals zero, each of the 40 terms in the *PVIFA* equals one and the *PVIF* also equals one. The market value of the bond is then:

$$MV = (40)(40) + 1,000$$
$$= 2,600$$

All of this theoretical upside potential belongs to the option owner. In any event, the most that the owner of the call option can lose is the $4 premium because the option is not exercised if the market value is less than the exercise price.

Writing a Call Option

The party on the other side of a call is the call writer or seller. Profits for this individual are the mirror image of profits for the call buyer. Figure 5–2 illustrates that the maximum profit for the call writer is the amount of the premium. Using the same exercise price and premium as in the previous example, as long as the market value is less than $95, the call owner does not exercise and the call writer keeps the $4 premium with no further obligation. As the price rises to more than $95, the likelihood of an exercise increases. When the market value of the bond rises above $99 prompting option exercise, the call writer must enter the market and purchase the bond at the going price and sell it to the call owner at $95. The profit for the call writer can be described as:

$$\text{Profit} = X + C - MV$$

The call writer receives X and C but must pay MV. To the extent that the market value is not bounded, neither are the losses for a call writer.

Buying a Put Option

A put option gives its owner the right to sell an asset. Figure 5–3 shows the profit for a put owner, assuming an exercise price of $95 and an option premium of $4. If the price of the bond in question is higher than $95, the owner has no incentive to exercise. Assuming the put owner already owns the bond, it would be more profitable to sell in the market rather than to exercise the option and sell at $95. Assuming that the put owner does not already own the bond, the investor would be forced to buy the bond in the market at a price higher than $95 and then sell it at $95. Under no circumstances will the option be exercised when the market value exceeds $95.

As the market value drops to less than $95, it becomes more profitable to exercise. For example, at $94, the put owner may enter the market, purchase

Figure 5–2.

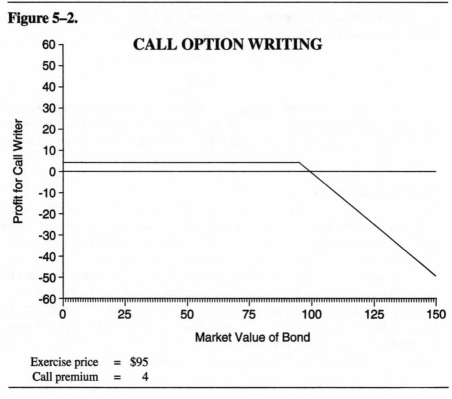

CALL OPTION WRITING

Exercise price = $95
Call premium =   4

the bond, exercise the option, and resell it to the put writer for $95. Of course, the $1 profit is offset by the $4 premium paid for the put writer, for a net loss of $3. At a market value of $91, the put owner breaks even, paying $91 for the bond, $4 for the premium, and receiving $95 on exercise of the option and resale of the bond. When the price declines to less than $91, the put owner realizes a profit. In general, the profit for the owner of a put option is

$$\text{Profit} = X - P - MV$$

where

$$P = \text{The value of the put option}$$

$$= \text{The put premium}$$

The put buyer receives the exercise price and pays the option premium and the market value of the underlying asset. In the event that the security

Figure 5–3.

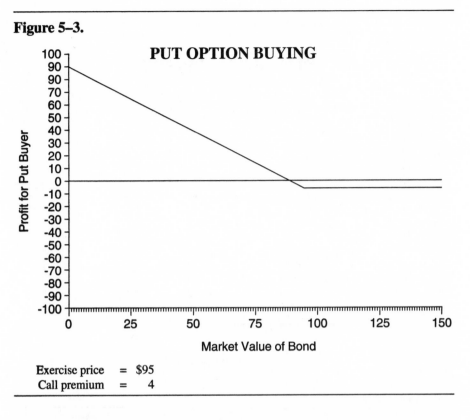

Exercise price = $95
Call premium = 4

becomes worthless, the maximum potential profit is the exercise price less the option premium or $91 in this case.

Writing a Put Option
The profits of a put option writer are the mirror image of the profits of the put option owner. The put writer gains no more than the option premium. If the price of the bond is more than the exercise price, the option is not exercised and the writer keeps the premium. As the market value declines below the exercise price, exercise becomes more likely. If the market value is $91, an exercise would mean that the put writer would purchase the bond at the $95 exercise price, retain the $4 premium, and sell the bond for $91 in the market. This is the put writer's break-even point. If the market price is lower than $91, the put writer sustains a loss. Profits for the put writer may be described as:

$$\text{Profit} \ = \ MV + P - X$$

Figure 5–4.

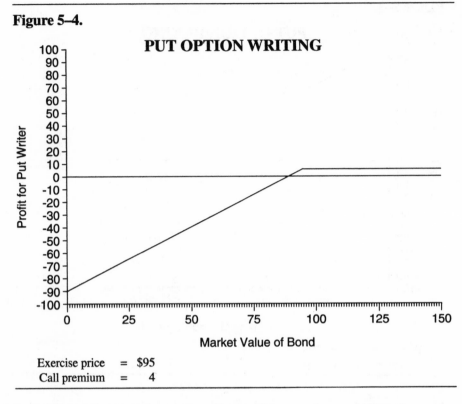

Exercise price   = $95
Call premium   =   4

The put writer receives the option premium and, on exercise, the market value less the exercise price. Should the security become worthless, the maximum loss is exercise price less option premium, $91 in this case.

THE NATURE OF EMBEDDED OPTIONS

Commercial bank portfolios contain options that are not separately disclosed. They are contained in the securities and loan portfolios and the deposit base:

➤ Government pass-through securities and mortgage loans.
➤ Callable bonds.
➤ Variable-rate loans.
➤ Deposits.

When the bank owns the option, it has a *long position*, that is, the option is an asset. If the underlying instrument is also an asset for the bank, the long option position adds to the market value of the asset. If the underlying instrument is a liability for the bank, the long option position reduces the market value of the liability.

When another party owns the option, the bank has a *short position*, that is, the option is a liability. If the underlying instrument is an asset for the bank, the short option position reduces the market value of the asset. If on the other hand, the underlying instrument is a liability, the short option position increases the market value of the liability.

These concepts may be summarized as follows:

Bank's Option Position	Effect on Market Value	
	Assets	**Liabilities**
Long	Increase	Decrease
Short	Decrease	Increase

Government Pass-Through Securities and Mortgage Loans

Government pass-through securities are securitized assets based on mortgage loans. Each month, investors in these securities receive their proportional share of interest and principal payments from the underlying securities. Banks receive principal and interest payments from borrowers directly from the mortgage loan portfolio.

The investors and lenders may not receive the promised cash flows, however, because of prepayments. The principal may be repaid faster than originally contracted. A borrower of one of the underlying mortgages has the right to buy back an entire mortgage, often at par, that is, with no prepayment penalty. This is a call option owned by the borrower. These prepayments can occur because current interest rates are substantially lower than the contracted mortgage rates. Prepayments also occur because the original borrowers sell their homes for other reasons such as upgrading to a larger home, employment relocation to a different city, or retirement.

While it is generally true that $1 received today is worth more than $1 received a year from now, these early payments can present problems for money managers.[1] If the payments are received after interest rates have declined, the investor in pass-through securities faces *reinvestment risk*; that is, faces the risk that it may not be possible to invest the early payments in as high a rate as is currently available.[1]

Table 5–1 gives a hypothetical example of a $100,000 pass-through security. The underlying mortgage is set up for 30 years at a mortgage rate of 10 percent. The general level of interest rates declines to 8 percent after the first five years (60 payments), but there are no prepayments. The calculations in the

---

Table 5–1.

TERMINAL VALUE OF A PASS-THROUGH SECURITY
WITHOUT PREPAYMENT

First 60 Payments

Reinvested at 10 percent through period 60
Reinvested at 8 percent for periods 61 through 360
    (300 periods)

$$877.57(FVIFA_{.10/12,60})(FVIF_{.08/12,300})$$
$$877.57(77.437072)(7.340176) \qquad \underline{\$498,812.31}$$

Remaining 300 payments

Reinvested at 8 percent for periods 61 through 360

$$877.57(FVIFA_{.08/12,300})$$
$$877.57(951.026395) \qquad \underline{834,592.23}$$
Total $\qquad \underline{\$1,333,404.54}$

Note: This security has an original term of 360 months and a coupon rate of 10 percent. The monthly payment is $877.57.

$$
\begin{aligned}
100,000 &= Pymt(PVIFA_{.10/12,360}) \\
100,000 &= Pymt(113.95082) \\
100,000/113.95082 &= Pymt \\
&= 877.57
\end{aligned}
$$

The reinvestment rate is assumed to be 10 percent during the first five years and 8 percent thereafter.

---

table are based on the assumption that the first 60 payments are reinvested at 10 percent until period 60 and at 8 percent thereafter. All the remaining 300 payments are reinvested at the 8 percent rate. Under these assumptions, the terminal value of this investment is $1,333,404.54.

Table 5–2 is the same mortgage pass-through under the assumption of refinancing at the end of period 60. As of the end of period 60, the balance of the loan is $96,574.15. This entire amount is refinanced in a new mortgage at 8 percent for the remaining 25 years (300 payments).[2] The new monthly payment is $745.37. The terminal value in this case consists of the same terminal value

Table 5–2.

TERMINAL VALUE OF A PASS-THROUGH SECURITY
WITH PREPAYMENT

First 60 Payments

Reinvested at 10 percent through period 60
Reinvested at 8 percent for periods 61 through 360
       (300 periods)

$$877.57(FVIFA_{.10/12,60})(FVIF_{.08/12,300})$$
$$877.57(77.437072)(7.340176) \qquad \underline{\$498,812.31}$$

Remaining 300 Payments

Reinvested at 8 percent for periods 61 through 360

$$745.37(FVIFA_{.08/12,300})$$
$$745.37(951.026395) \qquad \underline{708,866.54}$$
Total $\qquad\qquad \underline{\$1,207,678.85}$

Note: This security has an original term of 360 months and a coupon rate of 10 per-
        cent. The original monthly payment is $877.57.

$$
\begin{array}{rcl}
100,000 &=& Pymt(PVIFA_{.10/12,360}) \\
100,000 &=& Pymt(113.95082) \\
100,000/113.95082 &=& Pymt \\
&=& 877.57
\end{array}
$$

At the end of year 5, the remaining balance is refinanced at 8 percent. The balance
at year 5 is $96,574.15 and the new payment is $745.37.

Balance at the end of period 60:

$$
\begin{array}{rcl}
Balance_{60} &=& 877.57(PVIFA_{.10/12,300}) \\
&=& 877.57(110.047230) \\
&=& 96,574.15
\end{array}
$$

New payment:

$$
\begin{array}{rcl}
96,574.15 &=& Pymt(PVIFA_{.08/12,300}) \\
&=& Pymt(129.564522) \\
96,574.15/129.465522 &=& Pymt \\
&=& 745.37
\end{array}
$$

The reinvestment rate is assumed to be 10 percent during the first five years and 8
percent thereafter.

for the first 60 payments. However, because the last 300 payments are lower, their terminal value is lower. The total terminal value is $1,207,678.85. This amount is lower than the result in the first case by $125,725.72, or 9.4 percent.

$$\% \text{ decrease} = (1,207,678.85 - 1,333,404.57)$$
$$/1,333,404.57$$
$$= -125,725.72/1,333,404.57$$
$$= -.09429$$

The possibility of this situation is the nature of the risk for the bank. Because the bank's option position is short (the borrower owns the option), the option reduces the market value of mortgage pass-through securities and mortgage loans.

Callable Bonds

A callable bond also can be prepaid by the issuer. The bond issuer owns a call option and the bank faces reinvestment risk. Further, as interest rates increase, the market value of bonds increases. The upside potential for capital gains is limited by this option.

Figure 5–5 shows the value of a 20-year, 7 percent bond at various discount rates that range from 0 to 400 percent. At the higher end of the rate range, the bond is almost worthless. At a zero discount rate, the bond is worth $2,400. From a discount rate of 10 percent to a rate of 8 percent, the market value of the bond increases from $743 to $901, an increase of more than 20 percent. If the bond has a call provision, realization of such capital gains will be threatened depending on the specifics of the provision. The bond indenture contains the call price(s)—effectively the exercise price of the call option.

The commercial bank that owns a callable bond has a short option position. This option reduces the market value of the bond portfolio.

Variable-Rate Loans

Variable-rate loans have a market value close to book value because when the required market rate changes, so does the loan (coupon) rate of the loan. If the extent to which the loan rate can float is restricted, the virtual equality between book and market values is not sustained in all cases. The vehicles through which this restriction is accomplished are interest rate caps and interest rate floors.

Interest rate caps. If a loan has an interest rate cap, the borrower has the effective right to receive from the bank the stream of cash flows representing

Figure 5–5.

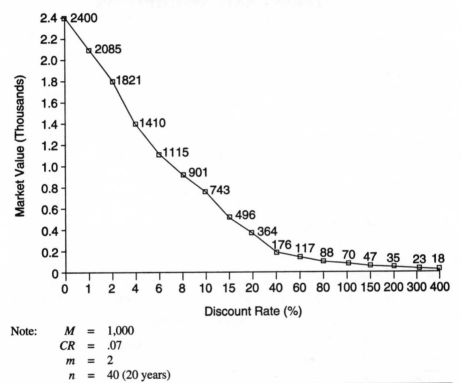

MARKET VALUE OF A BOND UNDER VARYING INTEREST RATE ASSUMPTIONS

Note: M = 1,000
        CR = .07
        m = 2
        n = 40 (20 years)

interest payments over the cap rate. These cash flows exactly offset the higher interest payments that the borrower would otherwise be required to make. Put another way, the borrower can call the interest payments above the cap level and eliminate that part of the obligation. The borrower owns a call option for which there is no exercise price. The call is automatically exercised when interest rates increase.

Figure 5–6 illustrates this point. The interest income from a $100 variable-rate loan increases linearly as market interest rates increase. If the loan has a 15 percent cap, the borrower calls the amount of interest payments above 15 percent. The bank has a short option position and the market value of the option reduces the market value of the loan.

Figure 5–6.

VARIABLE-RATE LOAN WITH A CAP AND A FLOOR: INTEREST INCOME UNDER VARYING INTEREST RATE ASSUMPTIONS

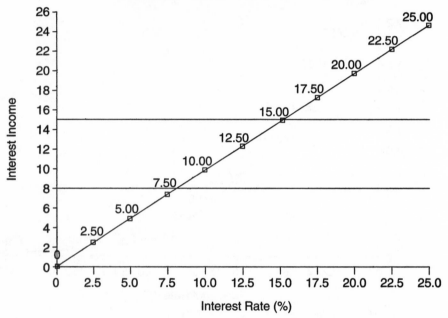

Note: This is the interest income per $100 of face value for a variable-rate loan with a 15 percent cap and an 8 percent floor.

Interest Rate Floors. An interest rate floor is the minimum interest rate that a variable-rate loan must pay. When a floor is associated with a variable-rate loan, the bank has the right to receive from the borrower the cash flows to replace the amounts not earned because of declining interest rates. In other words, the bank can put the interest payments below the floor and reinstate the obligation to pay a higher rate. In this case, the bank owns a put option. There is no exercise price and the option is automatically exercised when interest rates decline.

An 8 percent floor also is illustrated in Figure 5–6. The interest income that the bank would have lost below the 8 percent level is earned. The bank has a long put position causing the market value of the loan to increase.

Deposits

The most common option associated with deposits is the interest penalty for early withdrawal. The bank has the right to call some or all of the interest expense that would otherwise be payable. Figure 5–7 shows the effect of a 3-month interest penalty on 6-month and 12-month certificates of deposit. Instead of the interest expense increasing linearly from the date of deposit, the amount payable is zero if the deposit is withdrawn in the first 90 days. Only for withdrawals after 90 days does the bank have an interest expense liability. When the withdrawal is on the maturity date, the interest payable is accrued over the entire term.

The 6-month deposit has a 3.05 percent interest rate and the 12-month deposit 3.25 percent. The amount of interest payable is computed as follows (where n = days to maturity and t = day of withdrawal):

Day of withdrawal		Interest payable
From	**To**	
0	90	0
91	$n-1$	$100(1 + k)^{(t-90)/360} - 100$
n	n	$100(1 + k)^n$

Figure 5–8 contains similar illustrations of the interest expense associated with 2-year, 4-year, and 10-year certificates of deposit with a six-month interest penalty. The interest rates associated with these deposits are 3.85 percent, 4.75 percent, and 5.95 percent, respectively. The interest amounts payable are computed as follows (where n = years to maturity):

Month of withdrawal		Interest payable
From	**To**	
0	6	0
7	$12(n)-1$	$100(1 + k)^{(n)} - (100(1 + k)^5 - 100)$
$12(n)$	$12(n)$	$100(1 + k)^n$

Notice that the impact of the interest penalty declines with the maturity of the deposit. The interest penalty is a smaller percentage of total interest expense as the original deposit maturity grows. In each case, the bank has a long call position that decreases the value of deposit liabilities.

OPTION VALUATION

Market valuation quotations for traded options are readily available. Embedded options are, of course, not traded but many of the market valuation concepts for traded options apply.

Figure 5–7.

INTEREST EXPENSE FOR DEPOSITS WITH
THREE-MONTH PENALTY FOR EARLY WITHDRAWAL

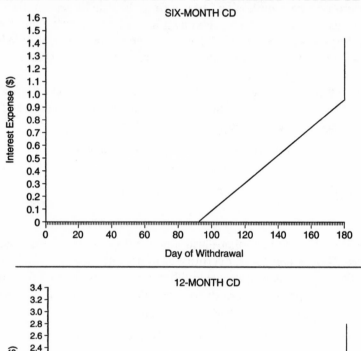

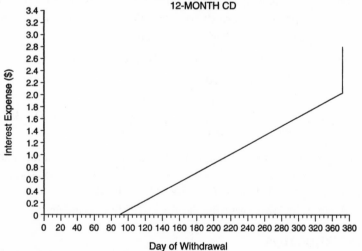

Note: These are six-month and one-year certificates of deposit with a three-month
            interest penalty for early withdrawal.

Figure 5–8.

INTEREST EXPENSE FOR DEPOSITS WITH SIX-MONTH PENALTY FOR EARLY WITHDRAWAL

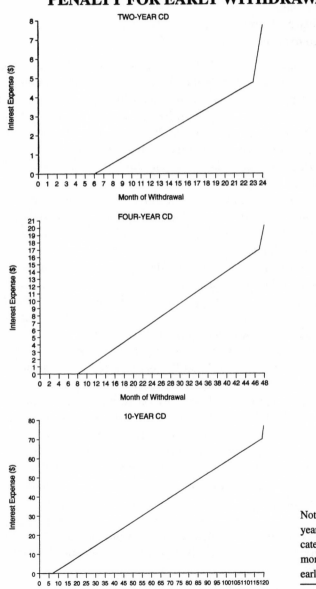

Note: These are 2-year, 4-year, and 10-year certificates of deposit with a six-month interest penalty for early withdrawal.

Factors that Affect Option Valuation
The factors that affect the value of options are:

➤ Market value of the underlying asset.
➤ Exercise price.
➤ Interest rates.
➤ Volatility of the price of the underlying asset.
➤ Time to maturity.

The *market value of an underlying asset* affects a call option and a put option in opposite ways. The higher the price, the more likely a call option will be in-the-money. Since the owner receives the difference between the market value and the exercise price, a higher price causes that difference to increase and, therefore, the value of the call option to increase. The owner of a put option receives the difference between the exercise price and the market value. The lower the price, the more likely the put option will be in-the-money and the more valuable the put option.

The *exercise price* of a call has a negative relationship to the value of a call option. A higher exercise price reduces the profits for a call owner. For a put option, a higher exercise price increases the profits for a put owner and thus has a positive relationship to put value.

When the *interest rate* increases, the value of a call also increases because the present value of the exercise price (cash outflow) declines. Since the put owner receives the exercise price, higher interest rates reduce the present value of future cash flows. Higher interest rates increase the value of a call option and decrease the value of a put option.

Greater *volatility of the price of the underlying asset* increases the value of a call option and a put option. Volatility is measured as the standard deviation of the rate of return of the underlying asset. The greater the volatility, the more likely the option is to be in-the-money because the price is more likely to increase (in the case of a call option) or decrease (in the case of a put option). Consider an underlying asset whose price never changes, (i.e., has a zero volatility). If the call option exercise price is more than the current market value or the put exercise price is less than the current market value, there is no possibility that either option will ever be in-the-money. A positive volatility increases the probability.

Time to maturity increases the value of call and put options because there is more of an opportunity for the market value of the underlying asset to move in an advantageous direction. There is a positive relationship between time to maturity and option value.

The two primary components of the value of an option are the *intrinsic value* and the *time value*. The intrinsic value of a call option is the difference between the current market value and the exercise price.

$$C = MV - X$$

If this difference is negative, the intrinsic value of the call is zero because the option cannot be exercised under these circumstances.

The intrinsic value of a put option is the difference between the exercise price and the current market value and will never be less than zero.

$$P = X - MV$$

The observed price of an option is almost always in excess of the intrinsic value because of the possibility that the price of the underlying asset moves in such a way as to bring the option in-the-money or more in-the-money.

Put-Call Parity

There is also a relationship between the value of a put and the value of a call. In general, the price of one places limits on the price of the other when both have the same exercise price and expiration date. Specifically, the price of a put must equal the price of a call plus the present value of the exercise price less the current market value of the underlying asset.

$$P = C + Xe^{-kt} - MV$$

where

$$X^{-kt} = \text{Continuously compounded present value of the exercise price}$$

To see that this relationship must hold, consider the following example. Two portfolios are constructed:

I: Long position in the put option.
II: Long position in the call option, one unit of the underlying asset sold short, and the present value of the exercise price invested at the risk free-rate[3].

Over the term of the option, the investment at the risk-free rate in portfolio II grows to X.

At the expiration date, the exercise price is either greater than, equal to, or less than the market value. The pay-offs of each portfolio are as follows (where $MV_1 = MV$ at expiration date):

Portfolio	$MV_1 \geq X$	$MV_1 < X$
I	—	$X - MV_1$
II	$MV_1 - X - MV_1 + X$	$-MV_1 + X$

For portfolio I, there is a payoff of $X - MV_1$ if the market value at the expiration date is less than the exercise price. Otherwise, the put option expires worthless. For portfolio II, if the market value at the expiration date is greater than the exercise price, then exercising the call option yields $MV_1 - X$. The short position is covered by buying the underlying asset in the market at MV_1 and the risk free investment yields X. Notice that when the market value of the asset is greater than or equal to the exercise price at expiration, the net cash flows of each portfolio equals zero. When the market value of the asset is less than the exercise price, each portfolio returns $X - MV_1$. Since both portfolios return the same cash flows, the two are equivalent.

Black-Scholes Option Pricing Model
The most widely used option pricing model is the Black-Scholes model:

$$C = (MV)N(d_1) - Xe^{-kt}N(d_2)$$

where

C	=	Value of a European call option
MV	=	Current market value of the underlying asset
X	=	Exercise price
k	=	Risk free rate of return
t	=	Time to option expiration
$N(y)$	=	The probability that an observation from a normal distribution will be less than or equal to y
	=	Cumulative normal probability distribution
d_1	=	$[ln(MV/X) + (k + \sigma^2/2)(t)]/\sigma(t^5)$
σ	=	Volatility of underlying asset
	=	Standard deviation of rate of return of underlying asset
d_2	=	$d_1 - \sigma(t^5)$

The intuition of the model is based on the fact that the owner of a call option receives market value of the underlying asset less the exercise price when a call option is exercised. The first term on the right side of the equation is market value, weighted by its probability of occurrence—$N(d_1)$. Notice that this probability depends on:

> ➤ The relationship of the current market value to the exercise price.
> ➤ The current level of interest rates.
> ➤ Volatility of return.
> ➤ Time to maturity.

These, of course, are the factors discussed earlier. The second term on the right side is the continuously compounded present value of the exercise price, weighted by its probability of occurrence—$N(d_2)$.[4]

The Black-Scholes model is based on four assumptions:

1. The volatility of the underlying asset is constant over the life of the option.
2. The risk-free interest rate does not change.
3. The underlying asset is a nondividend-paying stock.
4. The option is a European call option (i.e., it may not be exercised until maturity).

These assumptions affect the result of the Black-Scholes model when it is used for interest-sensitive, coupon-paying instruments such as bonds and loans.

With respect to volatility, over the life of a bond the volatility decreases because the market value approaches par value. However, as long as the time to bond maturity is substantially longer than the life of the option, the Black-Scholes result is reasonable.

The second assumption that interest rates are constant over the life of the option is not a material distortion of option value.

The third assumption is that the underlying asset pays no dividends. For either a dividend-paying stock or an interest-paying bond, the model may be adjusted by subtracting the present value of the interim payments from the market value.

The fourth assumption is that the option is European (i.e., may not be exercised before expiration). It has been shown that an American option paying interim payments (such as dividends or interest) is not exercised before option expiration as long as the present value of the exercise price exceeds the present value of the interim payments. This means that the value of the American option on such an instrument has the same value as a European option.

The Black-Scholes model for the value of a put option is as follows:

$$P = Xe^{-kt}N(-d_2) - (MV)N(-d_1)$$

$$N(-y) = \text{The probability that an observation}$$
$$\text{from a normal distribution will be less}$$
$$\text{than or equal to } -y$$

$$= 1 - N(y)$$

The intuition of this model is that on exercise, the owner of a put receives $X - MV$. The first term on the right side of the equation is the present value of the exercise price multiplied by its probability. The second term on the right side is the current market value multiplied by its probability of occurrence.

Black Futures Option Pricing Model
A model used to value a call option on a futures contract is the Black futures option pricing model:

$$C = E^{-kt}[(F)N(d_1) - (X)N(d)]$$

where

$$F = \text{Current market value of a futures}$$
$$\text{contract of the underlying asset}$$

$$t = \text{Life of the option}$$

The owner of an option on a futures contract exercises the option if the market value of the futures contract exceeds the exercise price of the option. On exercise, the owner of the option receives $F - X$. The pricing model measures this difference based on the current market value of the futures contract and weights each by its probability. The result is then discounted at the risk-free rate.

Similarly, the value of a put option on the futures contract is

$$P = e^{-kt}[(X)N(-d_2) - (F)N(-d_1)]$$

The owner of a put option will exercise if the exercise price is higher than the market value and will receive $X - F$. The model measures this difference, weights each by its probability, and discounts the result.

Application of the Black-Scholes Model
Consider a bond that pays interest semiannually with the next interest payment due six months from now. What are the values of put and call options on this bond if these options expire in 143 days?

Given: MV = 105; X = 103; t = 143/360 = .3972;
                                    price of a T-bill maturing in 143
                                    days = 98.63.

Because there are no interim interest payments before option expiration, the market value of the bond need not be adjusted for the present value of interest payments. The risk-free rate may be computed based on the T-bill price:

$$FV = PV(1 + k)^n$$

$$100 = 98.63(1 + k)^{143/360}$$

$$(100/98.63)^{360/143} - 1 = k$$

$$= .035$$

The Black-Scholes model also requires an estimate of the volatility of the underlying asset. This is accomplished by using the last 16 weeks as a basis for the calculations. The process is illustrated in Table 5–3. Recall that when using continuous compounding, the future value of a single amount is

$$FV = (PV)e^{kt}$$

$$FV/PV = e^{kt}$$

Substituting the end-of-week market value for FV and the beginning-of-week market value for PV, the continuously compounded weekly rate of return is computed as $\ln(MV_t/MV_{t-1})$. The average rate of return is based on rates of return for 15 weeks. The variance of these weekly returns is annualized by multiplying the weekly variance by 52. The volatility of the underlying asset is the standard deviation of the annualized variance, or .117117.

Using this information, the value of the call option is specified as:

$$C = (MV)N(d_1) - Xe^{-kt}N(d_2)$$

$$= (105)N(d_1) - (103)(e^{-(.035)(.3972)})N(d_2)$$

where

$$d_1 = [\ln(MV/X) + (k + \sigma^2/2)(t)]/\sigma(t^{.5})$$

$$= [.019231 + (.035 + .006858)$$

$$(.3972)]/(.117117)(.630238)$$

$$d_2 = d_1 - \sigma(t^{.5})$$

Table 5–3.

COMPUTING AN ESTIMATE OF VOLATILITY

Week	Price	X_t	$1n(X_t)$	$1n(X_t)-k$	$(1n(X_t)-k)^2$
1	$102.8626				
2	102.9655	1.001000	.0010	.000267	.000000071
3	103.3782	1.004008	.0040	.003267	.000010673
4	102.3701	.990248	−.0098	−.010533	.000110944
5	101.8697	.995112	−.0049	−.005633	.000031731
6	105.9211	1.039770	.0390	.038267	.001464363
7	106.2712	1.003305	.0033	.002567	.000006589
8	106.4837	1.002000	.0020	.001267	.000001605
9	108.1795	1.015925	.0158	.015067	.000227014
10	107.1245	.990248	−.0098	−.010533	.000110944
11	108.2011	1.010050	.0100	.009267	.000085877
12	106.9532	.988467	−.0116	−.002333	.000005443
13	108.1902	1.011566	.0115	.010767	.000115928
14	109.0156	1.007629	.0076	.006867	.000047156
15	105.1924	.964930	−.0357	−.036433	.001327363
16	104.0000	.988665	−.0114	−.012133	.000147210

Note:

$$X_t = MV_t / MV_{t-1}$$

$$1n(X) = \text{Continously compounded weekly rate of return}$$

$$\sum_{t=1}^{15} 1n(X_t)/15 = \text{Mean weekly rate of return}$$

$$= k$$

$$s^2 = \sum_{t=1}^{15} \left(1n(X_t) - k\right)^2 /14$$

$$= \text{Weekly variance}$$

$$= .000263779$$

$$52s^2 = \text{Annual variance}$$

$$= \sigma^2$$

$$= .013716508$$

$$\sigma = \text{Annual standard deviation}$$

$$= \text{Annual volatility}$$

$$= .117117$$

$$= .485791 - (.117117)(.630238)$$

$$= .411979$$

The values of $N(d_1)$ and $N(d_2)$ may be determined with reference to a cumulative normal distribution table (with appropriate interpolation) or to the polynomial approximation given in Figure 5–9. The approximation is accurate to four decimal places and facilitates a computer application of the Black-Scholes model. Using this approach for $N(d_1)$:

$$a = (.485791)^2$$

$$= .235992896$$

$$p = (1/(1+(.33267)(.485791)))$$

$$= .8608755$$

$$N(.485791) = 1 - (1/2.506628273)(.8886992)$$

$$(.375499775 - .089057005$$

$$+ .597996628)$$

$$= .686431134$$

Figure 5–9.

POLYNOMIAL APPROXIMATION OF CUMULATIVE NORMAL DISTRIBUTION FUNCTION

For $x \geq 0$:
$$N(x) \cong 1 - \left(1/(2\pi)^{.5}\right)\left(e^{-a/2}\right)\left(b_1 p + b_2 p^2 + b_3 p^3\right)$$
For $x < 0$:
$$N(x) \cong 1 - N(-x)$$

where $\pi = 3.14159265$
$\quad a = x^2$
$\quad b_1 = .4361836$
$\quad b_2 = -.1201676$
$\quad b_3 = .9372980$
$\quad p = \left(1/(1+cx)\right)$
$\quad c = .33267$
$\quad N(-x) = 1 - N(x)$

Following the same procedure for $N(d_2)$:

$$a = (.411979)^2$$
$$= .169726696$$
$$p = (1/(1+(.33267)(.411979)))$$
$$= .879466439$$
$$N(.411979) = 1 - (1/2.506628273)(.918637810)$$
$$(.383608837 - .092944978$$
$$+ .637581202)$$
$$= .659813536$$

Substituting these values, the market value of the call option is

$$C = 72.072 - 67.021$$
$$= 5.051$$

The value of the put option depends on $N(-d_1)$ and $N(-d_2)$.

$$N(-d_1) = 1 - N(d_1)$$
$$= 1 - .6864$$
$$= .3136$$
$$N(-d_2) = 1 - N(d_2)$$
$$= 1 - .6598$$
$$= .3402$$

The market value of the put option is

$$P = Xe^{-kt}N(-d_2) - (MV)N(-d_1)$$
$$= (103)(e^{-(.035)(.3972)})(.3402)$$
$$- (105)(.3136)$$
$$= 34.557 - 32.928$$
$$= 1.629$$

EMBEDDED OPTION VALUATION

The Black-Scholes option valuation model is useful for options associated with callable bonds. The Black futures options valuation model is appropriate for variable rate loans and deposits. The following section illustrates applications of embedded options in:

- ➤ Mortgage-related investments.
- ➤ Callable bonds.
- ➤ Variable-rate loans.

Mortgage-Related Investments

Neither the Black-Scholes model nor the Black model is appropriate to evaluate the options embedded in mortgage-related investments because exercise of the prepayment option will not necessarily be associated with changes in market interest rates. Thus, it is necessary to make an assumption about prepayments and then determine the net affect of these prepayments under various interest rate scenarios. The steps in the process are:

- ➤ Determine the cash flows of the portfolio under the assumption of no prepayments.
- ➤ Determine the cash flows of the portfolio with prepayments.
- ➤ Determine the value of the portfolio under both assumptions with one interest rate environment.
- ➤ Determine the difference between the market value of the portfolio with no prepayments and the market value under the prepayment assumption.
- ➤ Change the interest rate assumptions as many times as desired, revalue the portfolio with and without prepayments, and compute the difference in present value in each case.
- ➤ Estimate the probability of each interest rate scenario.
- ➤ Weight the present value differences by their respective probabilities to arrive at the value of the option.

An important element of this process is the prepayment assumption. In the example presented here, prepayments are assumed to occur at a constant rate, described as the *monthly prepayment rate*.[5]

$$MPR \;=\; 1 - (1 - CPR)^{1/12}$$

where

$$MPR = \text{Monthly prepayment rate}$$

$$CPR = \text{Constant annual prepayment rate}$$

Each month, prepayments are estimated as:

$$\text{prepayment}_t = MPR(UB_{t-1} - PR_t)$$

where

$$UB_{t-1} = \text{Unpaid mortgage balance at the end of month } t-1$$

$$PR_t = \text{Normal principal repayment in month } t$$

These prepayments also reduce the monthly payment.

$$P_t = \text{Mortgage payment in month } t$$

$$= (\text{original payment})(1 - MPR)^{t-1}$$

Table 5–4 contains excerpts of an amortization schedule for a $100,000 mortgage pass-through security with a mortgage rate of 8 percent and a servicing fee of .5 percent. There are no prepayments. The monthly payment is $733.76, based on the mortgage rate and 30 years to maturity. The servicing fee reduces the interest to the pass-through investor to 7.5 percent. Each month, the principal reduction is the $733.76 payment less interest and servicing fee.

Contrast this schedule to the schedule in Table 5–5. A 5 percent *CPR* is assumed or a .4265 percent *MPR*. .

$$MPR = 1 - (1 - .05)^{1/12}$$

$$= .004265$$

The payment is reduced at this rate each month and a prepayment column has been added. The net effect of these prepayments is that both interest and servicing fee are reduced.

	Without Prepayments	With Prepayments	Difference
Principal	$100,000.00	$100,000.00	—
Interest	153,895.60	90,950.87	$62,944.73
Subtotal	$253,895.60	$190,950.87	$62,944.73
Servicing	10,259.70	6,063.39	4,196.31
Total	$264,155.30	$197,0134.26	$67,141.04

Table 5–4.

MORTGAGE PASS–THROUGH AMORTIZATION SCHEDULE
WITH SERVICING FEE AND NO PREPAYMENTS

Payment Number	Interest	Service Fee	Principal Reduction	Unpaid Balance
0				100,000.00
1	625.00	41.67	67.10	99932.90
2	624.58	41.64	67.55	99865.36
3	624.16	41.61	68.00	99797.36
4	623.73	41.58	68.45	99728.91
5	623.31	41.55	68.91	99660.01
68	589.72	39.31	104.72	94251.23
69	589.07	39.27	105.42	94145.80
70	588.41	39.23	106.13	94039.68
71	587.75	39.18	106.83	93932.85
72	587.08	39.14	107.55	93825.30
140	529.49	35.30	168.97	84549.64
141	528.44	35.23	170.10	84379.54
142	527.37	35.16	171.23	84208.31
143	526.30	35.09	172.38	84035.93
144	525.22	35.01	173.52	83862.41
212	432.30	28.82	272.64	68896.12
213	430.60	28.71	274.46	68621.66
214	428.89	28.59	276.29	68345.37
215	427.16	28.48	278.13	68067.24
216	425.42	28.36	279.98	67787.26
284	275.49	18.37	439.90	43639.12
285	272.74	18.18	442.84	43196.28
286	269.98	18.00	445.79	42750.49
287	267.19	17.81	448.76	42301.73
288	264.39	17.63	451.75	41849.98
356	22.48	1.50	709.79	2886.89
357	18.04	1.20	714.52	2172.37
358	13.58	0.91	719.28	1453.09
359	9.08	0.61	724.08	729.01
360	4.56	0.30	729.01	0.00

Table 5–4. (Continued)

MORTGAGE PASS–THROUGH AMORTIZATION SCHEDULE
WITH SERVICING FEE AND NO PREPAYMENTS

Note: This is an amortization schedule for a 30-year mortgage pass-through with a
          servicing fee, assuming no prepayment.

$$L \; = \; \text{Loan amount} = 100{,}000$$

$$\text{Mortgage rate} \; = \; 8 \text{ percent}$$

$$\text{Payment} \; = \; 733.76$$

$$UB \; = \; \text{Unpaid balance}$$

$$\text{Servicing fee} \; = \; .5 \text{ percent}$$

$$= \; UB(.005/12)$$

$$\text{Interest} \; = \; UB(.075/12)$$

$$\text{Principal reduction}_t \; = \; PR_t$$

$$= \; 733.76 - UB_{t-1}(.075/12)$$
$$- UB_{t-1}(.005/12)$$

Notice that total cash flow to the investor is \$62,944.73 lower with pre-payments than without. Servicing fee (paid to a third party, often the original lender) is \$4,196.31 lower. The owner of this pass-through receives a decidedly different stream of cash flows than originally contracted.

Another element of risk is the reinvestment risk associated with early principal repayments. Should interest rates decline, the market value (present value) of the mortgage will change. Table 5–5 shows the market value of both mortgage pass-throughs under various interest rate assumptions. In each case, the market interest rate (discount rate) is 8.5 percent for the first half of the loan (payments 1–180). The difference among the cases is the market interest rate during the second half of the term of the loan (payments 181–360).

In the first case, the market interest rate is 7.5 percent during the second half of the term of the loan. Under this assumption, the difference in market value of the two pass-through securities is –\$1,852.97, that is, the pass-through without prepayments is worth less than the pass-through with prepayments. This occurs because the prepayments are worth more when they are received sooner rather than later.

Table 5–5.

MORTGAGE PASS–THROUGH AMORTIZATION SCHEDULE
WITH SERVICING FEE AND PREPAYMENTS

Payment Number	Payment Amount	Interest	Service Fee	Principal Reduction	Prepay	Unpaid Balance
0						100,000.00
1	733.76	625.00	41.67	67.10	426.21	99506.69
2	730.63	621.92	41.46	67.26	424.11	99015.32
3	727.52	618.85	41.26	67.42	422.01	98525.89
4	724.42	615.79	41.05	67.58	419.92	98038.39
5	721.33	612.74	40.85	67.74	417.84	97552.81
68	551.05	442.88	29.53	78.65	301.88	70479.62
69	548.70	440.50	29.37	78.83	300.26	70100.53
70	546.36	438.13	29.21	79.02	298.64	69722.87
71	544.03	435.77	29.05	79.21	297.03	69346.63
72	541.71	433.42	28.89	79.40	295.42	68971.81
140	405.08	292.31	19.49	93.28	199.07	46477.20
141	403.35	290.48	19.37	93.50	197.83	46185.87
142	401.63	288.66	19.24	93.73	196.58	45895.56
143	399.92	286.85	19.12	93.95	195.34	45606.27
144	398.21	285.04	19.00	94.17	194.11	45317.99
212	297.78	175.44	11.70	110.64	119.25	27840.34
213	296.51	174.00	11.60	110.91	118.27	27611.17
214	295.24	172.57	11.50	111.17	117.29	27382.71
215	293.98	171.14	11.41	111.43	116.31	27154.97
216	292.73	169.72	11.31	111.70	115.34	26927.93
284	218.90	82.19	5.48	131.23	55.52	12963.06
285	217.97	81.02	5.40	131.55	54.73	12776.79
286	217.04	79.85	5.32	131.86	53.93	12591.00
287	216.11	78.69	5.25	132.17	53.14	12405.69
288	215.19	77.54	5.17	132.48	52.35	12220.86
356	160.91	4.93	0.33	155.66	2.70	630.40
357	160.23	3.94	0.26	156.03	2.02	472.35
358	159.55	2.95	0.20	156.40	1.35	314.60
359	158.86	1.97	0.13	156.77	0.67	157.16
360	158.19	0.98	0.07	157.16	0.00	0.00

Table 5–5. (Continued)

MORTGAGE PASS–THROUGH AMORTIZATION SCHEDULE WITH SERVICING FEE AND PREPAYMENTS

Note: This is an amortization schedule for a 30–year mortgage pass–through with a servicing fee, assuming constant prepayment rate.

$$L = \text{Loan amount} = 100,000$$

$$\text{Mortage rate} = 8 \text{ percent}$$

$$\text{Constant prepayment rate} = CPR$$

$$= .05 \text{ annually}$$

$$\text{Monthly prepayment rate} = MPR$$

$$= \left(1 - (1 - CPR)^{1/12}\right)$$

$$= .004265$$

$$\text{Original payment} = 733.76$$

$$P_t = \text{Payment in month } t$$

$$= 733.76(1 - MPR)^{t-1}$$

$$UB = \text{Unpaid balance}$$

$$\text{Servicing fee} = .5 \text{ percent}$$

$$= UB(.005/12)$$

$$\text{Interest} = UB(.075/12)$$

$$\text{Principal reduction}_t = PR_t$$

$$= P_t - UB_{t-1}(.075/12) - UB_{t-1}(.005/12)$$

$$\text{Prepayment}_t = MPR\left(UB_{t-1} - PR_t\right)$$

In the second case, the discount rate in the second half of the term is 6.5 percent. This lower discount rate reduces the difference between the value of the two pass-through securities. The present value of the security without pre-payments increases by a larger percentage because it has a longer average maturity. Payments associated with the no-prepayments security are more

Table 5–6.

PRESENT VALUE OF MORTGAGE PASS–THROUGHS UNDER VARIOUS INTEREST RATE ASSUMPTIONS

Discount Rates for Periods 1–180	181–360	Value of Payments 1–180 at Time 0	Value of Payments 181–360 at Time 180	Value of Payments 181–360 at Time 0	Total Value at Time 0
INTEREST RATE DECLINES TO 7.5%					
Without Prepayments					
8.5	7.5	$70,578.93	$76,781.58	$21,551.80	$92,130.73
With Prepayments					
8.5	7.5	83,998.36	35,574.28	9,985.34	93,983.70
		Difference			(1,852.97)
INTEREST RATE DECLINES TO 6.5%					
Without Prepayments					
8.5	6.5	70,578.93	81,749.61	22,946.28	93,525.21
With Prepayments					
8.5	6.5	83,998.36	37,418.72	10,503.05	94,501.41
		Difference			(976.20)
INTEREST RATE DECLINES TO 5.5%					
Without Prepayments					
8.5	5.5	70,578.93	87,198.66	24,475.77	95,054.70
With Prepayments					
8.5	5.5	83,998.36	39,419.67	11,064.70	95,063.06
		Difference			(8.36)
INTEREST RATE DECLINES TO 4.5%					
Without Prepayments					
8.5	4.5	70,578.93	93,184.07	26,155.82	96,734.75
With Prepayments					
8.8	4.5	83,998.36	41,593.61	11,674.90	95,673.26
		Difference			1,061.49

evenly distributed over time while the payments of the other are skewed more toward the beginning of the term. The market value of both securities increases, but the market value of the no-prepayments security increases faster.

In the third case, the discount rate in the second 15 years is 5.5 percent and the difference in market value of the two is almost eliminated. In the fourth case, the discount rate is reduced to 4.5 percent. At this rate, the security without prepayments is worth more than the other.

This example includes four interest rate scenarios. The possible combinations, of course, are not limited. The simulation can be repeated for as many interest rate combinations and prepayment assumptions as desired. The important point to remember is that the difference between the market values of the securities is the value of the option in that state. To determine the market value of the option, probabilities must be assigned to each state, with the total of these probabilities summing to 1. In the example provided, four probabilities would be assigned because there are four interest rate combinations tested. The value of the option is then the sum of the individual option values weighted by their assigned probabilities.

This valuation approach allows prepayments to be included in the analysis. It also accommodates an analysis of interest rate sensitivity.

Callable Bonds

The call provision of a bond reduces the bond's market value. The relationship between callable bonds and noncallable bonds is

$$MV_N = MV_C + C$$

where

$$MV_N = \text{Market value of a noncallable bond}$$

$$MV_C = \text{Market value of a callable bond}$$

$$C = \text{Market value of a call option}$$

Put another way, a commercial bank that owns a callable bond has a long position in a noncallable bond and a short position in the call option.

$$MV_C = MV_N - C$$

The call price stipulated in the bond indenture is the exercise price of the call option.

Consider the following example of a bond with 10 years to maturity that is callable at 101 in six months. The option is valued over a six-month period to accommodate the assumption of constant volatility of the rate of return of the underlying asset over the life of the option.

Given: $MV = 107.79$; $X = $ call price $= 101$; $k = .05$; $t = .5$; $\sigma = .20$; $n = 20$.

$$C = (MV)N(d_1) - Xe^{-kt}N(d_2)$$
$$d_1 = [ln(MV/X) + (k + \sigma^2/2)(t)]/\sigma(t^{.5})$$
$$d_2 = d_1 - \sigma(t^{.5})$$

Substituting,

$$\begin{aligned} d_1 &= [ln(107.79/101) \\ &\quad + (.05 + (.04/2))(.5)]/(.20)(.5^{.5}) \\ &= [.065064373 + .035]/.141421356 \\ &= .707561968 \\ d_2 &= .707561968 - (.20)(.5^{.5}) \\ &= .566140612 \end{aligned}$$

Applying the polynomial approximation in Figure 5–9,

$$N(.707561968) = .7604$$
$$N(.566140612) = .7143$$

The value of the call option is

$$\begin{aligned} C &= (107.79)(.7604) \\ &\quad - (101)(e^{-(.05)(.5)})(.7143) \\ &= 81.963516 - 70.363051 \\ &= 11.600465 \end{aligned}$$

Thus,

$$\begin{aligned} MV_N &= 107.79 + 11.60 \\ &= 119.39 \end{aligned}$$

The bank has a long position in a noncallable bond worth $119.39 and a short position in a call option worth $11.60.

Variable-Rate Loans

When interest rate caps or floors are associated with variable-rate loans, these options have not been explicitly priced. From the bank's perspective, a cap is a short position in a call option. A floor is a long position in a put option. Both of these may be valued by use of the Black futures options model.

Call option:

$$C = e^{-kt}[(F)N(d_1) - (X)N(d_2)]$$

where

F = Current market value of futures contract of the underlying asset

t = Life of the option

= Time representing the fraction of the year between now and the next repricing

$$d_1 = [ln(F/X) + (\sigma_F^2/2)(t)]/\sigma(t^5)$$

$$d_2 = d_1 - \sigma_F(t^{.5})$$

Put option:

$$P = e^{-kt}[(X)N(-d_2) - (F)N(-d_1)]$$

When the models are applied to interest rate caps and floors,

F = The forward interest rate over the life of the option

X = The interest rate cap or floor

Thus, the value of the option is also a rate. It is the value of the option per dollar of loan balance that is covered by the cap or floor. The amount of loan balance that will be affected is the loan balance multiplied by the fraction of the year that represents the frequency of interest rate resets or repricing. Since the option covers a future period, this amount should be discounted to the present at the forward rate.

A = Amount subject to the cap or floor

= $\tau(L)/(1 + F(\tau))$

where

τ = Fraction of the year that represents the intervals between resets or repricing

F = Forward rate over the next repricing period

The following example illustrates the pricing of an interest rate cap (call option) for a three-month repricing period to begin in one year.

Given: L = loan amount = 10,000; k_{450} = annual risk free rate for a 450-day investment = .066; k_{360} = annual risk free rate for a one-year investment = .065; σ_F = volatility of the forward rate = .20; $t = 1$; $\tau = .25$; X = interest rate cap = .08.

The forward rate is implied by the term structure of interest rates.

$$
\begin{aligned}
F &= [(450)(k_{450}) - (360)(k_{360})]/90 \\
  &= [(450)(.066) - (360)(.065)]/90 \\
  &= [6.30]/90 \\
  &= .07
\end{aligned}
$$

The amount of the loan balance that will be affected by this cap is $2,500 and its present value is $2,457.

$$
\begin{aligned}
A &= \tau(L)/(1 + F(\tau)) \\
  &= (.25)(10,000)/(1 + (.07)(.25)) \\
  &= 2,500/1.0175 \\
  &= 2,457
\end{aligned}
$$

The value of the call is A multiplied by the value of the call per dollar of applicable loan balance.

$$
\begin{aligned}
C &= Ae^{-kt}[(F)N(d_1) - (X)N(d_2)] \\
d_1 &= [ln(F/X) + (\sigma_F^2/2)(t)]/\tau(t^{.5}) \\
d_2 &= d_1 - \sigma_F(t^{.5})
\end{aligned}
$$

Substituting,

$$
\begin{aligned}
d_1 &= [ln(.07/.08) + (.02)]/(.2) \\
    &= -.5677 \\
d_2 &= -.5677 - (.20) \\
    &= -.7677
\end{aligned}
$$

Solving for the cumulative probabilities,

$$
N(-.5677) = 1 - N(.5677)
$$

$$= \quad 1 - .7149$$

$$= \quad .2851$$

$$N(1.7677) \quad = \quad 1 - N(.7677)$$

$$= \quad 1 - .7787$$

$$= \quad .2213$$

Solving for the value of the call,

$$C \quad = \quad Ae^{-kt}[(F)N(d_1) - (X)N(d_2)]$$

$$= \quad 2,457(e^{-.065})[(.07)(.2851)$$

$$- (.08)(.2213)]$$

$$= \quad 2,457(.937067)[.019957$$

$$- .017704]$$

$$= \quad 2,302.37(.002253)$$

$$= \quad 5.19$$

SUMMARY OF OPTION VALUATION CONCEPTS

Table 5–7 is a summary of the option valuation models discussed in this chapter. It also contains a synopsis of the concepts that support the models and their application to commercial bank portfolios.

Table 5–7.

SUMMARY OF OPTIONS CONCEPTS

PROFITS FOR

Call buyer	$MV - X - C$
Call writer	$X + C - MV$
Put buyer	$X - P - MV$
Put writer	$MV + P - X$

RELATIONSHIP BETWEEN PARAMETERS AND OPTION VALUE

	Relationship to market valuation of	
Parameter	**Call**	**Put**
Market value of underlying asset	Positive	Negative
Exercise price	Negative	Positive
Interest rate	Positive	Negative
Volatility of underlying asset	Positive	Positive
Time to maturity	Positive	Positive

INTRINSIC VALUE OF OPTIONS

$$C = MV - X$$
$$P = X - MV$$

PUT–CALL PARITY

$$P = C + Xe^{-kt} - MV$$

BLACK–SCHOLES OPTION PRICING MODEL

$$C = (MV)N(d_1) - Xe^{-kt}N(d_2)$$

$$P = Xe^{-kt}N(-d_2) - (MV)N(-d_1)$$

where

C = Value of a European call option

MV = Current market value of the underlying asset

X = Exercise price

k = Risk free rate of return

t = Time to option expiration

Table 5–7. (Continued)

SUMMARY OF OPTIONS CONCEPTS

BLACK–SCHOLES OPTION PRICING MODEL (Concluded)

$N(y)$ = The probability that an observation from a normal

distribution will be less than or equal to y

= Cumulative normal probability distribution

$$d_1 = \left[\ln(MV/X) + \left(k + \sigma^2/2\right)(t)\right]/\sigma\left(t^{.5}\right)$$

σ = Volatility of underlying asset

= Standard deviation of rate of return of underlying asset

$$d_2 = d_1 - \sigma\left(t^{.5}\right)$$

$N(-y)$ = The probability that an observation from a normal

distribution will be less than or equal to $-y$

$$= 1 - N(y)$$

BLACK FUTURES OPTION PRICING MODEL

$$C = e^{-kt}\left[(F)N(d_1) - (X)N(d_2)\right]$$

$$P = e^{-kt}\left[(X)N(-d_2) - (F)N(-d_1)\right]$$

where

F = Current market value of futures contract of the

underlying asset

t = Life of the option

$$d_1 = \left[\ln(F/X) + \left(\sigma_F^2\right)(t)\right]/\sigma\left(t^{.5}\right)$$

$$d_2 = d_1 - \sigma_F\left(t^{.5}\right)$$

Table 5–7. (Continued)

SUMMARY OF OPTIONS CONCEPTS

POLYNOMIAL APPROXIMATION OF CUMULATIVE NORMAL DISTRIBUTION FUNCTION

For $x \geq 0$:

$$N(x) \cong 1 - \left(1/(2\pi)^{.5}\right)\left(e^{-a/2}\right)\left(b_1 p + b_2 p^2 + b_3 p^3\right)$$

For $x < 0$:

$$N(x) \cong 1 - N(-x)$$

where

$$\pi = 3.14159265$$

$$a = x^2$$

$$a = 2x$$

$$b_1 = .4361836$$

$$b_2 = -.1201676$$

$$b_3 = .9372980$$

$$p = \left(1/(1+cx)\right)$$

$$c = .33267$$

$$N(-x) = 1 - N(x)$$

EMBEDDED OPTIONS AND THEIR EFFECT ON BANK PORTFOLIOS

Underlying Instruments	Option	Position	Effect
Mortgage-related securities and loans	Call	Short	Reduces value of assets
Callable bonds	Call	Short	Reduces value of bonds
Variable-rate loans:			
Caps	Call	Short	Reduces value of loans
Floors	Put	Long	Increases value of loans
Deposits	Call	Long	Reduces value of deposits

Table 5–7. (Continued)

SUMMARY OF OPTIONS CONCEPTS

VALUING MORTGAGE–RELATED OPTIONS

➤ Determine the cash flows of the portfolio under the assumption of *no prepayments*.

➤ Determine the cash flows of the portfolio *with prepayments*.

➤ Determine the value of the portfolio under both assumptions with one interest rate environment.

➤ Determine the difference between the market value of the portfolio with no prepayments and the market value under the prepayment assumption.

➤ Change the interest rate assumptions as many times as desired, revalue the portfolio with and without prepayments, and compute the difference in present value in each case.

➤ Estimate the probability of each interest rate scenario.

➤ Weight the present value differences by their respective probabilities to arrive at the value of the option.

VALUING OPTIONS EMBEDDED IN CALLABLE BONDS

$$MV_N = MV_C + C$$

$$MV_C = MV_N - C$$

$$C = (MV)N(d_1) - Xe^{-kt}N(d_2)$$

where

MV_N = Market value of a noncallable bond

MV_C = Market value of a callable bond

C = Market value of a call option

X = Exercise price

= Call price of bond

Table 5–7. (Concluded)

SUMMARY OF OPTIONS CONCEPTS

VALUING OPTIONS EMBEDDED IN VARIABLE-RATE LOANS WITH CAPS AND FLOORS

$$C = Ae^{-kt}\left[(F)N(d_1) - (X)N(d_2)\right]$$

$$P = Ae^{-kt}\left[(X)N(-d_2) - (F)N(-d_1)\right]$$

where

F = Forward rate over the next repricing period

X = The interest rate cap or floor

t = Life of the option

= Time representing the fraction of the year between now and the next repricing

A = Amount subject to the cap or floor

$= \tau(L)/(1 + F(\tau))$

τ = Fraction of the year that represents intervals between resets or repricing

$$d_1 = \left[\ln(F/X) + \left(\sigma_F^2/2\right)(t)\right]$$

$$d_2 = d_1 - \sigma_F\left(t^{.5}\right)$$

SELECTED REFERENCES

Cox, John C., and Mark Rubinstein. *Options Markets.* Englewood Cliffs, N J: Prentice Hall, 1985.

Fabozzi, Frank J. *Fixed Income Mathematics.* Chicago: Probus Publishing, 1988.

Gibson, Rajna. *Option Valuation: Analyzing and Pricing Standardized Option Contracts.* New York: McGraw-Hill, 1991.

Howe, Donna M. *A Guide to Managing Interest-Rate Risk.* New York: New York Institute of Finance, 1992.

Hull, John. *Options, Futures, and Other Derivative Securities.* Englewood Cliffs, N J: Prentice Hall, 1989.

ENDNOTES

1   This refers to the time value of money. See Chapter 3.

2   This example ignores closing costs and points at the time of the original mortgage and at the time of refinancing.

3   A short sale of an asset involves selling an asset that is not owned. A short selling investor borrows the asset, sells it, and later buys the asset in the market to repay the borrowing. This is done when the investor expects that the price of the asset will decline. The profit is the net of the initial selling price and the subsequent, lower purchase price.

4   Note that the binomial approach is another alternative to option pricing. In this approach, the price of the underlying asset is assumed to either increase by u percent or decrease by d percent with some also assumed probabilities over a single period. For each subsequent period in the life of the option, these same percentage changes and probabilities apply. Each iteration produces a value for the call option, including, in some cases, zero when the call is out-of-the-money. The various values of the option are then weighted by their joint probabilities to arrive at an option value. Deficiencies of the model are:

  • There are abrupt changes in option value rather than continuous changes.
  • Percentage changes in the price of the underlying asset are restricted to only two values.
  • Probabilities of these price changes are set arbitrarily.

Further, when time to maturity is divided into an increasing number of sub-periods, the binomial result converges to the Black-Scholes result. Accordingly, the Black-Scholes model is used here rather than a binomial approach.

5   An alternative approach is the Public Securities Association schedule of prepayments which assumes that newly issued mortgages have a lower prepayment rate than older mortgages. The first month .2 percent of the mortgages prepay, the second month .4 percent, the third month .6 percent and so on.

CHAPTER 6

MEASURING THE GENERAL EFFECT OF INTEREST RATE CHANGES

INTRODUCTION

The market value of assets and liabilities is significantly influenced by the assumed required rate of return. In turn, market conditions, as well as the risk of the financial instrument, help determine the appropriate required rate. When market conditions change, so does the discount rate. This chapter examines:

➤ The effect of changing interest rates on market valuation of an asset.
➤ Investor returns when interest rates change.
➤ Future interest rate expectations.
➤ The exposure of bank portfolios to interest rate risk.

BOND THEOREMS

Theories that address the relationship between market value and interest rates most often are framed in terms of bonds. As long as financial instruments have finite lives with contractually determined cash flows, bond theorems apply to the financial instruments in asset and liability portfolios of commercial banks. Three fundamental theorems concern:

➤ The relationship between rate changes and market value changes.
➤ The differential reaction of long-term and short-term instruments to rate changes.
➤ The impact of coupon rate on interest rate sensitivity.

217

The Relationship between Changes in Rate and Changes in Market Value
Figure 6–1 shows the market value of a 15-year bond that pays 8 percent semi-annually when the discount rate ranges from 0 percent to 100 percent. At a zero rate of return, the bond is worth $2,200 [(40)(30) + 1,000] and at a 100 percent rate only $80. Each calculation is identical except for discount rate. To understand this phenomenon, consider the basic valuation formula that defines market value as the present value of all future cash flows.

$$MV = \sum_{t=1}^{n} CF_t \left(\frac{1}{(1+k)^t} \right)$$

Market value is the sum of n ratios of CF_t to $(1+k)^t$. Whenever k increases, the denominator of each of the n terms increases, causing each ratio and the sum of the ratios to decline.

The following bond theorem describes this relationship:

There is an inverse relationship between changes in required rate of return (or discount rate) and changes in market value.

The Maturity Date Effect
While it is true that increasing interest rates cause market value to decline and vice versa, the remaining time to maturity has an impact on the extent of the market value change. Figure 6–2 contains the market profiles of two bonds. Both bonds have a face value of $1,000 and a coupon rate of 8 percent paid semiannually. The difference between these bonds is their maturity dates—20 years for Bond A and 5 years for Bond B.

At a zero discount rate, Bond A is worth $2,600 [(40)(40) + 1,000] and Bond B, $1,400 [(40)(10) + 1,000]. At this discount rate, Bond A is worth more than Bond B because it will pay four times the number of coupon payments. At a 100 percent discount rate, however, the ranking is exactly reversed. The market value of Bond A is $80 and that of Bond B, $96.

$$MV = (PV \text{ of interest}) + (PV \text{ of maturity value})$$
$$MV_A = 80 + 0$$
$$= 80$$
$$MV_B = 79 + 17$$
$$= 96$$

Because Bond A cash flows are to be received further in the future, the present value is not as high. The 10 interest payments of Bond B are worth

Figure 6–1.

MARKET VALUE OF A BOND: DISCOUNT RATE EFFECT

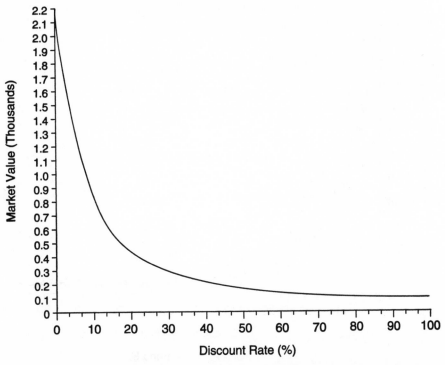

Note: Exhibit shows the market value of an 8 percent bond with a face value of $1,000 and 15 years to maturity with discount rates that range from 0 percent to 100 percent.

almost as much as the 40 interest payments of Bond A. Because it is received so far in the future, the maturity value of Bond A is worthless in present value terms when discounted at 100 percent.

Referring again to Figure 6–2, notice that the market value of both bonds equals $1,000 when the discount rate is 8 percent; that is, when the discount rate equals the coupon rate.[1] For discount rates less than 8 percent, Bond A is worth more than Bond B. For rates greater than 8 percent, the reverse is true. Despite the fact that Bond A actually pays a greater number of interest payments, its longer time to maturity causes the market value profile of Bond A to have a steeper slope (to decline more sharply) than Bond B.

Figure 6–2.

MARKET VALUE OF A BOND: MATURITY DATE EFFECT

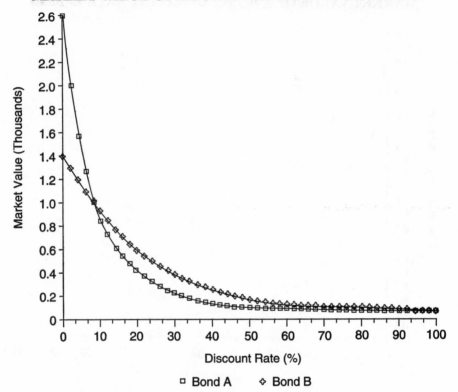

□ Bond A   ◇ Bond B

Note: Exhibit shows the market values of two bonds with discount rates that range
          from 0 percent to 100 percent. Both have a maturity value of $1,000 and a
          coupon rate of 8 percent paid semiannually. Bond A matures in 20 years, Bond
          B in 5 years.

The bond theorem is:

A given change in required rate of return will cause a greater percentage change in market value for longer-term bonds than for
shorter term bonds.

OR

Longer-term bonds are more price sensitive to changes in required
return than shorter term bonds.

The Coupon Rate Effect

Figure 6–3 contains the market value profiles of Bonds A and B, this time with the same maturity—10 years—but different coupon rates—10 percent for A and 6 percent for B. At a zero discount rate, the value of Bond A is $2,000 [(50)(20) + 1,000]. Because it has a lower coupon rate, the value of Bond B is $1,600 [(30)(20) + 1,000]. The difference in market value is $400. At a 100 percent discount rate, Bond A is worth only $100 and Bond B is worth $60, a difference of $40. In percentage terms, the value of Bond B, the lower-coupon bond, fell faster than the value of Bond A. A random sample of the market value changes shows this to be the case.

Discount Rate Change		Change in Market Value	
From	**To**	**Bond A**	**Bond B**
10%	12%	$(885 - 1000)/1000 = -.115$	$(656 - 751)/751 = -.126$
30	32	$(348 - 374)/374 = -.069$	$(229 - 249)/249 = -.080$
64	62	$(160 - 165)/165 = -.030$	$(97 - 101)/101 = -.040$
98	100	$(100 - 102)/102 = -.020$	$(60 - 62)/62 = -.032$

Bond B is the lower-coupon bond and its price changes were a larger percentage of market value than those of Bond A. The bond theorem that explains these observations is:

A given change in required rate of return will cause a greater percentage change in market value for lower-coupon bonds than for higher coupon bonds.

OR

Lower-coupon bonds are more price sensitive to changes in required return than higher-coupon bonds.

INTEREST RATE RISK AND INVESTOR RETURNS

Chapters 4 and 5 noted that prepayments of mortgage-related investments expose investors to *reinvestment risk;* that is the risk that it may not be possible to reinvest the proceeds of prepaying (or maturing) fixed-income securities at rates equivalent to those of the prepaying (or maturing) securities because of generally declining interest rates. Changes in interest rates also expose investors to *price risk* (i.e., the risk that the market value of a fixed-income security will decline when interest rates increase).

Figure 6–3.

MARKET VALUE OF A BOND: COUPON RATE EFFECT

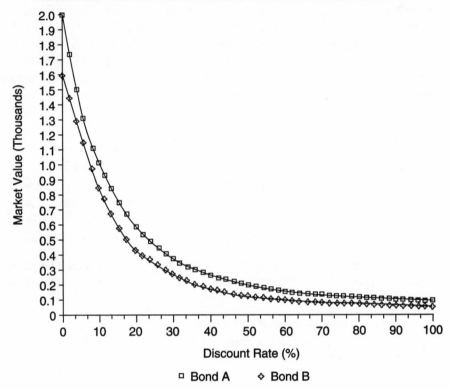

Note: Exhibit shows the market values of two bonds with discount rates that range
         from 0 percent to 100 percent. Both have a maturity value of $1,000 and mature
         in 10 years. The coupon rate of Bond A is 10 percent paid semiannually; Bond
         B, 6 percent paid semiannually.

Price risk can affect an investor's capital gains yield. The total rate of
return to a bondholder (or any investor in a fixed-income security) is composed
of the current yield and the capital gains yield.

$$k_B = CY + CGY$$

where

$$k_B = \text{Rate of return to a bond investor}$$

$$CY \;=\; \text{Current yield (interest payment as a percentage of}$$
$$\text{bond value at the beginning of the period)}$$

$$CGY \;=\; \text{Capital gains yield}$$

For a particular security, the current yield will depend on the bond's coupon rate and the value of the bond at the beginning of the holding period. Thus, the current yield for the year is a unique value that can be identified at the beginning of the year.

However, the capital gains yield, or percentage price change, depends on the market value of the bond at the end of the period. In turn, the end-of-period value depends on interest rate changes. For example, on January 1, a 10 percent coupon bond (Bond A) that pays interest annually and has a remaining maturity of two years with a required return of 12 percent sells at $966.21.

$$MV_0 \;=\; 100(PVIFA_{.12,2}) + 1,000(PVIF_{.12,2})$$
$$=\; 100(1.6901) + 1,000(.7972)$$
$$=\; 966.21$$

A 10-year bond (Bond B) with the same features, but a 12.5 percent required return sells for $861.59 on January 1.

The current yields of Bond A and Bond B are 10.35 percent [100/966.21] and 11.61 percent [100/861.59], respectively. The capital gains yields are functions of both beginning and ending prices, MV_0 and MV_1.

$$CGY \;=\; (MV_1 - MV_0)/MV_0$$
$$CGY_A \;=\; (982.14 - 966.21)/966.21$$
$$=\; 0.01649$$
$$CGY_B \;=\; (869.29 - 861.59)/861.59$$
$$=\; 0.00894$$

Thus, total return to an investor in Bond A during the year is 12.00 percent [10.35 + 1.65 percent]. The corresponding return on Bond B is 12.50 percent [11.61 + 0.89 percent]. Each bond yielded exactly the required return, even though the mix of current and capital gains yields is different.

Now suppose that interest rates decline during the year and required returns fall by 1 percentage point for all securities. In this case, end-of-year prices for Bonds A and B will be $990.99 and $918.53, respectively. The respective capital gains yields increase to 2.56 and 6.61 percent.

$$CGY_A = (990.99 - 966.21)/966.21$$
$$= .02556$$
$$CGY_B = (918.53 - 861.59)/861.59$$
$$= .06609$$

Total return from Bond A becomes 12.91 percent, 0.91 percentage point higher than before. However, total return for Bond B is 18.22 percent [11.61 + 6.61 percent], 5.72 percentage points higher.

Before the change in interest rates, the rate of return differential between the two bonds was 0.5 percentage point. After the decline, the differential is 5.31 percentage points. This example illustrates the price behavior of short-term versus long-term bonds in a declining interest rate environment, that is, long-term investments result in higher total rates of return.

As noted earlier, of course, should rates increase, the greater volatility of long-term bonds works to the disadvantage of the investor. Assuming an increase of 1 percentage point, end-of-year prices of Bonds A and B are $973.45 and $823.68, respectively. Resulting capital gains yield and total return for Bond A are 0.75 and 11.10 percent. Corresponding figures for Bond B are –4.40 and 7.21 percent.

While Bond A total return declined by 0.9 percentage point from that in the stable rate environment, Bond B total return is 5.29 percentage points lower. When interest rates increase, smaller declines in total rate of return result when shorter-term bonds are held.

INTEREST RATE BEHAVIOR
Because the return to an investor in fixed-income securities, including bonds and loans, can be so sensitive to interest rate changes, it is necessary to understand the mechanics of interest rate behavior.

The Term Structure of Interest Rates
A number of factors influence interest rates and changes in interest rates, but the term structure of interest rates, an important fundamental relationship, is frequently analyzed. The *term structure of interest rates* is defined as the relationship between time (term) and interest rates. The *yield curve* is an analytical tool that helps to describe this relationship. The yield curve is a graphic description of the relationship between time to maturity and yield to maturity for a given risk class of securities.

A yield curve plots the remaining time to maturity of a group of securities against yield to maturity.[2] The unique maturity date of each security in the group is represented by a point on the curve. As the objective of the analysis is to isolate the effect of time on yield, all characteristics of the securities besides maturity are held constant.

Corporate bonds and U.S. Treasury bonds, for example, would not be included in the same yield curve. Treasury bonds are considered free of default (nonrepayment) risk, corporate bonds are not. A yield curve including both bonds would mix up differences related to risk with the effects of time. It would be misleading as well to group corporate bonds with municipal bonds, even if they are in the same default risk class, because the two classes of bonds are subject to different income tax treatment, since municipal bond interest is not taxable. The differential tax treatment would be captured in such a combination, which also would distort the relationship between time to maturity and yield.

Figure 6–4 illustrates four possible yield curve shapes. All four types of yield curves have been observed in the United States at one time or another. The most common curve observed in the United States in fact has been the ascending yield curve that describes lower short-term yields relative to long-term yields, in an environment of generally low rates. The descending curve was observed from 1906 to 1929, then again in the late 1960s and early 1970s, when the general level of U.S. interest rates was higher. Humped Treasury yield curves also have been observed during periods of high interest rates, specifically around 1960 and during 1966–1970. Flat yield curves prevailed from 1901 to 1905, when interest rates fluctuated between their historical highs and lows.

Theories Explaining the Term Structure of Interest Rates

While the shape of these curves is objectively determined—maturity dates and yields are plotted on a graph—there are a number of differing theories that explain the reasons for the shapes. There are three basic theories explaining the term structure of interest rates:

➤ Unbiased expectations theory.
➤ Liquidity preference theory.
➤ Market segmentation theory.

Considerable academic research has tested each of these theories, but none of the evidence to date is conclusive enough to dismiss any of them. Each

Figure 6–4.

EXAMPLES OF YIELD CURVES

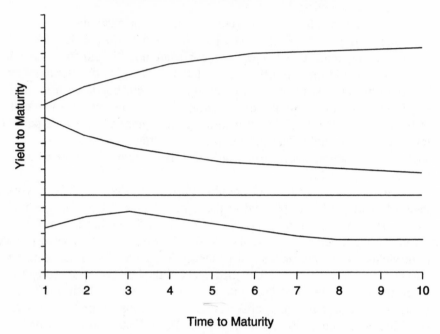

Note: Exhibit provides examples of four types of yield curves: ascending, descending, flat, and humped

theory in fact appears to contribute some insight into the behavior of interest rates and is therefore useful in combination with the others.

Unbiased Expectations Theory. The unbiased expectations theory assumes that the shape of the yield curve is explained by the market's consensus about future interest rates. That is, the yield curve is the result of both current and anticipated interest rates.

If the market as a whole believes that rates will rise, investors prefer shorter-term securities so that they do not lock themselves into a lower rate when they can make more money at a higher rate in the future. If interest rates are expected to rise, more investors want to invest only short term to take advantage of higher rates later. Also, when rates rise, prices of short-term securities are less volatile and suffer smaller percentage decreases than longer-term securities. These factors create strong demand for short-term securities that bid up short-term security prices and push their yields down. Of course, selling pressure on long-term securities at the same time creates the opposite effect on their prices and yields. The net effect, according to the unbiased expectations theory, is that the yield curve will slope upward.

The converse would be an expectation that interest rates will fall. In this case, investors want to invest in longer-term securities because longer-term investments appreciate more in such an environment than their short-term counterparts. Also, investors want to lock in the relatively high interest rates that are available today. This buying pressure causes the price of long-term bonds to increase and long-term yields to decline vis-à-vis short-term yields. The yield curve slopes downward.

Unbiased expectations theory suggests that the short-term interest rates implied by the yield curve are unbiased estimates of the market consensus of future rates. Specifically, long-term rates are a geometric average of current and anticipated future short-term rates.

$$(1 + {_0R_n})^n = (1 + {_0R_1})(1 + f_2)(1 + f_3) \ldots (1 + f_n)$$

where

$$_0R_n = \text{The long-term rate applicable for the period from time 0 to time } n$$

$$f_i = \text{The implied future one-year rate for year } i \, (i = 2, \ldots n)$$

Figure 6–5 is a hypothetical yield curve. The ascending curve begins at 7.50 percent for 1-year maturities and increases to 8.35 percent for 10-year maturities. All yields other than the one-year rate, $_0R_1$, are averages of implied future short-term rates. The rate for a two-year security, $_0R_2$, has a value of 7.80 percent and is a geometric average of 0R1 and the one-year rate during the second year, f_2.

$$(1 + {_0R_2})^2 = (1 + {_0R_1})(1 + f_2)$$

$$(1 + {_0R_2})^2 = (1 + {_0R_1})(1 + f_2)$$

$$(1.0780)^2 = (1.0750)(1 + f_2)$$

$$f_2 = 0.0810$$

The implied future one-year rate for year 2, f_2, is 8.10 percent. The same procedure is followed to determine the implied one-year rate for year 3, f_3, and

Figure 6–5.

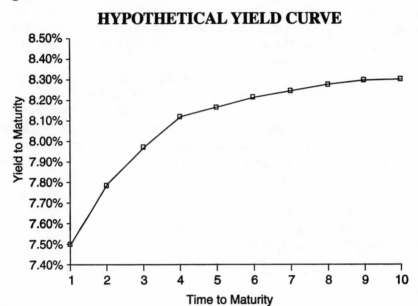

HYPOTHETICAL YIELD CURVE

Note: Exhibit represents hypothetical debt securities of the same risk class that are trading with several maturities outstanding.

Years to Maturity	Yield to Maturity
1	7.50%
2	7.80
3	7.99
4	8.15
5	8.20
6	8.25
7	8.29
8	8.32
9	8.34
10	8.35

all the other short-term rates; that is, increase the value of n by one year, substitute the values of known variables, and solve for f.

To streamline the process, note that all the terms on the right side of the equation that precede $(1 + f_n)$ are equivalent to $(1 + {_0}R_n - 1)^{n-1}$. Thus, dividing by $(1 + {_0}R_n - 1)^{n-1}$ and subtracting 1,

$$f_n = (1 + {}_0R_n)^n / (1 + {}_0R_{n-1})^{n-1} - 1$$

To find the one-year rate implied for year 10, substitute the yields to maturity for 10- and 9- year bonds, respectively, into the equation.

$$f_{10} = (1.0835)^{10} / (1.0834)^9 - 1$$

$$= 0.0844$$

The basic equation also may be used to infer yields for future multiyear periods. Suppose that the specific period of interest begins at time m and ends at time n, representing $(n - m)$ periods. Adapting the equation to these circumstances:

$$(1 + {}_0R_n)^n = (1 + {}_0R_1)(1 + f_2) \ldots$$

$$(1 + f_m)(1 + f_m + 1) \ldots (1 + f_n)$$

where

$$(m + 1) < n$$

Because time m is the end of year m, and

$$(1 + {}_0R_1)(1 + f_2) \ldots (1 + f_m) = (1 + {}_0R_m)^m$$

then

$$(1 + {}_0R_n)^n = (1 + {}_0R_m)^m (1 + {}_mR_n)^{(n-m)}$$

$$[(1 + {}_0R_n)^n / (1 + {}_0R_m)^m]^{1/(n-m)} - 1 = {}_mR_n$$

To illustrate, suppose that an investor wants to determine the yield to maturity during the four-year holding period beginning at time 6 (end of year 6) and that Exhibit 6–5 describes the yield curve. In this case, $m = 6$ and $(n - m) = 4$. The four-year yield implied by this curve is:

$$[(1.0835)^{10} / (1.0825)^6]^{1/4} - 1 = 0.0850$$

This is the estimated yield to maturity (average annual rate of return) for the four-year period beginning at the end of period 6. It is the geometric average of the short-term rates implied by the yield curve.

Under the assumptions of unbiased expectations theory, an investor should be indifferent between holding one long-term security and holding a series of one-year securities because the terminal value is the same in either case. All long-term rates are simply averages of short-term rates. Of course, in the real world, there are transactions costs associated with frequent buying and selling that work against true indifference.

Liquidity preference theory. Unbiased expectations theory assumes that everyone in the market correctly anticipates interest rate changes, so that each can make appropriate portfolio adjustments. Liquidity preference theory suggests that investors cannot be absolutely certain about future changes in the interest rate environment. To the extent that they hold long-term securities, investors' vulnerability to loss increases and they must be compensated for exposure to this additional risk.

As in an earlier example, Bonds A and B both have 10 percent coupon rates paid semiannually, but Bond A has only 2 years to maturity, while Bond B has 10 years remaining before it matures. Suppose that two investors attempt to assess their risk exposure when the appropriate discount rate for the bonds is 12 percent. In a 12 percent interest rate environment, the prices of Bonds A and B are $965.36 and $885.30. It is possible that one investor might expect interest rates to increase and therefore choose Bond A with two years to maturity. The other may think for some reason that interest rates will drop; this investor would choose Bond B with 10 years to maturity.

In the event that interest rates decline to 10 percent, the value of both bonds will increase to $1,000 (because they both have 10 percent coupon rates). While for the holder of Bond A, this represents a $34.64 increase (a 3.6 percent capital gain or increase in the market value of the bond), the holder of Bond B realizes a much greater increase of $114.70 (a 13 percent capital gain). Current yields (from interest income) further enhance profitability—10.4 percent for Bond A and 11.3 percent for Bond B.

If interest rates increase to 14 percent, the prices of Bonds A and B drop to $932.26 and $788.10. This results in a capital loss of 3.4 percent for Bond A that is offset by the current yield of 10.4 percent, for a net return of 7 percent despite the price decline. In the case of Bond B, the capital loss of 11 percent almost exactly offsets its 11.3 percent current yield. The longer-term Bond B places investors in greater jeopardy of *loss of principal* or exposes them to greater *price risk* than the shorter-term Bond A.

According to liquidity preference theory, compensation for this greater price risk is in the form of risk premiums that increase as time to maturity increases. This means that even if future one-year rates are all equal, the yield curve will be upward sloping.

$$(1 + {}_0R_n)^n \; = \; (1 + {}_0R_1)(1 + f_2 + L_2) \ldots (1 + f_n + L_n)$$

where

$$L_i \; = \; \text{The liquidity premium applicable to period } i, \text{ with}$$
$$L_n > L_{n-1} > \ldots > L_2 > 0$$

Liquidity preference theory rests on somewhat more subjective assumptions than unbiased expectations theory because liquidity premiums are not necessarily the same for everyone. The theory does, nevertheless, predict the shape of the yield curve that has been most common in the United States in the 20th century.

Market segmentation theory. Another approach to interest rate behavior is *market segmentation theory,* which suggests that investor time preferences involve more than price risk. That is, market participants operate essentially in one maturity band determined by their sources and uses of funds. Managers of insurance company and pension fund asset portfolios, for example, manage liabilities that typically are long-term in nature. If these managers invest in short-term asset portfolios, which are the least vulnerable to price risk, the company faces exposure to lower rates of return on investment that may be insufficient to service their liabilities. In other words, they face *reinvestment risk,* the potential loss of income.

According to market segmentation theory, other types of financial intermediaries (commercial banks, for example) need to maintain shorter average maturities of asset portfolios. Increases in their short-term cost of funds could quickly erode their profitability spread if long-term asset portfolios are locked in at lower rates.

Market segmentation theory suggests that interest rates in a maturity band depend on the supply of and demand for loanable funds with that maturity. Not everyone will prefer short-term securities or necessarily have a particular perception of future short-term vis-à-vis long-term rates.

The theory of *preferred habitat* is a compromise between market segmentation and unbiased expectations. This theory assumes that investors generally operate in the maturity class that is their preferred habitat, the maturity band in which they are most comfortable. Sufficiently high interest rates would lead them to switch to other maturities.

All of these theories contribute to the understanding of interest rate behavior. The yield curve may contain some information about the market's consensus of future short-term interest rates. There also may be a permanent element of upward bias in longer-term rates. In addition, conditions of supply and demand influence interest rate levels.

INTEREST RATE RISK AND THE BANK PORTFOLIO
Interest Rate Sensitivity
Bank assets and liabilities always are affected by changes in interest rates because of their respective fixed cash flows. Short-term instruments may be

associated with different interest rates as they mature and asset proceeds are reinvested or liabilities reissued. In some cases, instruments are *rate sensitive.* Their interest rates change at predetermined intervals; that is, they *float* with a specific publicly quoted rate or index. The rates earned and paid on rate-sensitive assets and liabilities change with market interest rates. These instruments have floating interest rates instead of fixed rates. If rate-sensitive assets and liabilities are significant in different portions of the bank balance sheet, earnings are volatile in an environment of changing interest rates.

Consider the hypothetical Security Bank. Referring to Table 6–1, notice that Security is well capitalized with 7 percent of average assets financed with equity. The exhibit also includes the average rates earned and paid on assets and liabilities. Loan rates range from 10.42 to 12.56 percent, while deposit rates are 8 percent or less. Even long-term borrowing costs are less than 10 percent. In the base case (before assuming any interest rate changes), interest income exceeds interest expense by $1.106 billion.

Note, too, that the 1993 assets include interest-bearing time deposits and federal funds that either have floating interest rates or are extremely short-term so as to almost immediately reflect rate changes. Also, a small portion of loans is rate sensitive. Total rate-sensitive assets equal $10.69 billion. The remaining assets ($22 billion) are considered fixed-rate assets, that is, a change in rates does not affect associated cash flows right away. On the other hand, most of Security's liabilities are highly rate sensitive ($25.078 billion).

If it is assumed that the bank's net noninterest expense is $636 million, 1993 income before taxes is $470 million in a stable interest rate environment [($1.106 billion) – ($636 million) = $470 million]. Should interest rates change, however, bank earnings could be subject to considerable volatility.

Table 6–2 illustrates the potential effect on bank earnings of a 1 percentage point change in short-term rates. For this example, assume instantaneous changes in the rates earned and paid on floating rate assets and liabilities. Thus, only rate-sensitive instruments are affected. Profit is measured for the full year.

When short-term rates increase by 1 percentage point, rate-sensitive assets earn more interest income than would have otherwise been the case. Since the average balance of these assets is $10.69 billion, projected interest income grows by $106.9 million. Similarly, rate-sensitive liabilities of $25.078 billion necessitate an additional $250.78 million in interest payments. Incremental interest income ($106.9 million) net of incremental interest expense ($250.78 million) produces a decrease in net interest income and earnings before taxes of $143.88 million. Under this assumption, the change in earnings is 30.6 percent.

Table 6–1.

SECURITY BANK: RATE SENSITIVITY 1993

	Average Balance (Millions)	Base Rates	Income or Expense (Millions)
Rate-Sensitive Assets			
Interest-bearing time deposits	$ 1,391	9.20%	$ 128
Federal funds sold and repos	600	7.60	46
Variable rate loans	8,699	10.42	906
	10,690		1,080
Fixed-Rate Assets			
Investment securities	$5,174	8.14	421
Fixed-rate loans	12,924	12.56	1,623
Cash and due from banks	2,252	—	—
Premises and other assets	1,699	—	—
	22,049		2,044
	$32,739		$3,124
Rate-Sensitive Liabilities			
Money market deposit accounts	$5,984	6.40	$ 383
Time deposits, $100,000 or more	8,548	7.90	675
Foreign time deposits	2,753	7.30	201
Short-term borrowings	7,532	7.65	576
Variable-rate LT borrowings	261	9.84	26
	25,078		1,861
Fixed-Rate Liabilities and Equity			
Interest-bearing transactions accounts	$500	5.20	26
Other time deposits	1,000	7.99	80
Savings deposits	720	5.35	39
Fixed-rate long-term borrowings	125	9.84	12
Demand deposits	2,200	—	—
Other liabilities	759	—	—
Equity	2,357		—
	7,661		157
	$32,739		$2,018

Table 6–2.

SECURITY BANK: PROFITABILITY ANALYSIS 1993
($ millions)

	Base Rates	1 Percent Increase	1 Percent Decrease
Interest Income			
Rate-sensitive assets	$1,080	$1,186.90[1]	$ 973.10[3]
Fixed-rate assets	2,044	2,044.00	2,044.00
Interest Expense			
Rate-sensitive liabilities	<1,861>	<2,111.78>[2]	<1,610.22>[4]
Fixed-rate liabilities	<157>	<157.00>	<157.00>
Net Interest Income	1,106	962.12	1,249.88
Net Noninterest Expense	<636>	<636.00>	<636.00>
Earnings before Taxes	$ 470	$ 326.12	$ 613.88
Percentage Change in Earnings		<30.6%>	+30.6%

[1] $1,080 plus 0.01($10,690) = $1,186.90
[2] $1,861 plus 0.01($25,078) = $2,111.78
[3] $1,080 minus 0.01($10,690) = $973.10
[4] $1,861 minus 0.01($25,078) = $1,610.22

When short-term rates are assumed to decrease by 1 percentage point, the reverse is true. Projected interest expense declines more than interest income. Security Bank profits climb by $143.88 million or 30.6 percent.

Gap

Gap and gap ratio. The projected volatility of Security's earnings is directly related to the difference between its rate-sensitive assets and liabilities. This difference is the bank's gap.[3] Gap is the difference between rate-sensitive assets and liabilities. Gap may be measured in absolute dollar terms.

$$GAP = A_s - L_s$$

where

A_s = Rate-sensitive assets

L_s = Rate-sensitive liabilities

Gap also may be measured in relative terms.

$$GAP \text{ ratio} = A_s/L_s$$

Security Bank. Applying the gap equation, Security Bank's gap is a negative $14.388 billion, that is, rate-sensitive liabilities exceed rate-sensitive assets by $14.388 billion. An assumed 1 percentage point increase in short-term rates produced earnings declines of 1 percent of gap.

$$\Delta NII = \Delta k(GAP)$$

where

ΔNII = Change in net interest income (interest income less interest expense)

Δk = Change in short-term interest rates

Generally, increasing interest rates has a negative effect on earnings when rate-sensitive liabilities exceed rate-sensitive assets. Conversely, lower rates relieve the interest expense burden more than they reduce interest income, and earnings improve.

A positive gap (more rate-sensitive assets than liabilities) creates, opposite reactions to short-term rate changes. Increasing rates will boost interest income more than interest expense and profits will improve. However, when rates drop, deteriorating interest income more than offsets lower interest expense and profits slump.

The gap ratio measures the amount of rate-sensitive assets for every dollar of rate-sensitive liabilities, that is, it measures rate-sensitive assets as a percentage of liabilities. Security Bank's gap ratio is 0.426 [$10,690/$25,078 = 0.42627]. The bank's rate-sensitive assets represent less than one-half of corresponding liabilities.

Whenever the gap is negative, the gap ratio will be less than 1.0. Similarly, a gap ratio that is greater than 1.0, implies a positive dollar value gap. Theoretically, when the gap and gap ratio are zero and 1.0, respectively, earnings volatility (attributable to interest rate changes) is minimized.

First National Bank. In practice, a zero gap is difficult to maintain. However, it is possible to achieve a smaller gap than Security's. Security Bank and First National Bank, another hypothetical institution, are comparable in a number of ways. Total asset levels and rates earned and paid on specific categories are identical. Their net noninterest expense is even assumed to be the same. The primary difference between the two banks is the mix of assets and liabilities. Specifically, First National holds more rate-sensitive assets and fewer rate-sensitive liabilities.

As can be seen in Table 6–3, First National's rate-sensitive assets also are less than liabilities. However, the difference is smaller than that noted with Security. First National's gap is a negative $3.24 billion [($16.208 billion) – ($19.448 billion) = $3.24 billion] and its gap ratio is 0.833. In the base case, projected interest income and expense are $3.01 billion and $1.874 billion, respectively. After deducting net noninterest expense of $636 million, earnings before tax equal $500 million.

Again assuming a 1 percentage point interest rate change, the nonzero gap produces earnings volatility (Table 6–4). A 1 percentage point increase in short-term rates reduces profits by the same percentage (1 percent) of gap, or $32.4 million. However, because the gap (on the same asset base) is smaller, both the aggregate change and the percentage change (negative 6.48 percent) are smaller than was true for Security Bank. Similarly, if short-term rates decline, the improvement in earnings is smaller.

Gap Applications
These two examples illustrate the manner in which bank portfolios can be constructed to minimize earnings variability when assets and liabilities are classified as either rate sensitive or fixed rate. Practically, however, this classification scheme often is more involved than it may first appear.

Strictly speaking, maturing assets and liabilities expose banks to as much earnings volatility as do rate-sensitive instruments. So, items subject to *repricing* include both variable rate instruments and those fixed-rate instruments that mature in the near term. Table 6–5 shows the time periods within which First National's assets and liabilities are either due to be repriced (rate-sensitive instruments) or mature (fixed rate).

Measurements of gap occur in each time period analyzed. In the first 90 days, liabilities exceed assets. Thus, there is a negative gap of $2.776 billion with a corresponding gap ratio of 0.845. In the 91–180 day period, the gap is a positive $88 million and the gap ratio is 1.096. However, this positive gap is not large enough to offset the negative gap in the 0–90 day period. Cumulatively, that is, for the first 180 days, First National has a negative gap of $2.688 billion and a gap ratio of 0.857.

The 181–365 day period (second six months of the year) also has a positive gap that, again, is not large enough to offset the negative gap of the first 90 days. The greatest gap exposure is in the 0–90 day period. Whether the bank attempts to modify this position depends on its customer base, interest rate expectations, and its inclination to use other financial instruments to hedge the balance sheet.

Table 6–3.

FIRST NATIONAL BANK: RATE SENSITIVITY 1993

	Average Balance (Millions)	Base Rates(%)	Income or Expense (Millions)
Rate-Sensitive Assets			
Interest-bearing time deposits	$ 1,391	9.20%	$ 128
Federal funds sold and repos	895	7.60	68
Variable rate loans	13,922	10.42	1,450
	16,208		1,646
Fixed-Rate Assets			
Investment securities	$4,879	8.14	397
Fixed-rate loans	7,701	12.56	967
Cash and due from banks	2,252	—	—
Premises and other assets	1,699		—
	16,531		1,364
	$32,739		$3,010
Rate-Sensitive Liabilities			
Money market deposit accounts	$ 4,984	6.40	$ 319
Time deposits, $100,000 or more	6,544	7.90	517
Foreign time deposits	1,753	7.30	128
Short-term borrowings	6,037	7.65	462
Variable-rate LT borrowings	130	9.84	13
	19,448		1,439
Fixed-Rate Liabilities and Equity			
Interest-bearing transactions accounts	$ 1,500	5.20	78
Other time deposits	3,004	7.99	240
Savings deposits	1,720	5.35	92
Fixed rate long-term borrowings	256	9.84	25
Demand deposits	3,695	—	—
Other liabilities	759	—	—
Equity	2,357		—
	13,291		435
	$32,739		$1,874

Table 6–4.

FIRST NATIONAL BANK: PROFITABILITY ANALYSIS 1993
($ millions)

	Base Rates	1 Percent Increase	1 Percent Decrease
Interest Income			
Rate-sensitive assets	$ 1,646	$1,808.08[1]	1,483.92[3]
Fixed rate assets	1,364	1,364.00	1,364.00
Interest Expense			
Rate-sensitive liabilities	<1,439>	<1,633.48>[2]	<1,244.52>[4]
Fixed rate liabilities	<435>	<435.00>	<435.00>
Net Interest Income	1,136	1,103.60	1,168.40
Net Noninterest Expense	<636>	<636.00>	<636.00>
Earnings before Taxes	$ 500	$ 467.60	$ 532.40
Percentage Change in Earnings		<6.48%>	+6.48%

[1] $1,646 plus 0.01($16,208) = $1,808.08
[2] $1,439 plus 0.01($19,448) = $1,633.48
[3] $1,646 minus 0.01($16,208) = $1,483.92
[4] $1,439 minus 0.01($19,448) = $1,244.52

Gap Strategies

Bank management's reaction to a negative gap will vary. If First National's management believes that interest rates are likely to decline, it may not attempt to eliminate the gap. To do so would eliminate potentially higher earnings, as interest expense declines more than interest income. If short-term rates decline by 1 percentage point in the first 90 days, earnings will be $27.8 million higher than would otherwise be the case.[4] To the extent possible, the bank may decide to make the gap even more negative. Emphasizing fixed-rate loans and/or issuing more floating-rate or short-term deposits would accomplish this. New longer-term loans with fixed rates would fall outside shorter-term gapping periods. Effectively, First National could attempt to lock in the now available higher rates on assets. Interest paid on new variable-rate or short-term deposits would decrease when short-term rates fall.

Table 6–5.

FIRST NATIONAL BANK: GAP ANALYSIS 1993
($ millions)

	INTEREST SENSITIVITY PERIOD				
	0–90 Days	91–180 Days	181–365 Days	Over One Year	Total
Assets					
Money market instruments[1]	$ 1,990	$ 195	$ 101	—	$ 2,286
Investment securities	496	375	534	$ 3,474	4,879
Loans	12,696	433	874	7,690	21,623
Other assets[2]	—	—	—	3,951	3,951
Total	$15,112	$1,003	$1,509	$15,115	$32,739
Liabilities and Equity					
Noninterest bearing deposits[3]	—	—	—	$ 3,695	$ 3,695
Interest bearing deposits[4]	$11,799	$ 897	$1,211	5,598	19,505
Short-term borrowings	5,980	10	47	—	6,037
Long-term borrowings	109	8	13	256	386
Other liabilities	—	—	—	759	759
Equity	—	—	—	2,357	2,357
Total	$17,888	$ 915	$1,271	$12,665	$32,739
GAP	<2,776>	88	238	2,450	
GAP ratio	0.845	1.096	1.187	1.193	
Cumulative GAP	<2,776>	<2,688>	<2,450>	0	
Cumulative GAP ratio	0.845	0.857	0.878	1.000	

[1] Interest-bearing time deposits, federal funds sold, and repurchase agreements.
[2] Cash and due from banks, premises, allowance for possible credit loss, and other assets
[3] Demand deposits
[4] Money-market deposit accounts, time deposits > $100,000, foreign time deposits, interest-bearing transactions accounts, other time deposits, and savings accounts.

Thus, it is clear from this example that a negative gap may be desirable if bank management anticipates falling interest rates. At the end of an expansionary economic cycle, during which short-term interest rates have reached relatively high levels, a negative gap enhances profitability as rates decline to more normal levels.

On the other hand, if the economy is poised at the beginning of a period of anticipated economic expansion, during which interest rates are expected to increase, a positive gap may be advisable. For First National, reversing its near-term negative gap might involve offering more variable-rate loans or stressing short-term loans and investments to position the bank to take advantage of subsequent repricing at higher rates. At the same time, locking in longer-term deposits would result in less exposure on the liability side.

Creating or increasing a negative gap when management expected interest rates to decline and taking the opposite approach when future expectations are for higher rates are theoretically sound, but highly speculative, strategies. If management is to succeed in these attempts, projections of future interest rates must be accurate. If actual rate movements are in the opposite direction, earnings could deteriorate seriously. Accurate interest forecasting is an imprecise science, at best. Making deliberate, substantial changes in the bank's gap to widen it in one direction or the other can be a risky proposition. It amounts to gambling the bank's capital, and perhaps its solvency, on management's interest rate projections. This is clearly not sound management.

Even if management could predict interest rates with certainty, bank customers may not be anxious to accommodate the necessary changes in interest rate exposure. When the market consensus is that rates will decline, the appropriate bank strategy is to increase rate-sensitive liabilities relative to rate-sensitive assets. This may mean asking bank clients to accept fixed-rate loans. Yet if clients have the same rate expectations, fixed-rate loans appear unattractive to them. Likewise, variable rate or extremely short-term deposits are not particularly appealing.

These gap strategies are feasible only to a certain extent. They are, at best, difficult to achieve and, at worst, speculative and may threaten the bank's soundness. The difficulty of predicting interest rates complicates administration of the schemes. The financial sophistication of bank clients can preclude necessary portfolio adjustment.

INTEREST RATE RISK AND BANK CAPITAL

In addition to the practical limitations of gap management, there are more fundamental problems associated with gap analysis.

Interest Rate Changes and Net Worth

Adjusting the timing of asset and liability repricing to achieve a zero gap does not necessarily protect an institution from adverse changes in net worth. Net worth is the difference between the market values of assets and liabilities.[5] The simple example in Table 6–6 will help to illustrate. Suppose that two banks, A and B, each have total assets of $100 million, liabilities of $95 million, and net worth of $5 million.

Table 6–6.

ANTICIPATED CASH FLOWS: BANKS A AND B

($ millions)

	Year				
	1	2	3	4	5
Bank A					
Loans	12	12	12	12	112
Certificates of Deposit	0	0	0	0	<152.998>
Bank B					
Loans	0	0	0	0	176.234
Certificates of Deposit	0	0	0	0	<152.998>

MARKET VALUE OF LOANS AND DEPOSITS:

	Bank	Instrument	Percent Rate	Value at Year Zero
Before Interest Rate Change:				
	A and B	Loans	12.0%	$100.00
	A and B	CDs	10.0	95.00
After Interest Rate Change:				
	A	Loans	11.5	101.82
	B	Loans	11.5	102.26
	A and B	CDs	9.5	97.19

Each bank holds fixed-rate loans that mature in five years on the same date. Liabilities consist of five-year certificates of deposit that mature on the same date as the loans. In all gapping periods up to year 5, there are no potential repricings. Since all repricings occur on the same date in year 5, each bank has a positive $5 million gap in that period and a gap ratio of 1.05.

$$GAP = \$100 \text{ million} - \$95 \text{ million}$$
$$= \$5 \text{ million}$$
$$GAP \text{ ratio} = 100/95$$
$$= 1.0526$$

The only difference in the portfolios of Banks A and B is the type of loans held. Bank A's loans pay 12 percent interest each year on the face amounts, with principal due at maturity. Bank A plans to receive $12 million per year until the maturity date, at which time the last interest payment and principal repayment will be received.

Bank B's 12 percent loans, however, will be completely repaid in year 5. The bank will receive no cash flows until maturity, at which time its customers will repay all accrued interest and principal.[6] Given these terms, loan repayments for Bank B will total $176.234 million [$100 million $(1.12)^5$ = $176.234 million].

The 10 percent certificates of deposit (CDs) are identical. At the end of five years, each bank will pay a total of $152.998 million to depositors [$95 million $(1.10)^5$ = $152.998 million]. Notice that at required loan and CD rates of 12 and 10 percent, respectively, the present values also are identical. Loans are valued at $100 million, CDs at $95 million. Net worth, of course, is $5 million.

Now, assume that interest rates decline by 50 basis points across the board. Loan and CD rates fall to 11.5 and 9.5 percent, respectively. Anticipated cash flows will not change, but their present values will. Since there is an inverse relationship between interest rate changes and changes in market value, present values increase.

The present value of CDs increases to $97.19 million for both banks. However, changes in loan market values are not equal. Bank B loans increase more in value than those held by Bank A. After the rate change, loan portfolios of Banks A and B are worth $101.82 million and $102.26 million, respectively. Bank B's loan portfolio value increases more because of the time pattern of its cash flows. All cash flows occur in year 5, making it similar to a zero-coupon bond. Bank B's loan portfolio will be more rate sensitive since Bank A receives a portion of its cash flows in the interim years 1 through 4, that is, Bank A's loan portfolio is similar to a higher-coupon bond.

Note, too, that these different changes in asset values cause the net worth of the two banks to differ after interest rates decline.[7] The market value of equity drops from \$5 million to \$4.63 million for Bank A [\$101.82 million − 97.19 million] and increases to \$5.07 million for Bank B [\$102.26 million − 97.19 million]. Gap analysis does not satisfactorily explain this phenomenon because the technique does not consider the time value of money.

Duration
Gap analysis considers only dates of maturity or repricing. The objective of gap analysis is to measure the impact on earnings of mismatched combinations of rate-sensitive assets and liabilities. It does not address the issue of changes in the market value of assets and liabilities. So gap analysis necessarily does not address the change in net worth noted in the prior example. The market value of assets and liabilities depends not only on maturity or repricing dates but also on the timing of future cash flows.

Duration is a concept that measures a financial instrument's *average life* or the *weighted-average time of cash receipt*. The time of each cash receipt is weighted by the proportion of total present value which that cash flow represents.

$$D = \frac{\left[\sum_{t=1}^{n} \left(\frac{(CF_t)(t)}{(1+k)^t} \right) \right]}{\sum_{t=1}^{n} \left(\frac{CF_t}{(1+k)^t} \right)}$$

where

D = Duration

CF_t = Cash flow in time t

t = Number of periods before CF_t occurs

k = Appropriate discount rate for the instrument

n = Number of periods before instrument matures

To the extent that the durations of two financial instruments differ, their price sensitivities to interest rate changes differ. Table 6–7 illustrates duration calculations for Banks A and B. Bank A will receive interest payments prior to year 5. So the weighted-average time of cash receipt, duration, is less than five years. On the other hand, Bank B loans generate no interim cash flows and, as

Table 6–7.

DURATION ANALYSIS: BANKS A AND B

($ millions)

(1) Instrument	(2) Bank	(3) Year	(4) CF	(5) PVCF	(6) (3)x(5)	(7) Duration (Years)
Loan (12%)	A	1	$ 12	$ 10.71	10.71	
		2	12	9.57	19.14	
		3	12	8.54	25.62	
		4	12	7.63	30.52	
		5	112	63.55	317.75	
				100.00	403.74	4.0374
Loan (12%)	B	1	0	0	0	
		2	0	0	0	
		3	0	0	0	
		4	0	0	0	
		5	176.234	100	500	
				100	500	5.0
CD (10%)	A&B	1	0	0	0	
		2	0	0	0	
		3	0	0	0	
		4	0	0	0	
		5	153.998	95	475	
				95	475	5.0

Note: Duration equals the total of column (6) divided by the total of column (5).

a direct result, these loans have a duration of exactly five years. The same is true for both banks' CDs.

Just as the stated maturity of a financial instrument suggests its degree of price sensitivity to yield changes, duration also helps to describe price sensitivity. The following formula uses duration to estimate the percentage price change that will be associated with a particular change in rates.

$$\Delta MV/MV = -D(\Delta k/(1+k))$$

where

MV = Market value of financial instrument

ΔMV = Change in market value of financial instrument

D = Duration

$$k = \text{Appropriate discount rate}$$

$$\Delta k = \text{Change in discount rate}$$

The algebraic sign of the percentage change in market value is inversely related to the algebraic sign of the change in rates, that is, the relationship between price and rate changes is inverse. Note, too, that the longer an instrument's duration, the greater will be the absolute value of its change in market value for a given change in rate. This is consistent with the concept of greater price volatility for longer-term instruments. This equation works well for relatively small changes in rates.

Referring again to Banks A and B, the durations of their loan portfolios are 4.0374 years and 5 years, respectively. For Bank A, the duration prediction is a positive 1.802 percent change in price $[\Delta\ MV/MV = -\ 4.0374(-.005/1.12) = 0.018024]$. The actual change was 1.820 percent. Similarly, the predicted change for Bank B's loan portfolio is 2.232 percent $[\Delta\ MV/MV = -\ 5(-.005/1.12) = 0.022321]$, while the actual change was 2.260 percent. In general, when rates decline, the predicted price increase is less than the actual increase. When rates increase, the duration prediction produces a greater percentage price decline than actually occurs. However, for very small rate changes, the error also is small.

Duration and Net Worth
The most significant implication of duration analysis is that bank asset and liability portfolios with the same duration have similar market value sensitivity to interest rate changes. The process of matching durations of asset and liability portfolios can significantly reduce interest rate risk. However, this matching does not necessarily eliminate the risk.

Notice that when interest rates declined, the net worth of Bank A declined from $5 million to $4.63 million and that the capital ratio fell from 5 to 4.55 percent $[4.63/101.82 = 0.04547]$. However, the corresponding results for Bank B were less severe. After the rate change, net worth was $5.07 million and the capital ratio only fell to 4.96 percent $[5.07/102.26 = 0.04958]$. That is, the interest rate risk to net worth was reduced by matching the duration of assets and liabilities but was not eliminated.

When the durations of two instruments are equal and the instruments are discounted by the same rate, the duration prediction of $\Delta\ MV/MV$ suggests that a given change in interest rate will produce equivalent percentage changes in their respective market values. Further, the difference between the values of the two instruments should change by the same percentage. If both conditions had existed, the net worth of Bank B would have increased by this same percentage.

However, we note that for Bank B this was not the case. This result is attributable to the differential rates at which loans and CDs were discounted. The 0.5 percentage point decline in rates represented a larger percentage change in deposit rates than in loan rates. In essence, the present value of the liabilities changed by a greater percentage than the present value of loans.

Notice from the equation for Δ *MV/MV* the percentage change in market value has an inverse relationship with rate level prior to any change in rates. Thus, a 50-basis-point decline produces a greater proportional change for a 10 percent financial instrument than a 12 percent instrument. Bank B's CDs increased by 2.30 percent, loans by only 2.26 percent. Thus, the capital ratio declined by 0.4 percentage points.

The case of Bank A is further complicated by the unmatched durations of loans and CDs. Bank A's aggregate CD value also increased by 2.30 percent, but loan values only increased by 1.82 percent because the duration of the loan portfolio was just over four years. The combination of shorter asset duration and differential discount rates resulted in a larger decline in net worth than would have been true if durations were matched and both assets and liabilities discounted at more similar rates.

Certain points should be remembered when applying duration analysis.

➤ Unless the instrument involved is a zero-coupon instrument (no cash flows until maturity), duration will not equal time to maturity.

➤ Duration changes as time passes and as market interest rates change.

➤ If the instruments have any embedded options that may alter the future cash flows, the objective of duration analysis can be frustrated. An example of such an embedded option is a mortgage prepayment option that can severely shorten the future cash flow stream of a mortgage loan.

➤ If interest rate changes for assets do not equal interest rate changes for liabilities, matched durations do not help at all.

CONVEXITY

Figure 6–6 shows the difference between the duration prediction of market value and the actual market value for a $1,000 bond with 10 years to maturity and an 8 percent coupon rate paid semiannually. The base computation uses a 16 percent discount rate; the resulting market value is $607.27.

Figure 6–6.

MARKET VALUE PREDICTIONS BY DURATION

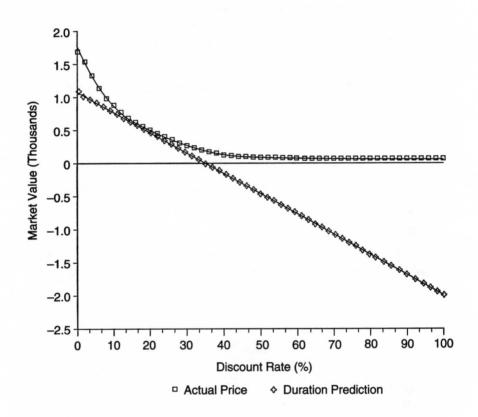

Note: For an 8 percent coupon bond paying interest semiannually and maturing
         in 10 years, exhibit shows: Actual market value of a fixed-rate bond and
         market value predicted by duration

Calculations are performed using the base market value of $607.27 at a 16 percent discount
rate. Market value is recomputed at interest rate intervals of 2 percentage points. Notice
that the actual market value is a convex function of rate while the duration prediction is a
linear function.

The actual market value changes in a nonlinear fashion producing a *convex function*. This quality is referred to as the bond's *convexity*. On the other hand, the duration prediction of market value is a linear function. The formula to compute the duration prediction is

$$MV_D = MV - (MV)(D)(\Delta k/(1 + k))$$

where

MV_D = Market value predicted by duration after interest rate change

MV = Market value before interest rate change

= 607.27

D = Duration

Δk = Change in discount rate

k = Discount rate used in base calculation

= .16

Notice that the duration prediction is a good approximation for small changes in rate. However, as the Δk increases, the approximation is not very accurate. There is an adjustment to compensate for this, also called *convexity*.

$$c = [\sum_{t=1}^{n} t(t+1)(CF_t)/(1 + k/m)^t]$$

$$/[(1 + k/m)^2 \sum_{t=1}^{n} CF_t/(1 + k/m)^t)]$$

c = Convexity in periods

t = Period t

n = Number of periods before maturity

k = Discount rate

m = Number of times per year interest is paid

Like duration, convexity is measured in time. To convert convexity in periods to convexity in years, c is divided by m^2.

$$c' = c/m^2$$

$$= \text{Convexity in years}$$

The percentage change in market value that is predicted by convexity is

$$\Delta MV/MV = (.5)(c')((\Delta k)^2)$$

The dollar amount of change in market value predicted by convexity is

$$\Delta MV_C = MV(.5)(c')((\Delta k)^2)$$

where

$$\Delta MV_C = \text{Price change due to convexity}$$

This result is added to the duration results for a new prediction of market value after the interest rate changes.

$$MV_{DC} = \text{Market value predicted by duration and convexity after interest rate change}$$

$$= MV_D + \Delta MV_C$$

$$= MV - (MV)(D)(\Delta k/(1 + k))$$

$$+ MV(.5)(c')((\Delta k)^2)$$

The convexity measure works well in compensating for small changes from the current market yield. The prediction of market values after changes in rate of ± 200 basis is improved by using convexity. Beyond 300- to 400-basis-point changes, however, the best approach is to use the valuation formula for the underlying instrument.

SUMMARY OF INTEREST SENSITIVITY CONCEPTS

Table 6–8 summarizes the concepts described in this chapter. Included are the bond theorems, interest rate theories, and interest sensitivity measures.

Table 6–8.

SUMMARY OF INTEREST SENSITIVITY CONCEPTS

Bond Theorems

➤ There is an inverse relationship between changes in required rate of return (or discount rate) and changes in market value.

➤ A given change in required rate of return will cause a greater percentage change in market value for longer term bonds than for shorter-term bonds.

OR

➤ Longer-term bonds are more price sensitive to changes in required return than shorter-term bonds.

➤ A given change in required rate of return will cause a greater percentage change in market value for lower coupon bonds than for higher-coupon bonds.

OR

➤ Lower-coupon bonds are more price sensitive to changes in required return than higher-coupon bonds.

Bondholder Returns

$$k_B = CY + CGY$$

where k_B = Rate of return to a bond investor

CY = Current yield (interest payment as a percentage

of bond value at the beginning of the period)

CGY = Capital gains yield

Table 6–8. (Continued)

SUMMARY OF INTEREST SENSITIVITY CONCEPTS

Term Structure of Interest Rates

$$\left(1+{}_0R_n\right)^n = \left(1+{}_0R_1\right)\left(1+f_2\right)\left(1+f_3\right)...\left(1+f_n\right)$$

where ${}_0R_n$ = The long-term rate applicable for the period from time 0 to time n

f_i = The implied future one-year rate for year i $(i = 2,...n)$

$$f_n = \left(1+{}_0R_n\right)^n / \left(1+{}_0R_{n-1}\right)^{n-1} - 1$$

$${}_mR_n = \left[\left(1+{}_0R_n\right)^n / \left(1+{}_0R_m\right)^m\right]^{1/(n-m)} - 1$$

where ${}_mR_n$ = Long-term rate applicable for the period from time m to time n

$$\left(1+{}_0R_n\right)^n = \left(1+{}_0R_1\right)\left(1+f_2+L_2\right)...\left(1+f_n+L_n\right)$$

where L_i = The liquidity premium applicable to period i, with

$$L_n > L_{n-1} > ... > L_2 > 0$$

Gap

$$GAP = A_S - L_S$$

where A_S = Rate-sensitive assets

L_S = Rate-sensitive liabilities

$$\Delta NII = \Delta k(GAP)$$

where ΔNII = Change in net interest income (interest income less interest expense)

Δk = Change in interest rate

Table 6–8. (Continued)

SUMMARY OF INTEREST SENSITIVITY CONCEPTS

Duration

$$D = \left[\sum_{t=1}^{n} \left((CF_t)(t)/(1+k)^t \right) \right] / \sum_{t=1}^{n} \left(CF_t /(1+k)^t \right)$$

where D = Duration

CF_t = Cash flow in time t

t = Number of periods before CF_t occurs

k = Appropriate discount rate for the instrument

n = Number of periods before instrument matures

$$\Delta MV / MV = -D\left(\Delta k /(1+k) \right)$$

where MV = Market value of financial instrument

ΔMV = Change in market value of financial instrument

D = Duration

k = Appropriate discount rate

Δk = Change in discount rate

$$MV_D = MV - (MV)(D)\left(\Delta k /(1+k) \right)$$

where MV_D = Market value predicted by duration after interest rate change

MV = Market value before interest rate change

D = Duration

Δk = Change in discount rate

k = Discount rate used in base calculation

Table 6–8. (Concluded)

SUMMARY OF INTEREST SENSITIVITY CONCEPTS

Convexity

$$c = \left[\sum_{t=1}^{n} t(t+1)(CF_t)/(1+k/m)^t \right] \left/ \left[(1+k/m)^2 \left(\sum_{t=1}^{n} CF_t/(1+k/m)^t \right) \right] \right.$$

where $c =$ Convexity in periods

$t =$ Period t

$n =$ Number of periods before maturity

$k =$ Discount rate

$m =$ Number of times per year interest is paid

$c' = c/m^2$

= Convexity in years

$\Delta MV/MV = (.5)(c')\left((\Delta k)^2\right)$

= Percentage change in market value predicted by convexity

$\Delta MV_C = MV(.5)(c')\left((\Delta k)^2\right)$

= Dollar price change predicted by convexity

$MV_{DC} =$ Market value predicted by duration and convexity after
interest rate change

$= MV_D + \Delta MV_C$

$= MV - (MV)(D)\left(\Delta k/(1+k)\right) + MV(.5)(c')\left((\Delta k)^2\right)$

SELECTED REFERENCES

Bierwag, Gerald O. *Duration Analysis; Managing Interest Rate Risk.* Cambridge, MA: Ballinger Publishing, 1987.

Grumball, Clive. *Managing Interest Rate Risk.* Westport, CT: Quorum Books, 1987.

Nelson, Charles R. *The Term Structure of Interest Rates.* New York: Basic Books, 1972.

ENDNOTES

1 See Chapter 4 for the bond theorem describing the relationships of market value, coupon rate, and discount rate.

2 The yield to maturity is the average annual rate earned by an investor who holds a security until it matures. Alternatively, yield to maturity is the discount rate that causes the present value of the future cash flows to exactly equal the market price. (See Chapter 3.)

3 Gap should not be confused with GAAP, generally accepted accounting principles.

4 This amount is 1 percent of GAP.

5 In this context, net worth is to be distinguished from GAAP-defined shareholders' equity and from RAP-defined capital. GAAP and RAP are acronyms for generally accepted accounting principles and regulatory accounting principles.

6 We assume that both banks assessed loan origination fees sufficient to cover all operating expenses during the five-year period.

7 In the discussion of duration, net worth and capital ratio refer to the market value concept of these terms. Neither GAAP-reported capital nor RAP-defined capital change.

CHAPTER 7

THE IMPACT OF CHANGING INTEREST RATES ON THE MARKET VALUE OF SPECIFIC BALANCE SHEET CATEGORIES

INTRODUCTION

The market value of a commercial bank portfolio is vulnerable to interest rate risk. The same principles that drive the bond theorems are relevant for bank assets and liabilities.

➤ There is an inverse relationship between interest changes and changes in market value.

➤ The market value of longer-term financial instruments is more sensitive to changes in interest rates.

➤ The market value of interest-paying financial instruments is less sensitive to interest rate changes than that of interest-only or single-payment (zero-coupon) financial instruments. In other words, lower-coupon instruments are more sensitive to rate changes than higher-coupon instruments.

This chapter analyzes specific asset and liability categories of a commercial bank balance sheet in the face of interest rate changes. The examples of Chapters 4 and 5 are extended to consider the impact of:

➤ 200-basis-point (b.p.) increase in the discount rate.

➤ 200-basis-point (b.p.) decrease in the discount rate.

All interest rates are assumed to change to the same extent. In other words, the yield curve simply shifts up or down by the specified number of basis points. An analysis of market value changes follows the calculations for each category:

➤ Temporary investments.
➤ Investment securities.
➤ Loans.
➤ Liabilities.

TEMPORARY INVESTMENTS
Temporary investments include:

➤ Interest-bearing time deposits in other banks.
➤ Federal funds sold.
➤ Term federal funds sold.
➤ Securities purchased under agreement to resell.

Interest-Bearing Time Deposits in Other Banks
The valuation model for a time deposit is

$$MV = D(1 + k_c)^n/(1 + k)^n$$

where

$$D = \text{Deposit}$$

$$k_c = \text{Contractual (coupon) rate}$$

An example of a time deposit from Chapter 4 is the six-month CD with a market value of $100,000.

Given: $D = \$100,000$; $k_c = .05$; $k = .05$; $n = .5$.

Assumed: 200 b.p. increase; $k = .07$.

$$MV = 100,000(1.05)^{.5}/(1.07)^{.5}$$

$$= 99,061.01$$

Change in MV: −.9390 percent

Assumed: 200 b.p. decrease; $k = .03$.

$$MV = 100,000(1.05)^{.5}/(1.03)^{.5}$$

$$= 100,966.21$$

Change in MV: .9662 percent

Federal Funds Sold

The valuation model for federal funds sold is almost identical to that for time deposits.

$$MV = FF(1+k_c)^n/(1+k)^n$$

where

$$FF = \text{Federal funds}$$

One of the original examples is an overnight sale with a market value of $1,000,000.

Given: $FF = 1,000,000$; $k_c = .04$; $k = .04$; $n = 1/365$.

Assumed: 200 b.p. increase; $k = .06$.

$$MV = 1,000,000(1.04)^{1/365}/(1.06)^{1/365}$$

$$= 999,947.81$$

Change in MV: $-.0052$ percent

Assumed: 200 b.p. decrease; $k = .02$.

$$MV = 1,000,000(1.04)^{1/365}/(1.02)^{1/365}$$

$$= 1,000,053.20$$

Change in MV: $.0053$ percent

Term Federal Funds Sold

The only difference between this asset and the federal funds noted above is the time to maturity of the agreement. The original example is a one-month agreement valued at $999,593.52.

Given: $FF = 1,000,000$; $k_c = .04$; $k = .045$; $n = 31/365$.

Assumed: 200 b.p. increase; $k = .065$.

$$MV = 1,000,000(1.04)^{31/365}/(1.065)^{31/365}$$

$$= 997,984.56$$

Change in MV: $-.1610$ percent

Assumed: 200 b.p. decrease; $k = .025$.

$$MV = 1,000,000(1.04)^{31/365}/(1.025)^{31/365}$$

$$= \quad 1,001,234.66$$

Change in *MV*:   .1642 percent

Securities Purchased under Agreement to Resell

The market value of this asset includes the value of any coupon payments received before the agreement ends.

$$MV = [\sum_{t=1}^{n} CP_t/((1 + k/m)^t)]$$

where

CP_t = Coupon paid in period t

SP = Selling price specified in resale agreement

m = Number of times per year interest is paid

The example is an agreement valued at $1,051,344.75.

Given: $SP = \$1,050,000$; $k = .045$; $n =$ one six-month period; $m = 2$;
$M = \$1,000,000$; $CR = .05$; semiannual coupon payment = 25,000.

Assumed: 200 b.p. increase; k = .065.

$$MV = 25,000/(1.0325) + 1,050,000/(1.0325)$$

$$= 1,041,162.23$$

Change in *MV*:   −.9658 percent

Assumed: 200 b.p. decrease; k = .025.

$$MV = 25,000(1.0125) + 1,050,000/(1.0125)$$

$$= 1,061,728.40$$

Change in *MV*:   .9876 percent

Analysis

Significant changes in interest rates do not affect the market value of this category of short-term assets to a great extent, as shown in Table 7–1. For interest-bearing time deposits and securities purchased under agreement to resell—instruments with six months to maturity in this case—the change is not even 1 percent of original market value. For term federal funds sold, a one-month

Table 7–1.

VARIABILITY OF TEMPORARY INVESTMENTS

Instrument	Years to Maturity	Percent Change in Value after 200 Basis Point	
		Increase	Decrease
Interest-bearing time deposits with other banks	.5	–.9390%	.9662%
Federal funds sold	1/365	–.0052	.0053
Term federal funds sold	31/365	–.1610	.1642
Securities purchased under agreement to resell	.5	–.9685	.9876

transaction, the percentage change is less than 25 basis points and the change for overnight federal funds is not even 1 basis point. This pattern is directly related to the very short-term nature of these assets.

INVESTMENT SECURITIES
The investment securities category of assets is longer term than temporary investments and includes

- ➤ Treasury bills.
- ➤ Treasury notes.
- ➤ Treasury bonds.
- ➤ Mortgage pass-through certificates.
- ➤ Noncallable municipal bonds.
- ➤ Callable municipal bonds with advance refunding.
- ➤ Zero-coupon bonds.

Treasury Bills
Treasury bills are instruments with less than one year of original maturity. They have no interim cash flows and are traded on a discount basis.

$$MV = M - M(k)(N/360)$$

$$M = \text{Maturity value}$$

$$N = \text{Days to maturity}$$

One of the examples in Chapter 4 is of a six-month T-bill with 100 days left to maturity and a market value of $9,888.89.

Given: $M = 10,000$; $k = 04$; $k = .04$; $N = 100$.

Assumed: 200 b.p. increase; $k = .06$.

$$MV = 10,000 - 10,000(.06)(100/360)$$
$$= 10,000 - 166.67$$
$$= 9,833.33$$

Change in MV: $-.5618$ percent

Assumed: 200 b.p. decrease; $k = .02$.

$$MV = 10,000 - 10,000(.02)(100/360)$$
$$= 10,000 - 55.56$$
$$= 9,944.44$$

Change in MV: $.5618$ percent

Treasury Notes

Treasury notes pay interim interest payments and have original maturities of 1 to 10 years. The market value is based on the maturity value and the annuity of interest payments.

$$MV = [\sum_{t=1}^{n} \{(M)(CR)/m\}/((1+k/m)^t)]$$
$$+ [M/(1+k/m)^n]$$

where

$$CR = \text{Coupon rate}$$

Consider the example of a Treasury note with three years to maturity and a market value of $102,800.75.

Given: $M = 10,000$; $CR = .05$; $m = 2$; $k = .04$; $k = .04$; $n = 6$. (three years)

Assumed: 200 b.p. increase; $k = .06$.

$$MV = 2,500(PVIFA_{.06/2,6})$$
$$+ 100,000(PVIFA_{.06/2,6})$$
$$= 2,500(5.417191444)$$

$$+ 100,000 \ (.837484257)$$

$$= \ 97,291.41$$

Change in MV: -5.3592 percent

Assumed: 200 b.p. decrease; $k = .02$.

$$MV = 2,500(PVIFA_{.06/2,6})$$

$$+ 100,000 \ (PVIFA_{.06/2,6})$$

$$= 2,500(5.795476475)$$

$$+ 100,000(.942045235)$$

$$= 108,693.21$$

Change in MV: 5.7319 percent

Treasury Bonds

The valuation model for Treasury bonds is the same as for Treasury notes. The difference is that Treasury bonds are longer-term instruments with 10 to 30 years of original maturity. The example is of a bond with 28 years to maturity and a \$111,636.63 market value.

Given: $M = 100,000$; $CR = .085$; $m = 2$; $k = .075$; $n = 56$ (28 years).

Assumed: 200 b.p. increase; $k = .095$.

$$MV = 4,250(PVIFA_{.0475,56})$$

$$+ 100,000(PVIF_{.0475,56})$$

$$= 4,250(19.48703228)$$

$$+ 100,000(.074365967)$$

$$= 90,256.48$$

Change in MV: -19.1515 percent

Assumed: 200 b.p. decrease; $k = .055$.

$$MV = 2,500(PVIFA_{.0275,56})$$

$$+ 100,000(PVIF_{.0275,56})$$

$$= 4,250(28.40415454)$$

$$+ 100,000(.21888575)$$

$$= 142,606.24$$

Change in MV: 27.7414 percent

Mortgage Pass-Through Certificates

Mortgage pass-through certificates also are long-term investments. These mortgage-backed securities carry the risk of prepayment. In this example, the risk of such prepayments is incorporated into a higher discount rate. Future cash flows are set equal to payments originally promised. The alternative approach of estimating the prepayment rate is discussed in a later section of the chapter. The value of the instrument is the present value of future cash flows.

$$MV = \sum_{t=1}^{n} CF_t/((1+k/m)^t)$$

The original example is a 30-year pass-through with a market value of $836,164.82.

Given: $M = 1,000,000$; $CR = .08$; $m = 12$; $k = .10$; $n = 360$;
        monthly payment $= 7,337.92$.

Assumed: 200 b.p. increase; $k = .12$.

$$MV = 7,337.92(PVIFA_{.01,360})$$

$$= 7,337.92(97.21833108)$$

$$= 713,380.34$$

Change in MV: −14.6842 percent

Assumed: 200 b.p. decrease; $k = .08$.

$$MV = 7,337.92(PVIFA_{.0066667,360})$$

$$= 7,337.92(136.2783152)$$

$$= 1,000,000$$

Change in MV: 19.5936 percent

Noncallable Municipal Bonds

The valuation formula for noncallable municipal bonds is the same as for Treasury bonds.

$$MV = [\sum_{t=1}^{n} \{(M)(CR)/m\}/((1+k/m)^t)]$$
$$+ [M/(1+k/m)n)]$$

The example used here is a portfolio of bonds with a market value of $60,508.65 and 15 years to maturity.

Given: $M = 50,000$; $CR = .07$; $m = 4$; $k = .05$; $n = 60$.

Assumed: 200 b.p. increase; $k = .07$.

$$MV = 875(PVIFA_{.0175,60})$$
$$+ 50,000(PVIFA_{.0175,60})$$
$$= 875(36.96398552)$$
$$+ 50,000(.353130254)$$
$$= 50,000$$

Change in *MV*: −17.3672 percent

Assumed: 200 b.p. decrease; $k = .03$.

$$MV = 875(PVIFA_{.0075,60})$$
$$+ 50,000(PVIFA_{.0075,60})$$
$$= 875(48.17337352)$$
$$+ 50,000(.638699699)$$
$$= 74,086.68$$

Change in *MV*: 22.4398 percent

Callable Municipal Bonds with Advance Refunding

When there is an advance refunding of a bond, the time to maturity is effectively shortened. Only those interest payments up to the first call date and the call price should be used to value the bond.

$$MV = [\sum_{t=1}^{c} \{(M)(CR)/m\}/((1+k/m)^t)]$$
$$+ [CP/((1+k/m)^c)]$$

$$c \;=\; \text{Number of periods before first call date}$$

$$CP \;=\; \text{Call price}$$

The example in Chapter 4 assumes that the same municipal bond noted above is callable in five years at 103. At a 5 percent discount rate, the portfolio of bonds is worth \$55,569.85.

Given: $M = 50,000$; $CR = .07$; $m = 4$; $k = .05$; $n = 60$; $c = 20$; $CP = 51,500$.

Assumed: 200 b.p. increase; $k \;=\; .07$.

$$
\begin{aligned}
MV \;&=\; 875(PVIFA_{.0175,20}) \\
&\quad + 51,500(PVIF_{.0175,20}) \\
&=\; 875(16.7528813) \\
&\quad + 51,500(.706824577) \\
&=\; 51,060.24
\end{aligned}
$$

Change in MV: -8.1152 percent

Assumed: 200 b.p. decrease; $k \;=\; .03$.

$$
\begin{aligned}
MV \;&=\; 875(PVIFA_{.0075,20}) \\
&\quad + 51,500(PVIF_{.0075,20}) \\
&=\; 875(18.50801969) \\
&\quad + 51,500(.861189852) \\
&=\; 60,545.80
\end{aligned}
$$

Change in MV: 8.9544 percent

Zero Coupon Bonds

When bonds pay only a maturity value, they are referred to as zero-coupon bonds. The value of a zero-coupon bond is the present value of that single future pay-off.

$$MV \;=\; M/((1+k)^n)$$

The original portfolio is composed of 30-year bonds worth \$23,137.75. Given: $M = 100,000$; $k = .05$; $n = 30$.

Assumed: 200 b.p. increase; k = .07.

$$MV = 100,000(1/(1.07)^{30})$$

$$= 100,000(.131367117)$$

$$= 13,136.71$$

Change in MV: -43.2239 percent

Assumed: 200 b.p. decrease; k = .03.

$$MV = 100,000(1/(1.03)^{30})$$

$$= 100,000(.41198676)$$

$$= 41,198.68$$

Change in MV: 78.0583 percent

Analysis

The market value of investment securities is more sensitive to interest rate changes than that of temporary investments, with the exception of Treasury bills. The percentage change in T-bill value is less than 100 basis points.

For all other categories, however, Table 7–2 shows that the market value fluctuations exceed 500 basis points. In general, these shifts are directly related to the time to maturity of the assets. Treasury notes and callable municipal bonds with advance funding have time to maturity (or effective time to maturity) of three years and five years, respectively. Percentage shifts in market value for these categories are between 500 and 850 basis points.

For longer-term instruments, the changes are even larger. Among these changes, however, the coupon effect is noticeable. Mortgage pass-through certificates have 30 years to maturity and noncallable municipal bonds, 15 years. All other things being equal, the pass-throughs should reflect greater volatility. However, the reverse is true. The reason is that the pass-throughs return principal as well as interest; that is, they have a higher coupon than the municipals. As a result, the market value of the 15-year noncallable municipals is more volatile than the value of the 30-year pass-throughs. The 28-year Treasury bonds are still more volatile because of their relatively lower coupon vis-à-vis pass-throughs. Of course, the extreme case of the coupon effect is the zero-coupon bonds with fluctuations between 4,300 and 7,800 basis points.

Table 7–2.

VARIABILITY OF INVESTMENT SECURITIES

Instrument	Years to Maturity	Percent Change in Value After 200 Basis Point	
		Increase	Decrease
Treasury bills	100/360	−.5618%	.5618%
Treasury notes	5	−5.3592	5.7319
Treasury bonds	28	−19.1515	27.7414
Mortgage pass-through certificates	30	−14.6842	19.5936
Noncallable municipal bonds	15	−17.3672	22.4398
Callable municipal bonds with advance refunding	5	−8.1152	8.9544
Zero-coupon bonds	30	−43.2239	78.0583

Clearly, investment securities can contribute significantly to volatility of the market value of bank assets. If liabilities are equally volatile, the effect can be offset. To the extent that the market value of liabilities does not change in this way, the volatility of investment securities is absorbed by bank equity.

LOANS

Like investment securities, loans can contain long-term instruments that are very sensitive to interest rate changes. The sections that follow address four broad classifications of loans:

➤ Commercial loans.
➤ Mortgage loans.
➤ Consumer loans.
➤ Lease financing.

Commercial Loans

The pattern of cash flows of commercial loans can vary significantly. However, most patterns conform to one of the following:

➤ Bullet loans.
➤ Working capital lines of credit.
➤ Term installment loans.
➤ Term interest-only loans.

Bullet loans. A bullet loan pays no interest and principal until maturity. The market value is the present value of that single future payoff.

$$MV = L((1+k_L/m)^n)/((1+^k/m)^n)$$

where

$$L = \text{Loan amount}$$

$$k_L = \text{Loan (coupon) rate}$$

Consider the example of a bullet loan with five years to maturity and a market value of $243,943.42.

Given: $L = 250,000; k_L = .075; m = 4; k = .08; n = 20.$

Assumed: 200 b.p. increase; $k = .10.$

$$MV = 250,000(1 + .075/4)^{20}/(1 + .10/4)^{20}$$

$$= 250,000(1.449948026)/(1.63861644)$$

$$= 221,215.29$$

Change in *MV:*   −9.3170 percent

Assumed: 200 b.p. decrease; $k = .06.$

$$MV = 250,000(1 + .075/4)^{20}/(1 + .06/4)^{20}$$

$$= 250,000(1.449948026)/(1.346855007)$$

$$= 269,135.88$$

Change in *MV:*   10.3272 percent

Working capital lines of credit. Working capital lines of credit earn interest on the amount of the line actually used and commitment fees on the amount not used.

$$MV = [A((1+k_{LC})^n) + (MX - A)((1+k_{CF})^{n-1})]/(1+k)^n$$

where

$$A = \text{Actual borrowings}$$

$$k_{LC} = \text{Interest rate for portion of line of credit used}$$

$$MX = \text{Maximum credit available}$$

$$k_{CF} = \text{Commitment fee}$$

The portfolio of lines of credit used to illustrate this model has an average maturity of nine months and a market value of $2,014,059.64.

Given: $A = 2,000,000;\ MX = 5,000,000;\ k_{LC} = .10;\ k_{CF} = .01;$
$k = .105;\ n = .75.$

Assumed: 200 b.p. increase; $k = .125.$

$$
\begin{aligned}
MV &= [2,000,000(1.10)^{.75} \\
&\quad + (3,000,000((1.01)^{.75} - 1)]/(1.125)^{.75} \\
&= [2,148,199.00 + 22,471.99] \\
&\quad /(1.092356486) \\
&= 2,170,670.99/(1.092356486) \\
&= 1,987,145.24
\end{aligned}
$$

Change in MV: -1.3363 percent

Assumed: 200 b.p. decrease; $k = .085.$

$$
\begin{aligned}
MV &= [2,000,000(1.10)^{.75} \\
&\quad + (3,000,000((1.01)^{.75} - 1)] \\
&\quad /(1.085)^{.75} \\
&= 2,170,670.99/(1.063095558) \\
&= 2,041,839.96
\end{aligned}
$$

Change in MV: 1.3793 percent

Term installment loans. Term installment loans provide for periodic payments of principal and interest, with each payment amortizing a part of the unpaid balance. When the last of these equal payments is made, the unpaid balance of the loan is zero. The market value of these loans is the present value of the annuity of equal payments.

$$MV = [L/PVIFA_{k/m,n}][PVIFA_{k/m,n}]$$

where

$$L/PVIFA_{k/m,n} = \text{The loan amount divided by the } PVIFA$$
$$\text{based on the loan rate and the number}$$
$$\text{of periods}$$
$$= \text{Periodic payment}$$

The example given is a three-year loan with quarterly payments and a market value of $1,007,556.73.

Given: $L = 1,000,000$; $k_L = .11$; $k = .105$; $m = 4$; $n = 12$.

Assumed: 200 b.p. increase; $k = .125$.

$$MV = [1,000,000/(PVIFA_{.11/4,12})]$$
$$[PVIFA_{.125/4,12}]$$
$$= [1,000,000/10.10420366]$$
$$[9.880136654]$$
$$= [98,968.71][9.880136654]$$
$$= 977,824.38$$

Change in MV: -2.9509 percent

Assumed: 200 b.p. decrease; $k = .085$.

$$MV = [1,000,000/(PVIFA_{.11/4,12})]$$
$$[PVIFA_{.085/4,12}]$$
$$= [98,968.71][10.49461045]$$
$$= 1,038,638.06$$

Change in MV: 3.0848 percent

Term interest-only loans. These loans repay interest on principal during the term of the loan and the entire principal at the end of the term. In this sense, they are similar to bonds. The market value is the sum of the present values of (1) the annuity of interest payments and (2) the single principal payment.

$$MV = [L(k_L/m)(PVIFA_{k/m,n})]$$
$$+ [L/((1+k/m)^n)]$$

In the illustration of this lending arrangement, the interest is paid semiannually over a three-year period and the market value is $1,012,588.40.

Given: $L = 1,000,000$; $k_L = .11$; $k = .105$; $m = 2$; $n = 6$;
interest payment = 55,000.

Assumed: 200 b.p. increase; k = .125.

$$MV = [55,000(PVIFA_{.125/2,6})]$$
$$+[1,000,000/(1 + .125/2)^6]$$
$$= [55,000(4.878935737)]$$
$$+ [1,000,000/(1.438711226)]$$
$$= 963,407.99$$

Change in *MV:*   −4.8569 percent

Assumed: 200 b.p. decrease; k = .085.

$$MV = [55,000(PVIFA_{.085/2,6})]$$
$$+[1,000,000/(1 + .085/2)^6]$$
$$= [55,000(5.199739996)$$
$$+ [1,000,000/(1.283678838)]$$
$$= 1,064,996.75$$

Change in *MV:*   5.1757 percent

Mortgage Loans

Mortgage loans can either be residential or commercial. This distinction is important in assigning appropriate discount rates and predicting future cash flows. However, in both cases, the impact of interest rate changes is determined in the same way. The examples in this section illustrate four types of mortgage loans:

➤ Fixed-rate mortgages.
➤ Graduated payment mortgages.
➤ Balloon mortgages—interest-only.
➤ Balloon mortgages—amortizing.

The possibility of prepayments is an option held by borrowers. This option is discussed in a later section of the chapter.

Fixed-rate mortgages. The market value of fixed-rate mortgages is based on the future contractual cash flows that amortize the principal in much the same way as term installment loans in the commercial loan portfolio.

$$MV = (L/PVIFA_{k/m,n})(PVIFA_{k/m,n})$$

The example of this is a 25-year mortgage with a market value of $176,602.32.

Given: $L = 150,000$; $k_m = .10$; $k = .08$; $n = 300$;
monthly payment = 1,363.05.

Assumed: 200 b.p. increase; $k = .10$.

$$MV = 1,363.05(PVIFA_{.10/12,300})$$

$$= 1,363.05(110.0472301)$$

$$= 150,000$$

Change in MV: -15.0634 percent

Assumed: 200 b.p. decrease; $k = .06$.

$$MV = 1,363.05(PVIFA_{.06/12,300})$$

$$= 1,363.05(155.206864)$$

$$= 211,554.72$$

Change in MV: 19.7916 percent

Graduated payment mortgages. Graduated payment mortgages are fixed-rate loans that allow for lower payments in the early years of the loan. The difference between the normal payments and the graduated payments is added to the unpaid balance to be amortized over the later years. The market value of this type of mortgage is the present value of the future payments—both graduated and level.

$$MV = \sum_{t=1}^{g} \{(L/PVIFA_{k/m,n}) - PR_t\}/(1+k/m)^t]$$
$$+ \{[(L/PVIFA_{k/m,n})(PVIFA_{k/m,n-g})$$
$$+ \sum_{t=1}^{g} PRt]/PVIFA_{k/m,n-g}\}$$
$$(PVIFA_{k/m,n-g})(1/((1+_{k/m})^g)$$

where

g = Periods with graduated payments

PR_t = Payment reduction in period t

$$L/PVIFA_{k/m,n} = \text{Normal monthly payment}$$

$$\sum_{t=1}^{g} PR_t = \begin{array}{l}\text{Total amount of payment reductions to be}\\\text{added to the unpaid balance at period } g\end{array}$$

The example given in Chapter 4 involves a 25-year mortgage with 5 years of graduated payments. Its market value was \$175,782.37.

Given: $L = 150{,}000$; $k_m = .10$; $k = .08$; $m = 12$; $n = 300$; monthly $PR = 150$ in year 1, 200 in year 2, 150 in year 3, 100 in year 4, and 50 in year 5; monthly payment = 1,113.05 in year 1, 1,163.05 in year 2, 1,213.05 in year 3, 1,263.05 in year 4, and 1,313.05 in year 5; unpaid loan balance at the end of year 5 = 150,245.54; monthly payment after year 5 = 1,449.90.

Assumed: 200 b.p. increase; $k = .10$.

$$
\begin{aligned}
MV = \ & 1{,}113.05(PVIFA_{.10/12,12}) \\
& + 1{,}163.05(PVIFA_{.10/12,12})(PVIF_{.10/12,12}) \\
& + 1{,}213.05(PVIFA_{.10/12,12})(PVIF_{.10/12,24}) \\
& + 1{,}263.05(PVIFA_{.10/12,12})(PVIF_{.10/12,36}) \\
& + 1{,}313.05(PVIFA_{.10/12,12})(PVIF_{.10/12,48}) \\
& + 1{,}449.90(PVIFA_{.10/12,240})(PVIF_{.10/12,60}) \\
= \ & 1{,}113.05(11.37450843) \\
& + 1{,}163.05(11.37450843)(.90521243) \\
& + 1{,}213.05(11.37450843)(.819409543) \\
& + 1{,}263.05(11.37450843)(.741739704) \\
& + 1{,}313.05(11.37450843)(.671431999) \\
& + 1{,}449.90(103.6246187)(.607788592) \\
= \ & 147{,}943.36
\end{aligned}
$$

Change in MV: -15.8372 percent

Assumed: 200 b.p. decrease; $k = .06$.

$$MV = 1{,}113.05(PVIFA_{.06/12,12})$$

$$+ 1,163.05(PVIFA_{.06/12,12})(PVIF_{.06/12,12})$$

$$+ 1,213.05(PVIFA_{.06/12,12})(PVIF_{.06/12,24})$$

$$+ 1,263.05(PVIFA_{.06/12,12})(PVIF_{.06/12,36})$$

$$+ 1,313.05(PVIFA_{.06/12,12})(PVIF_{.06/12,48})$$

$$+ 1,449.90(PVIFA_{.06/12,240})(PVIF_{.06/12,60})$$

$$= 1,113.05(11.61893207)$$

$$+ 1,163.05(11.61893207)(.941905340)$$

$$+ 1,213.05(11.61893207)(.887185669)$$

$$+ 1,263.05(11.61893207)(.835644919)$$

$$+ 1,313.05(11.61893207)(.787098411)$$

$$+ 1,449.90(139.5807717)(.741372196)$$

$$= 212,474.12$$

Change in *MV:*   20.8734 percent

Balloon Mortgages—Interest-Only. Balloon mortgages represent more short-term assets. The interim payments are composed of interest payments only until the loan due date at which time the entire balance is payable. In other words, the cash flow stream is similar to that of a bond.

$$MV = \sum_{t=1}^{n} [\Delta(L)(k_m/m)/((1+k)^t)]$$
$$+ L/((1+k/m)^t)$$

where

$$(L)(k_m/m) = \text{Periodic interest payment}$$

The example involves a five-year loan with a market value of \$98,080.15.

Given: $L = 100,000$; $k_m = .09$; $k = .095$; $m = 1$; $n = 5$;
annual interest payment = 9,000.

Assumed: 200 b.p. increase; $k = .115$.

$$MV = 9,000(PVIFA_{.115,5})$$
$$+ 100,000(PVIF_{.115,5})$$

$$= 9{,}000(3.649877847)$$

$$+ 100{,}000(.580264048)$$

$$= 90{,}875.30$$

Change in *MV*: -7.3459 percent

Assumed: 200 b.p. decrease; k = .075.

$$MV = 9{,}000(PVIFA_{.075,5})$$

$$+ 100{,}000(PVIF_{.075,5})$$

$$= 9{,}000(4.045884902)$$

$$+ 100{,}000(.69558632)$$

$$= 106{,}068.83$$

Change in *MV*:   8.1451 percent

Balloon Mortgages—Amortizing. Often balloon mortgages include a provision for payments of principal and interest that are computed as if the mortgage is to be repaid over a longer time period. The balloon payment (balance of the mortgage) is, however, scheduled long before the time implied by these payments.

$$MV = (L/PVIFA_{k/m,n})(PVIFA_{k/m,b})$$

$$+ B/((1+k/m)^{b})$$

where

B = Amount of balloon payment

b = Number of periods before
        balloon payment

Consider the balloon mortgage worth \$90,326.54, with monthly payments as if amortized over 30 years and a balloon payment at the end of the fifth year.

Given: $L = 100{,}000$; $k_{m} = .07$; $k = .095$; $n = 360$; $b = 60$; monthly payment = 665.30; loan balance at the end of period 60 = 94,131.24.

Assumed: 200 b.p. increase; k = .115.

$$MV = 665.30(PVIFA_{.115/12,60})$$

$$+ 94,131.24(PVIF_{.115/12,60})$$

$$= 665.30(45.46982461)$$

$$+ 94,131.24(_{.564247514})$$

$$= 83,364.39$$

Change in *MV*: -7.7078 percent

Assumed: 200 b.p. decrease; $k = .075$.

$$MV = 665.30(PVIFA_{.075/12,60})$$

$$+ 94,131.24(PVIF_{.075/12,60})$$

$$= 665.30(49.90530818)$$

$$+ 94,131.24(.688091824)$$

$$= 97,972.94$$

Change in *MV*:   8.4653 percent

Consumer Installment Loans

Consumer installment loans are relatively short-term, especially as compared to mortgage loans. Often the loans are used to finance automobile purchases and have an original maturity of three to five years. The market value is the present value of the payment annuity.

$$MV = (L/PVIFA_{k/m,n})(PVIFA_{k/m,n})$$

where

$L/PVIFA_{k/m,n}$ = Loan amount divided by *PVIFA* computed with the loan (coupon) rate

The example in Chapter 4 is a four-year auto loan valued at \$20,747.74.

Given: $L = 20,000$; $k_L = .15$; $k = .13$; $n = 48$; monthly payment $= 556.61$.

Assumed: 200 b.p. increase; $k = .15$.

$$MV = 556.61(PVIFA_{.15/12,48})$$

$$= 556.61(35.93148091)$$

$$= 20,000$$

Change in *MV*: -3.6040 percent

Assumed: 200 b.p. decrease; k = .11.

$$MV = 556.61(PVIFA_{.11/12,48})$$
$$= 556.61(38.69142114)$$
$$= 21,536.03$$

Change in MV: 3.7994 percent

Lease Financing

Lease financing is similar to an installment loan. The difference is that the borrower does not obtain title to the property being financed unless the borrower pays the residual value at the end of the term of the loan. The value of these loans is the present value of the periodic payments and the residual value.

$$MV = (L/PVIFA_{k/m,n})(PVIFA_{k/m,n})$$
$$+ R(1/(1+k/m)^n)$$

where

L = Loan amount (to be amortized)

R = Residual value

The lease illustrated in Chapter 4 is a five-year commercial lease valued at \$1,350,837.45.

Given: L = 1,000,000; R = 500,000; k_L = .12; k = .10; n = 60; monthly payment = 22,244.45.

Assumed: 200 b.p. increase; k = .12.

$$MV = 22,244.45(PVIFA_{.12/12,60})$$
$$+ 500,000(PVIF_{.12/12,60})$$
$$= 22,244.45(44.9550384)$$
$$+ 500,000(.550449616)$$
$$= 1,275,224.81$$

Change in MV: −5.5975 percent

Assumed: 200 b.p. decrease; k = .08.

$$MV = 22,244.45(PVIFA_{.08/12,60})$$

$$+ 500,000(PVIF_{.08/12,60})$$
$$= 22,244.45(49.3184333)$$
$$+ 500,000(.671210444)$$
$$= 1,432,666.64$$

Change in MV: 6.0577 percent

Analysis

As shown in Table 7–3, the working capital line of credit is the least volatile loan category because it is the most short term. The fixed-rate and graduated payment mortgages are the most volatile because they represent the longest term loans with 25 years to maturity. Notice, however, that the graduated payment mortgage is slightly more volatile than the regular fixed-rate mortgages because of the coupon effect. Early payment reductions in the graduated payment loans are loaded to the back end of the mortgage, making this instrument a somewhat lower-coupon loan than the regular fixed-rate mortgage.

The coupon effect is noticeable in other categories with comparable maturities. In commercial loans, term installment loans due in three years are less sensitive to interest rate changes than term interest-only loans of the same maturity. (Notice also that the consumer installment loan is slightly more sensitive than the commercial installment loan because the consumer loan maturity is longer by one year.) Five-year commercial bullet loans with no interim payments are far more volatile than five-year lease financing arrangements with monthly payments that amortize the loan amount. The amortizing balloon mortgage is somewhat more sensitive to interest rate changes because its monthly payment of $665.30 ($7,983.60 annually) is smaller than the $9,000 annual payment associated with the interest-only balloon mortgage. The small amount of principal reduction associated with the amortizing balloon mortgage is not enough to offset the difference.

The most interest-sensitive components of the bank portfolio are the mortgage loans. However, any sort of long-term financing, including 15- to 20-year commercial loans, have the same effect. Likewise, intermediate-term loans that do not amortize principal add significantly to market value variability.

LIABILITIES

Bank liabilities are composed primarily of deposits and borrowed funds. Transactions and savings accounts are due on demand or effectively due on

Table 7–3.

VARIABILITY OF LOANS

Instrument	Years to Maturity	Percent Change in Value after 200 Basis Point	
		Increase	Decrease
Commercial:			
Bullet loans	5	–9.3170%	10.3271%
Working capital lines of credit	.75	–1.3363	1.3793
Term installment loans	3	–2.9509	3.0848
Term interest-only loans	3	–4.8569	5.1757
Mortgage:			
Fixed-rate mortgages	25	–15.0634	–19.7916
Graduated payment mortgages	25	–15.8372	20.8734
Balloon mortgages— interest-only	5	–7.3459	8.1451
Balloon mortgages— amortizing	5	–7.7078	8.4653
Consumer installment loans	4	–3.6040	3.7994
Lease financing	5	–5.5975	6.0577

demand; this causes market value to equal book value. The market value of time deposits can change, however, with changing interest rates. These deposits are analyzed in this section.

Long-term borrowings most often are subordinated notes and debentures with an original maturity of at least seven years. They are valued in the same way as Treasury bonds or municipal bonds and exhibit the same sort of variability as interest rates change.

Short-term borrowed funds include federal funds purchased, securities sold under agreement to repurchase, and commercial paper. Both federal funds purchased and securities sold under agreement to repurchase are the counterparts of the assets discussed earlier. The market value of these instruments is not very sensitive to changes in interest rates. Commercial paper is analyzed later.

Time Deposits
Time deposits can be small-denomination accounts or accounts in excess of $100,000. Maturities can be as short as seven days or as long as 10 years. The market value of a time deposit is the present value of the maturity value.

$$MV = D(1+k_D)n/((1+k)^n)$$

where

$$D = \text{Deposit amount}$$

$$k_D = \text{Deposit rate}$$

The example in Chapter 4 is a two-year CD worth $990,202.16.

Given: $D = 1,000,000$; $k_D = .06$; $k = .065$; $m = 4$; $n = 8$.

Assumed: 200 b.p. increase; $k = .085$.

$$MV = 1,000,000(1.015)^8(PVIF_{.085/4,8})$$

$$= 1,126,492.59(.845168775)$$

$$= 952,076.36$$

Change in MV: −3.8503 percent

Assumed: 200 b.p. decrease; $k = .045$.

$$MV = 1,000,000(1.015)^8(PVIF_{.045/4,8})$$

$$= 1,126,492.59(.914390537)$$

$$= 1,030,054.16$$

Change in MV: 4.0246 percent

Commercial Paper
Commercial paper always has an original maturity of no more than 270 days and is issued on a discounted basis. The market value is face value minus the discount.

$$MV = M - M(k)(N/360)$$

where

$$N = \text{Number of days before maturity}$$

The example used in Chapter 4 is a new 270-day issue valued at $966,250.

Given: $M = 1,000,000$; $k = .045$; $N = 270$.

Assumed: 200 b.p. increase; k = .065.

$$MV = 1,000,000$$

$$- 1,000,000(.065)(270/360)$$

$$= 1,000,000 - 48,750$$

$$= 951,250$$

Change in MV: −1.5524 percent

Assumed: 200 b.p. decrease; k = .025.

$$MV = 1,000,000$$

$$- 1,000,000(.025)(270/360)$$

$$= 1,000,000 - 18,750$$

$$= 981,250$$

Change in MV: 1.5524 percent

Analysis
The liabilities shown here (and summarized in Table 7–4) are typical of the majority of funding sources for a commercial bank in terms of maturity. As noted earlier, many deposit liabilities are due on demand and their market value equals book value; changing interest rates have no impact. Those liabilities that are not due on demand are frequently concentrated in instruments with maturities of two years or less. Only subordinated notes and debentures (with pricing and volatility comparable to Treasury bonds) are capable of offsetting the volatility of bank asset portfolios in the face of interest rate changes. Subordinated notes and debentures, however, are a relatively small part of total liabilities and capital for the typical bank.[1] This means that bank equity absorbs most of the fluctuations of bank assets in a changing interest rate environment.

EMBEDDED OPTIONS
Chapter 5 contains an example of several types of embedded options. The mortgage-related investment is analyzed under different interest rate scenarios to arrive at an estimate of the value of the prepayment option. To determine the effect of changes in the base rate, the calculations should be redone at the

Table 7–4.

VARIABILITY OF LIABILITIES

		Percent Change in Value after 200 Basis Point	
Instrument	Years to Maturity	Increase	Decrease
Time deposits	2	–3.8503%	4.0246%
Commercial paper	.75	–1.5524	1.5524

assumed rates. That is, the contractual mortgage rate remains the same, but the group of interest rates used to compute the present value of the payments under various scenarios changes.

In the case of callable bonds and interest rate caps and floors, there are two reasonable approaches:

➤ Recompute options values with the new interest rate using either the Black-Scholes option pricing model or the Black futures option pricing model. Current market rates (Black-Scholes and Black) should be increased or decreased as desired and the calculations repeated. The forward rate also should be increased by the same number of basis points since all rates are assumed to change by the same number of basis points.

➤ Use delta (the change in option price per dollar of change in the value of the underlying instrument) and gamma (the change in delta per dollar of change in the value of the underlying instrument) to estimate the new option value.

The following sections illustrate the application of both of these approaches in the case of the callable bond in Chapter 5.

Recomputing Option Values

The example in Chapter 5 is a callable bond that matures in 10 years with the first call date in six months.

Given: $MV = 107.79$; $X =$ call price $= 101$; $k = .05$; $t = .5$; $\sigma = .20$; n = 20.

Under these circumstances, the call option is valued at $11.60, composed of an intrinsic value of $6.79 ($MV - X = 107.79 - 101.00$) and a time value of $4.81.

Assuming a 200-basis-point increase in rates. With a 200-basis-point increase in rates, both the required return and the risk-free rate rise to 7 percent and the new price of the bond, assuming a 6 percent coupon paid semiannually, is \$92.89, or 13.8 percent lower.[2]

$$MV_{bond} = 3(PVIFA_{.07/2,20}) + 100(PVIF_{.07/2,20})$$
$$= 3(14.21403) + 100(.502566)$$
$$= 92.89$$

The Black-Scholes model used to value the call option is:

$$C = (MV)(N(d_1)) - Xe^{-kt}N(d_2)$$

where

$$d_1 = [ln(MV/X) + (k + \sigma^2/2)(t)]/\sigma(t^{.5})$$
$$d_2 = d_1 - \sigma(t^{.5})$$

$N(y)$ = Probability that an observation from the normal distribution will be less than or equal to y

= Cumulative normal distribution function

Solving for d_1 and d_2,

$$d_1 = [ln(92.89/101)$$
$$+ (.07 + .04/2)(.5)]/(.20)(.5^{.5})$$
$$= [-.083704519 + .045]/.141421356$$
$$= -.273682279$$
$$d_2 = -.273682279 - .20(.5^{.5})$$
$$= -.273682279 - .141421356$$
$$= -.415103635$$

Using the polynomial approximation of the cumulative normal distribution function (see Figure 5–9) to solve for $N(d_1)$ and $N(d_2)$,

$$N(d_1) = N(-.273682279)$$

$$= 1 - N(.273682279)$$
$$= 1 - .607836089$$
$$= .3922$$
$$N(d_2) = N(-.415103635)$$
$$= 1 - N(.415103635)$$
$$= 1 - .660988345$$
$$= .3390$$

Substituting these values into the call pricing model, the new market value of the call is \$3.37.

$$C = (92.89)(.3922)$$
$$- (101)(e^{-(.07)(.5)})(.3390)$$
$$= 36.431458$$
$$- (101)(.965605416)(.3390)$$
$$= 3.37$$

Notice that at a market value of \$92.89 for the underlying bond, the intrinsic value of the call option is zero (the bond issuer would not call the bonds with a 6 percent coupon and then reissue at 7 percent), but the time value is \$3.37. Thus, an increase of 200 basis points greatly reduces the probability of exercise; that is, the option is now out-of-the-money. Likewise, the value of the option falls from \$11.60 to \$3.37, a 71 percent decline.

Assuming a 200-basis-point decrease in rates. With a 200-basis-point decrease in rates, the required return is 3 percent and the price of the bond increases to \$125.75, or 16.7 percent higher.

$$MV_{bond} = 3(PVIFA_{.03/2,20}) + 100(PVIF_{.03/2,20})$$
$$= 3(17.168639) + 100(.742470)$$
$$= 125.75$$

The parameters of the Black-Scholes model are

$$d_1 = [ln(125.75/101)$$

$$+ (.03 + .04/2)(.5)]/(.20)(.5^{.5})$$

$$= [.219175292 + .025]/.141421356$$

$$= 1.726580051$$

$$d_2 = 1.726580051 - .20(.5^{.5})$$

$$= 1.726580051 - .141421356$$

$$= 1.585158695$$

Again applying the polynomial approximation of the cumulative normal distribution function, to solve for $N(d_1)$ and $N(d_2)$,

$$N(d_1) = N(1.726580051)$$

$$= .9579$$

$$N(d_2) = N(1.585158695)$$

$$= .9437$$

Based on these parameters, the new market value of the call is $26.56.

$$C = (125.75)(.9579)$$

$$- (101)(e^{-(.03)(.5)})(.9437)$$

$$= 120.455925$$

$$- (101)(.98511194)(.9437)$$

$$= 26.56$$

When the market interest rate declines to 3 percent, the option is more in-the-money than when the rate is 5 percent, causing the value of the option to increase. The $26.56 value of the option includes an intrinsic value of $24.75 ($125.75 − 101.00) and a time value of $1.81. Altogether, a 200-basis-point increase caused the value of the option to increase from $11.60 to $26.56, or by 129 percent.

Delta and Gamma
An alternative approach is to use the measures of delta (Δ) and gamma (Γ), parameters of the Black-Scholes option pricing model, to estimate the new option values. Delta is the change in the value of an option per dollar of change in the value of the underlying asset. Gamma is the change in delta per dollar of change in the value of the underlying asset.[3]

$$\Delta \ = \ (\text{Change in } C)/(\text{change in } MV)$$

$$\Gamma \ = \ (\text{Change in } \Delta)/(\text{change in } MV)$$

The relationship among the variables is

$$C_{new} \ = \ C + [\text{Change in } MV]$$
$$[\Delta + (\Gamma)(\text{change in } MV)]$$

where

$$(\Gamma)(\text{change in } MV) \ = \ [(\text{Change in } \Delta)$$
$$/(\text{Change in } MV)] \ (\text{change in } MV)$$

$$= \ \text{Change in } \Delta$$

$$\Delta + (\Gamma)(\text{change in } MV) \ = \ \text{Original } \Delta + \text{Change in } \Delta$$

$$= \ \Delta_{new}$$

Substituting,

$$C_{new} \ = \ C + [\text{change in } MV][\Delta_{new}]$$

$$= \ C + [\text{change in } MV]$$

$$[(\text{New change in } C)/(\text{change in } MV)]$$

$$= \ C + \text{new change in } C$$

Delta and *gamma* are computed as follows:

$$\Delta \ = \ N(d_1) \text{ for a call option}$$

$$= \ N(d_1) - 1 \text{ for a put option}$$

$$\Gamma \ = \ (1/(2\pi)^5)e^{-y^2/2}/(MV)(\sigma)(t^5) \text{ for call and put options}$$

where

$$d_1 \ = \ [ln(MV/X) + (k + \sigma^2/2)(t)]/\sigma(t^5)$$

$$N(d_1) \ = \ \text{Cumulative normal distribution function}$$

$$y \ = \ d_1$$

$$\pi \ = \ 3.14159265$$

Using Delta and Gamma to Compute Option Values

Using delta and gamma to compute option values after interest rates change requires several steps:

➤ Determine the change in market value of the underlying instrument.
➤ Determine d_1.
➤ Calculate Γ.
➤ Determine the original delta.
➤ Calculate Δ_{new} (Δ after the value of the underlying instrument changes).
➤ Combine the terms to arrive at C_{new} (C after the market value of the underlying instrument changes).

Change in the market value of the underlying bond. As noted earlier, a 200-basis-point increase in rates pushes down the market value of the bond from $107.79 to $92.89. A 200-basis-point decrease raises the market value to $125.75.

$$\text{Change in } MV = -14.90 \text{ for a 200 b.p. increase}$$

$$= 17.96 \text{ for a 200 b.p. decrease}$$

Determining d_1. The calculation of d_1 is the same as in the original calculation of the option value. The logic for this approach is that delta and gamma are useful because they allow a calculation of a new option value from a base case ($MV = \$107.79$ and $k = .05$), without directly recomputing option value as was done in the earlier section.

$$d_1 = .707561968$$

This is the same d_1 computed for this bond in Chapter 5.

Calculating gamma and the change in delta. Gamma is based on the square of d_1.

$$\Gamma = (1/(2\pi)^{.5})e^{-y/2}/(MV)(\sigma)(t^{.5})$$

where

$$y = d_1^2$$

$$= .500643939$$

Substituting,

$$\Gamma = (1/2.506628273)(e^{-.500643939/2})$$

$$/(107.79)(.20)(.5^{.5})$$

$$= (.398942281)(.778550073)$$

$$/15.24380799$$

$$= .020375259$$

A \$1 change in the value of the underlying asset will produce a \$.02 change in the value of delta. The changes in delta are linear in gamma; that is, a \$2 change in the value of the underlying asset produces a \$.04 change in delta, a \$3 change in the underlying asset produces \$.06 change in delta, and so on.

Assuming a 200-basis-point increase and a new MV of the underlying bond of \$92.89, the change in delta is negative \$.303591365.

$$\Gamma = \text{(Change in } \Delta)/(\text{change in } MV)$$

$$.020375259 = \text{(Change in } \Delta)/(92.89 - 107.79)$$

$$= \text{(Change in } \Delta)/(-14.90)$$

$$\text{change in } \Delta = .020375259(-14.90)$$

$$= -.303591359$$

A 200-basis-point decrease causes the value of the MV of the underlying bond to increase to \$125.75 and delta increases by .365939652.

$$\Gamma = \text{(Change in } \Delta)/(\text{change in MV})$$

$$.020375252 = \text{(Change in } \Delta)/(125.75 - 107.79)$$

$$= \text{(Change in } \Delta)/(17.96)$$

$$\text{change in } \Delta = .020375259(17.96)$$

$$= .365939652$$

Determining the original delta. The original delta is $N(d_1)$ and in the case of this bond equals .7604.

$$d_1 = .707561968$$

$$N(d_1) = .7604$$

$$= \Delta$$

Calculating the new delta. The variables delta, gamma, and change in MV of the underlying bond determine Δ_{new}. For the 200-basis-point increase, Δ_{new} is .456808641.

$$\Delta_{new} = \Delta + \Delta \text{ (change in } MV)$$
$$= \Delta + \text{(change in } \Delta)$$
$$= .7604 - .303591359$$
$$= .456808641$$

This value means that every dollar of decrease in value of the underlying instrument results in a \$.457 decrease in the value of the option.

The Δ_{new} for a 200-basis-point decrease in rates is 1.126339652.

$$\Delta_{new} = \Delta + \Gamma \text{(change in } MV)$$
$$= \Delta + \text{(change in } \Delta)$$
$$= .7604 + .365939652$$
$$= 1.126339652$$

This means that each dollar increase in the value of the underlying bond increases the value of the call option by \$1.126.[4]

Calculating the new value of the call option. C_{new} depends on C, Δ_{new}, and change in MV of the underlying instrument. For the 200-basis-point increase, C_{new} is \$4.79.

$$C_{new} = C + (\Delta_{new})\text{(change in } MV)$$
$$= 11.60 + (.456808641)(-14.90)$$
$$= 11.60 - 6.81$$
$$= 4.79$$

Because the market value of the underlying asset is \$92.89 (i.e., below the call (exercise) price of \$101), the option has no intrinsic value but does have a time value of \$4.79.

Under the assumption of a 200-basis-point decrease, C_{new} equals \$31.83.

$$C_{new} = C + (\Delta_{new})\text{(change in } MV)$$
$$= 11.60 + (1.126339652)(17.96)$$
$$= 11.60 + 20.23$$
$$= 31.83$$

Because the market value of the underlying asset is $124.75 and the call price is $101, the intrinsic value of the option is $24.75. The time value of the option is $7.08.

Analysis
The two approaches for valuing the embedded option after interest rate changes lead to different results. Table 7–5 shows that when interest rates increase and the value of the underlying asset declines, using delta and gamma produces a smaller decline in option value and a higher ending option value. When rates decrease, using delta and gamma produces a larger increase in option value and, again, a higher ending option value.

Table 7–5.

VARIABILITY OF EMBEDDED OPTIONS

Underlying Instrument		Option			
Market Value	**Call Price**	**Market Value**	**Percent Change**	**Intrinsic Value**	**Time Value**
ORIGINAL VALUATION:					
$107.79	$101.00	$11.60	—	$6.79	$4.81
ASSUMING 200-BASIS-POINT INCREASE:					
Recalculating Option Value					
92.89	101.00	3.37	–70.9%	—	3.37
Using Δ and Γ					
92.89	101.00	4.79	–58.7	—	4.79
ASSUMING 200-BASIS-POINT DECREASE:					
Recalculating Option Value					
125.75	101.00	26.56	129.0	24.75	1.81
Using Δ and Γ					
125.75	101.00	31.83	174.4	24.75	7.08

Essentially, the approach of completely recalculating option value leads to more conservative end results; that is, the value of the options is smaller and has less impact on portfolio valuation. Also, recalculating option value makes it possible to change any assumed parameters of the model such as underlying instrument price volatility and interest rate, for example, before making the calculation. Using delta and gamma does not permit this since the two measures only address an instantaneous change in price. In this sense, recalculating option values provides more accurate information. Delta and gamma can be useful for quick estimates, however.

SUMMARY
Market valuation of commercial bank assets and liabilities is an important element in helping render bank operations more transparent to investors, depositors, and regulators. The impact of changing interest rates is no less critical in assessing the viability of a financial institution.

SELECTED REFERENCES
Fabozzi, Frank J. *Fixed Income Mathematics*. Chicago: Probus Publishing, 1988.

Howe, Donna M. *A Guide to Managing Interest-Rate Risk*. New York: New York Institute of Finance, 1992.

Hull, John. *Options, Futures, and Other Derivatives Securities*. Englewood Cliffs, NJ: Prentice Hall, 1989.

ENDNOTES
1   In 1991, subordinated notes and debentures were only 3.4 percent of total commercial bank liabilities.

2   The required return and risk-free rate are assumed to be equal to simplify the example. The process can be modified easily to accommodate a higher required rate of return of the bond.

3   Technically, Δ is the first derivative of the option pricing model with respect to value of the underlying asset. Γ is the second derivative.

4   Practically speaking, Δ will not exceed 1. That is, when an option is in-the-money, a \$1 increase in the value of the underlying asset will result in a \$1 increase in the value of the option. Theoretically, however, Δ is not bounded by 1, as this example illustrates.

CHAPTER 8

MARKET VALUATION MODELS FOR OFF-BALANCE-SHEET ITEMS AND DERIVATIVES

INTRODUCTION

Off-balance-sheet items cover a wide spectrum of activities. The importance of these categories cannot be ignored when assessing a bank's market value. At year-end 1994, total U.S. banking industry assets amounted to $3.9 trillion. As of the same date, the off-balance-sheet total reported to federal regulators was $14.9 trillion or 382 percent of industry assets! Of this total off-balance-sheet exposure, notional amounts of swaps (both interest rate and foreign exchange) represented $4.8 trillion. Ignoring these notional amounts, the off-balance-sheet exposure of the banking industry still stood at $10.1 trillion or 259 percent of industry assets. Some of these off-balance-sheet items are extensions of traditional lending services and investments, while others are derivative securities that are exchange-traded financial instruments. The basic categories discussed in this chapter are:

➤ Unused commitments.
➤ Letters of credit.
➤ Loans transferred with recourse.
➤ When-issued securities.
➤ Interest rate derivatives.

UNUSED COMMITMENTS

A *loan commitment* is a lender's agreement to make a loan at a quoted rate for a specified time. The loan commitment may be documented in a *commitment let-*

ter from the bank indicating willingness to lend to a borrower under specified conditions. This letter is a common notice when lending is secured by real estate, including home equity lines of credit and second mortgages. In the commitment letter, the borrower may be protected against interest rate increases via a *lock-in period,* usually 30 to 60 days. However, the commitment letter often specifies that the offer to lend may be rescinded in the event of adverse changes in the borrower's financial condition.

To the extent that these loan commitments are outstanding but not yet funded, these *unused commitments* represent a liability for the bank. The correct valuation of these off-balance-sheet liabilities is to find their expected value, that is, the sum of the individual commitments multiplied by their probabilities of being funded.

$$MV = \sum_{i=1}^{n} p_i UC_i$$

where

p_i = Probability that the loan commitment to client i will be funded

UC_i = Amount of the unused loan commitment to client i

Probabilities that the loan commitment will be funded must be subjectively determined based on past experience, current interest rate environment, and the specific financial circumstances of the bank client.

LETTERS OF CREDIT

A *letter of credit (L/C)* is slightly different from a loan commitment in that the L/C usually guarantees payment to a third party on behalf of the bank's client. Essentially, a letter of credit substitutes the credit of the issuing bank for the credit of the client. For example, an importer or exporter is authorized to write drafts up to a specified amount that are payable by the issuing bank.[1] L/Cs are widely used in banking in connection with trade financing.

The extent of the bank's commitment with respect to letters of credit is determined by several factors.

➤ An *irrevocable L/C* cannot be canceled before a specified date without agreement by all parties involved. On the other hand, a *revocable L/C* may be amended at any time by the issuing bank.

➤ A *confirmed L/C* has been endorsed, guaranteeing all payment of all drafts written against it, while an *unconfirmed L/C* does not carry these guarantees.

➤ A *standby L/C* is contingent on the bank client's failure to perform under terms of a contract, such as the client's issuance of commercial paper.

The valuation of these off-balance-sheet liabilities of the bank should be determined by using the same approach as for unused loan commitments. However, the probabilities used differ depending on the L/C involved. For example, a ranking of these L/Cs in descending order of probability of being funded by the bank may be:

➤ Confirmed L/C.
➤ Unconfirmed irrevocable L/C.
➤ Unconfirmed revocable L/C.
➤ Standby L/C.

The appropriate specific probabilities depend on the bank's past experience and current circumstances surrounding the underlying transactions.

LOANS TRANSFERRED WITH RECOURSE

Bank loans may be sold to third parties either (1) *without recourse,* implying no further obligation if the original borrower prepays or defaults; or (2) *with recourse,* giving the purchaser of the loans the right to receive payment from the seller of the loans (bank) for failure of the original borrower(s) to pay when due or for prepayments. If the loans are sold without recourse, the bank has no further liability. However, if the loans are sold with recourse, the bank has a contingent or off-balance-sheet liability.[2]

Statement of Financial Accounting Standards No. 77 stipulates that certain items must recorded by the seller of the loans at the date of sale:

➤ Probable adjustments for probable credit losses, effects of prepayments, and defects in the eligibility of the transferred loans (to be recorded as a liability).
➤ As applicable, a deferral of that portion of the sales price that represents servicing fees for future periods (to be recorded as a liability).
➤ As applicable, an intangible asset representing excess prepaid servicing fees.

Under generally accepted accounting principles (GAAP), after the date of sale, the recourse liability related to probable adjustments will be charged with any actual losses incurred and an expense for the period recorded. In the case of the unearned servicing fees, an appropriate amount of income will be recorded for normal servicing fees, reducing the liability.

Note that under regulatory accounting principles (RAP), a sale of loans may be considered a borrowing, and the assets remain on the books with a corresponding liability for the cash proceeds. Any of the following necessitate this treatment under RAP:

> ➤ A put option owned by the purchaser of the loans allowing the resale to the bank.
> ➤ Sale secured by a credit arrangement issued by the selling bank or by a third party with risk falling back to the selling bank.
> ➤ Sale secured by an insurance contract in which the selling bank indemnifies the insurance company against loss.
> ➤ Sale of a short-term loan that is part of a long-term credit commitment by the bank (a strip participation).

However, the above-mentioned RAP treatment does not apply to a sale of mortgage loans to the Government National Mortgage Association (Ginnie Mae), Federal National Mortgage Association (Fannie Mae), or Federal Home Loan Mortgage Corporation (Freddie Mac).

In valuing loans transferred with recourse, the critical question is whether the existing liability that has been established for probable adjustments is:

> ➤ Reasonably stated (no adjustment necessary).
> ➤ Excessive (market value is lower than book value).
> ➤ Deficient (market value is greater than book value).

Two primary factors that should be considered are past experience (with respect to default) and the current interest rate environment (with respect to prepayments).

WHEN-ISSUED SECURITIES

The *when-issued securities* market involves the conditional trading in government bonds or other securities in the interval between the announcement date and the date of actual issue; that is, before the effective listing date. For U.S. Treasury securities, this trading begins immediately after the formal announcement of new bills, notes, and bonds. Initially, when-issued trading is done on a discount basis for bills and on a coupon (yield) basis for notes and bonds. Once the auction results for notes or bonds have been announced, however, when-issued trading in these securities is done on a price basis. Settlement dates are the settlement dates for the respective auctions.

When-issued securities must be valued on the basis of their commitments to purchase and commitments to sell. In the case of a commitment to purchase, the net value of the transaction is the market value of the when-issued security less the purchase price.

$$MV = MV_{WI} - PP$$

where

$$MV_{WI} = \text{Market value of the when-issued security}$$

$$PP = \text{Purchase price}$$

For a commitment to sell, the net value of the transaction is the sale price of the when-issued security less its market value.

$$MV = SP - MV_{WI}$$

where

$$SP = \text{sale price}$$

INTEREST RATE DERIVATIVES

An interest rate derivative is a contract that involves an interest-sensitive product or the exchange of interest rates on a specified underlying position. Some are negotiated between two counterparties, while others are exchange-traded contracts. The major classifications for interest rate derivatives discussed in this chapter are swaps futures and forwards.[3]

Swaps

An *interest rate swap* contract is an agreement between two counterparties to exchange interest payments for a specified time at predetermined intervals. Swap contracts do not involve purchasing financial market instruments. Instead, the rights to future cash flows are exchanged. Alternatively, the obligations to pay future cash may be exchanged. The fundamental concept is to exchange a fixed-rate cash flow stream with a floating-rate stream.

Swap contracts. The most basic interest rate swap is a *coupon swap* in which a floating rate is exchanged for a fixed rate. For example, a financial institution may hold a large portfolio of fixed-rate loans while most of its deposit liabilities are floating-rate CDs. Another bank may hold considerable variable rate investments with fixed-rate obligations. To minimize interest rate risk, the two institutions may agree to swap interest payments on liabilities.

The two banks agree on a *notional principal*, or the amount of liabilities for which interest rates will be swapped. Note that this notional amount does not change hands but is simply the basis for interest rate calculations. The swap agreement also establishes the maturity date of the swap and the frequency of payments. When the swap arrangement involves exchanges of interest rates on assets, it is called an *asset swap*. When the exchange is on liabilities, it is a *liability swap*. For example, Bank C (with fixed-rate liabilities) may enter a liability swap that stipulates a $50 million notional amount for four years with payments made semiannually.

If its fixed rate on liabilities is 4 percent, Bank C may agree to swap the fixed 4 percent for a floating rate of Treasury bill plus 1.5, meaning 1.5 percentage points or 150 basis points above the Treasury bill rate.[4] Bank C:

➤ Has agreed to pay T-bill plus 1.5.
➤ Has agreed to receive 4 percent.
➤ Is referred to as the *floating-rate payor.*
➤ Is said to have sold a swap and has a short position in the swap market.

Of course, Bank C's counterparty:

➤ Has agreed to pay 4 percent.
➤ Has agreed to receive T-bill plus 1.5.
➤ Is referred to as the fixed-rate payor.
➤ Is said to have bought a swap and has a long position in the swap market.

The swap agreement does not change the way Bank C pays or records its interest expense on liabilities. Bank C continues to pay its fixed-rate obligations on the notional principal as would otherwise be the case every six months (in thousands).

	DR	CR
Interest expense	$1000	
Cash		$1000

The effect of the swap agreement is recorded via a separate entry. If Treasury bill plus 1.5 is 4.75 percent, Bank C loses .75 percent or 75 basis points on an annual basis for the 6-month period because Bank C must pay the 4.75 percent and receive only 4 percent. The 75-basis-point difference for six months on $50 million is $187,500 [$50 million × .0075 × .5]. When Bank C makes the payment to its counterparty, the following entry is made (in thousands).

	DR	CR
Interest expense	$187.5	
Cash		$187.5

Bank C pays this amount to its counterparty in the swap and its own interest expense is increased.

If Treasury bill plus 1.5 is 3.95 percent in the following six-month period, the first entry is the same (in thousands).

	DR	CR
Interest expense	$1000	
Cash		$1000

But Bank C has saved .05 percent or 5 basis points, amounting to $12,500 [$50 million × .0005 × .5] because Bank C pays 3.95 percent and receives 4 percent. Bank C receives this amount from its counterparty and records it in the following entry (in thousands):

	DR	CR
Cash	$12.5	
Interest expense		$12.5

This entry reduces the net interest expense of Bank C to $987,500 ($1 million – $.125 million).

Swap valuation. The value of a swap is the present value of the differential interest payments (a negative $187,500 in the first example and a positive $12,500 in the second example). Each of these payments should be discounted at the appropriate rate that applies to a zero-coupon instrument of the same duration.

The difficulty with this process is that, for the most part, the variable-rate payments are not known with certainty at any given time. The exception to this is the next floating-rate payment. This payment is known because the interest rate is set at the beginning of the period. However, it is also true that on the next reset date for the floating-rate side, the rate that is set for the subsequent period will exactly equal the market rate. That is, the floating-rate side will have a market value equal to the notional amount on the next reset date. Thus, instead of projecting future variable payments, it is necessary only to find the present value of the next floating-rate payment and the notional amount, using the currently prevailing market rate as the discount rate.

$$V_{FL} = \frac{NA\left(\frac{k_{FL'}}{m}\right) + NA}{(1+k_{FL})^t}$$

where

$$V_{FL} = \text{Value of the floating-rate side of swap}$$

$$NA = \text{Notional principal}$$

$$k_{FL}' = \text{Floating rate established at last reset date}$$

$$k_{FL} = \text{Current level of the swap floating rate}$$

$$t = \text{Time to next reset date}$$

Theoretical Spot Rate Yield Curve. The market value of the fixed-rate portion of the swap presents a different type of challenge. There is no doubt as to the amount of each of these payments, but it is necessary to establish the correct discount rate to be used. The amount of each payment is the notional amount multiplied by the fixed rate specified in the swap contract. This fixed rate (coupon rate) is normally set to the *swap yield* at the time that the swap is created (trade date) so that the fixed-rate side will be valued at par (notional amount). At the trade date, the fixed rate is generally set equal to a Treasury yield of a specified maturity plus a spread. After the trade date, the appropriate swap yield will change when the specified Treasury yield changes.

To price the fixed payments it is appropriate to consider each payment as a zero-coupon bond and to discount each payment by the zero-coupon rate that is appropriate for the date on which the payment will be received. Technically, the term structure of interest rates is the relationship between yield on zero-coupon Treasury securities and their maturities. A noncallable Treasury security can be considered a package of zero-coupon securities, with the date of each coupon payment being its respective maturity date. If the yields on such a package of zero-coupon securities are not the same as the yields available on an equivalent coupon-paying bond, arbitrage profits are possible.[5] However, the zero-coupon, spot-rate curve must be constructed, rather than derived from observed stripped Treasury securities (maturity value separated from coupon payments, creating a zero-coupon bond), because:

➤ The conventional Treasury market is more liquid than the stripped Treasury market.
➤ Yields in certain maturity segments of the stripped Treasury market are distorted by investors who find the strips attractive, bidding up the price and driving down the yield.
➤ Accrued interest on stripped Treasury securities is taxed, creating a tax disadvantage vis-à-vis coupon-paying Treasury. This disadvantage is reflected in the market yield.

Since this yield curve is constructed, it is called the *theoretical spot-rate yield curve* or the *theoretical zero-coupon yield curve.*

Thus, the theoretical spot rate curve is constructed using the conventional Treasury yield information. However, it is necessary to adjust the conventional Treasury yield information because the implied yields in the Treasury yield curve are lower than the theoretical zero-coupon rates. It can be shown that a long-term Treasury security that is selling at par will have a value greater than par when each of the coupon payments is discounted at the yield to maturity (YTM) for Treasury securities that mature on the same date that the coupon payment is made. (For example, a coupon payment that is due two years from now will be discounted at the YTM on a two-year Treasury security.) This is true because the calculation of YTM assumes reinvestment of all interim cash flows at the YTM. For a zero-coupon security, there is no interim cash flow and no reinvestment prior to maturity. The theoretical spot rates must be higher to compensate for this difference. It can also be shown that when all cash flows of the Treasury bond (selling at par) are discounted at the theoretical spot rates, the calculated value is also par value.

The *theoretical spot rates* are the rates that cause the present value of each of the payments associated with a Treasury security to equal the current market price of the security.

$$P_0 = \sum_{t=1}^{n} \left(\frac{CF_t}{(1+k_t)^t} \right)$$

where

P_0 = Current market price of Treasury security

CF_t = Cash flow in period t

n = Number of periods to maturity

s_t = Theoretical spot rate for period t

Since each calculation depends on the theoretical spot rates of both the current period and the previous periods, it is necessary to derive the earlier spot rates first and progress period-by-period in the derivation of subsequent theoretical spot rates.

Table 8–1 illustrates the calculation of theoretical spot rates for a two-year yield curve as of February 1995. Since coupon interest is paid on a semi-annual basis, there are four periods in this two-year time frame.

The first observed Treasury security on the time line is a six-month T-bill, a zero-coupon instrument, with a yield of 6.33 percent. Since this is a zero-

Table 8–1.

THEORETICAL TREASURY SPOT RATES

Maturity Date	To Maturity Years	To Maturity Periods	Coupon	Price	YTM[1]	Semiannual Theoretical Spot Rate[1]
Aug 95	.5	1	0	$96.87	.03165	.03165
Feb 96	1.0	2	4 5/8	97.90625	.03395	.034187095
Aug 96	1.5	3	7 1/2	100.28125	.0353	.03661406
Feb 97	2.0	4	4 3/4	95.46875	.0360	.036163055

[1] Rates in decimal form.

Note: Prices and yields to maturity are as of February 1995.

coupon security, no adjustment is necessary and the semiannual theoretical spot rate is the same as the observed rate, that is, 3.165 percent.

The observed Treasury note that matures in one year has a coupon rate of 4.625 percent, an asked price of 97:29 or 97.90625, and a YTM of 6.79 percent.[6] The theoretical spot rate for the second semiannual period is that rate which causes the present value of the future cash flows to equal the price, given a theoretical spot rate of 3.165 percent in the first semiannual period.

$$97.90625 = \frac{2.3125}{1.03165} + \frac{102.3125}{(1+s_2)^2}$$

$$97.90625 - 2.241554791 = \frac{102.3125}{(1+s_2)^2}$$

$$95.66469521 \, (1+s_2)^2 = 102.3125$$

$$s_2 = \left(\frac{102.3125}{95.66469521}\right)^{\frac{1}{2}} - 1$$

$$= .034187095$$

The theoretical spot rates for periods 3 and 4 are calculated using the specific prices and coupon rates associated with observed Treasury securities with 1.5 years to maturity and 2 years to maturity.

$$100.2185 = \frac{3.75}{1.036165} + \frac{3.75}{(1.034187095)^2} + \frac{103.75}{(1+s_3)^3}$$

$$s_3 = .03661406$$

Similarly

$$95.4685 = \frac{2.375}{1.036165} + \frac{2.375}{(1.034187095)^2}$$

$$+ \frac{2.375}{(1.034187095)^3} + \frac{102.375}{(1+s_4)^4}$$

$$s_4 = .036163055$$

In general, the formula to find the theoretical spot rates is

$$s_n = \left(\frac{(M+I)}{\left(P_0 \sum_{t=1}^{n-1} \frac{I}{(1+s_t)^t} \right)} \right)^{\frac{1}{n}} - 1$$

Table 8–2 verifies these results. When the coupon payments and maturity of the two-year Treasury note are discounted using the theoretical spot rates, the sum of their present values is 95.468850098 versus the actual observed market price of 95.46875, a difference of only .0001.

These theoretical spot rates then form the basis for determining the present value of the fixed interest payments associated with a swap. For example, if the fixed rate at trade date was Treasury plus 1, meaning the relevant Treasury rate plus 100 basis points on an annual basis, then 50 basis points should be added to each of the semiannual theoretical spot rates derived above.

The value of the fixed-rate side of the swap is the sum of all future fixed payments discounted at the appropriate rate of theoretical spot rate plus spread.

$$V_{FX} = \sum_{t=1}^{n} \frac{CF_t}{\left(1 + (s_t + \alpha)^t\right)}$$

where

V_{FX} = Value of fixed rate side of swap

s_t = Theoretical spot rate for period t based on Treasury rates

α = Spread over Treasury rate

Table 8–2.

TREASURY BOND VALUATION USING
THEORETICAL SPOT RATES

Periods	Semiannual YTM[1]	Coupon	Semiannual Spot Rate	PVIF	Present Value Using Spot
1	.03165	2.375	.03165	.969320991	2.302137354
2	.03395	2.375	.034187095	.934978818	2.220574693
3	.0353	2.375	.03661406	.897736152	2.132123361
4	.0360	102.375	.036163055	.867536163	88.814014690
Price based on theoretical spot rates					95.468850098
Actual market price					95.46875
Difference					.000100098

[1]   Rates in decimal form.

The value of the swap will be the difference between the value of the floating-rate side and the value of the fixed-rate side. For the floating-rate payor, the value of the swap is the difference between the value of the fixed-rate side (cash flows being received) and the floating-rate side (cash flows being paid).

$$M_V = V_{FX} - V_{FL}$$

For the fixed-rate payor, the value of the swap is the difference between the value of the floating-rate side (cash flows being received) and the fixed-rate side (cash flows being paid).

$$MV = V_{FL} - V_{FX}$$

Futures and Forwards
An *interest rate futures contract* is a publicly traded agreement to exchange a standard quantity of a fixed-income security at a specified date in the future at a predetermined price. An *interest rate forward contract* is similar to a futures except that the agreement is not exchange-traded and the quantity of the underlying asset is not standardized.

The following list includes the most common interest rate futures contracts traded in the United States on the Chicago Board of Trade (CBT), MidAmerica Commodity Exchange (MCE), Financial Instrument Exchange (FINEX, a division of the New York Cotton Exchange), and the International Monetary Market at the Chicago Mercantile Exchange (IMM).

Instrument	Denomination	Exchange
Treasury bonds	$100,000	CBT
Treasury bonds	$50,000	MCE
Zero-coupon		
Treasury bonds	$100,000	CBT
10-yr. Treasury notes	$100,000	CBT
5-yr. Treasury notes	$100,000	CBT
5-yr. Treasury notes	$250,000	FINEX
2-yr. Treasury notes	$200,000	CBT
2-yr. Treasury notes	$500,000	FINEX
90-day Treasury bills	$1 million	IMM
90-day Treasury bills	$500,000	MCE
30-day Federal funds	$5 million	CBT
1-month LIBOR	$3 million	IMM
Mortgage-backed bonds	$100,000	CBT
Municipal bond index	$1,000 times	CBT
	Bond Buyer MBI	CBT

Treasury bond and Treasury bill futures have historically been the most actively traded.

The buyer of a futures contract is entitled to purchase the underlying asset at a future date at a specified price. In the interim, if the value of the underlying asset increases, the value of the futures contract also increases. If the purchaser chose to sell the contract instead of taking delivery of the underlying asset, that purchaser would realize a profit.

An institution (or individual) also may enter the market and sell a futures contract that obligates the seller to sell the underlying instruments at some specified date and price. In the interim, if the value of the underlying asset decreases, the value of the futures contract also declines. If the seller purchased an offsetting contract (at the now lower price) instead of delivering the underlying asset, that party would again realize a profit.

These basic principles make the use of futures a viable method of hedging against portfolio loss. For example, a securities portfolio manager for a bank may be concerned that the value of the bank's portfolio of Treasury bonds will decline if rates increase. The holdings of Treasury bonds are in the cash market—the market of actual transactions in stocks and bonds. The appropriate hedge would be to take the opposite position in the hedge market, in this case, the futures markets. Since the bank holds Treasury bonds, it is said to have a long position (asset) in bonds in the cash market. Accordingly, the bank portfolio manager would take a short position in the futures market by selling Treasury bond futures contracts (liability) for subsequent delivery.

Should rates increase, the long portfolio of Treasury bonds in the cash market declines in value. However, the futures position can be closed by buying an offsetting contract (settling the liability) at a now lower price. The profit in the futures market works to offset the loss in the cash market.

The valuation of futures contracts is based on the premise that prices in the futures market and the cash market for a particular interest rate instrument will not provide an opportunity for arbitrage profits. The two scenarios in Table 8–3 illustrate the minimum and maximum prices for interest rate futures contracts, with the following assumptions:

k_C = Coupon rate of underlying bond, with a face value of 100[7]

k_L = Lending interest rate, for example, the Treasury bill rate

k_B = Borrowing interest rate, for example, the Federal funds rate

$k_B > k_L$

t = Time to futures contract expiration

F = Futures price

P_0 = Current price of underlying bond

Both scenarios assume that time zero (today) is immediately after a bond coupon payment and both scenarios ignore (1) transactions costs and (2) initial and variation margins on the futures contracts.

Scenario I involves a long position in the futures market and a short position in the bond market. At time zero, a bond futures contract is purchased, requiring no cash outflow. At the same time, in the cash market, the proceeds of a short sale of the bond are lent in money markets at the rate k_L. When the futures contract expires, the futures price and accrued interest on the underlying bond are paid. The bond that is delivered in the futures market is used in the cash market to cover the short position. Also in the cash market, the short-term investment including interest is received. The net cash flow represents the profit in this transaction. To eliminate the possibility of arbitrage profits, this profit must be zero.

Table 8–3.

INTEREST RATE FUTURES PRICING

SCENARIO I CASH FLOWS	Time Zero	Futures Expiration Date
Buy Futures Contract		
No cash flow at time 0	0	
Pay contract price at expiration		$-F$
Pay accrued interest on bond		$-100(k_C)(t)$
Sell Bond Short		
Receive price of bond	P_0	
Lend proceeds of short sale	$-P_0$	
Deliver bond (from futures)		
to cover short		0
Receive proceeds from lending:		
Principal		P_0
Interest		$P_0(k_L)(t)$
Net cash flow:	0	$-F - 100(k_C)(t)$
		$+ P_0 + P_0(k_L)(t)$

SCENARIO II CASH FLOWS	Time Zero	Futures Expiration Date
Sell Futures Contract		
No cash flow at time 0	0	
Receive contract price at expiration		F
Receive accrued interest on bond		$100(k_C)(t)$
Buy Bond		
Borrow price of bond	P_0	
Purchase bond	$-P_0$	
Deliver bond to cover futures		0
Repay borrowing:		
Principal		$-P_0$
Interest		$-P_0(k_B)(t)$
Net cash flow	0	$F + 100(k_C)(t)$
		$-P_0 - P_0(k_B)(t)$

Table 8–3. (Concluded)

INTEREST RATE FUTURES PRICING

Given:

k_C = Coupon rate of underlying bond with a face value of 100

k_L = Lending interest rate, for example, the Treasury bill rate

k_B = Borrowing interest rate, for example, the Federal funds rate

$k_B > k_L$

t = Time to futures contract expiration

F = Futures price

P_0 = Current price of underlying bond

Note: It is assumed that time zero is immediately after bond coupon payment.

$$0 = -F - 100(k_c)(t) + P_0(k_L)(t)$$
$$F = P_0 + P_0(k_L)(t) - 100(k_c)(t)$$
$$F = P_0[1 + (k_L)(t)] - 100(k_c)(t)$$

Thus, the price of an interest rate futures contract is bounded on the lower end by the relationship between the bond price, the bond coupon rate, and the lending rate.

Scenario II involves a short position in the futures market and a long position in the bond market. At time zero, a bond futures contract is sold, resulting in no cash inflow. At the same time, in the cash market, a bond is purchased with borrowed funds, at the interest rate of k_B. When the futures contract expires, the bond that was purchased in the cash market is delivered to the futures market and the futures price plus accrued interest are received. Also in the cash market, the short-term loan including interest is paid. The net cash flow also represents the profit in this transaction. Again, to eliminate the possibility of arbitrage profits, this profit must be zero.

$$0 = F + 100(k_c)(t) - P_0 - P_0(k_B)(t)$$
$$F = -P_0 - P_0(k_B)(t) + 100(k_c)(t)$$
$$F = P_0[1 + (k_B)(t)] - 100(k_c)(t)$$

The price of an interest rate futures contract is bounded on the upper end by the relationship between the bond price, the bond coupon rate, and the borrowing rate.[8]

The value of *interest rate forward contracts* can be approximated by the valuation formulas for futures contracts. The differences between the two contracts are related primarily to the markets in which they are offered:

➤ Futures contracts are standardized, traded on organized exchanges, and have a liquid secondary market. Forwards are not standardized in denomination, are not traded, and have virtually no secondary market.

➤ More than 90 percent of futures contracts are not settled by delivery but, instead, by offsetting futures contracts. Forward contracts are settled by delivery.

➤ Futures contracts are marked-to-market (variation margins), while forward contracts are not.

➤ There is credit risk for counterparties in forward contracts, but almost none with futures contracts because the exchanges on which futures are traded assume credit risk.

Beyond these differences, the futures and forward contracts are similar in construction and the same arbitrage logic is appropriate for both.

A COMPLETE ASSESSMENT OF VALUE

Market valuation of commercial banks is a concept with important implications for investors, depositors, and regulators. These models can assist in the valuation of the off-balance-sheet positions of a bank. The goal in each case is to arrive at an objective measurement of value to properly assess the overall financial position of the bank. Together with valuation models for the balance sheet, this approach to valuation provides not only a rational assessment of the value of the institution in total but also insights into how the bank's value can be maximized in the future.

SELECTED REFERENCES

Battley, Nick, ed. *The World's Futures & Options Markets*. Chicago: Probus Publishing, 1993.

Fabozzi, Frank J. *Bond Markets, Analysis and Strategies*. Englewood Cliffs, NJ: Prentice Hall, 1993.

Fitch, Thomas. *Dictionary of Banking Terms*. Hauppauge, NY: Barron's Educational Series, 1990.

Howe, Donna M. *A Guide to Managing Interest-Rate Risk*. New York: New York Institute of Finance, 1992.

Hull, John. *Options, Futures, and Other Derivative Securities*. Englewood Cliffs, NJ: Prentice Hall, 1989.

Johnson, Hazel J. *Financial Institutions and Markets: A Global Perspective*. New York: McGraw-Hill, 1993.

Jones, Frank J., and Frank J. Fabozzi. *The International Government Bond Markets: An Overview and Analysis of the World's Leading Public Debt Markets*. Chicago: Probus Publishing, 1992.

Konishi, Atsuo, and Ravi E. Dattatreya, eds. *The Handbook of Derivative Instruments*. Chicago: Probus Publishing, 1991.

Pavel, Christine A. *Securitization: The Analysis and Development of the Loan-Based/Asset-Backed Securities Markets*. Chicago: Probus Publishing, 1989.

ENDNOTES

1 A draft is a payment order that directs a second party to pay a specified amount to a third party (the payee). Although similar to a bill of exchange, the term draft is generally used when the second party is a bank. A check is a sight draft (due when presented). A time draft is due at a future date.

2 The Financial Accounting Standards Board has established certain criteria for this off-balance-sheet treatment. To be recognized as a sale and removed from the balance sheet, a transfer of assets must meet each of the following conditions:

   • Transferor (bank as seller) surrenders control of the future cash flows associated with the loans, with no option to repurchase at a later date.

- It must be possible to reasonably estimate the obligations of the transferor in the case of sale with recourse.

- The transferee (purchaser) may not require the transferor to repurchase the loans, except when the amount of the remaining unpaid loans is quite small (a clean-up call).

When one of the preceding conditions is not met, the transaction is not a sale, but a secured borrowing. The loans remain on the books of the bank, and the cash proceeds of the transfer are recorded as a liability. The discussion in this section assumes that these conditions have been met and that the loans are no longer recorded as assets.

3   The valuation of interest rate options and interest rate caps is discussed in Chapter 5, "Embedded Options." Options are discussed in connection with callable bonds. Interest rate caps are discussed in the context of variable-rate loans.

4   A basis point is one-hundredth of 1 percent.

5   Arbitrage is the process of buying a security at a lower price in one market and selling it at a higher price in another market. In efficient markets, market participants bid up the price in the lower-priced market, eliminating arbitrage profits.

6   The fractional portion of the price for Treasury notes and bonds is expressed in 32nds of a point, such that 1/32 equals .03125.

7   The term bond is used to signify any fixed-income instrument that accrues interest on its face value.

8   Notice that this is the upper boundary because $k_B > k_L$.

Appendix A–1

FUTURE VALUE OF $1

$$FVIF = (1+k)^n$$

Periods	1%	2%	3%	4%	5%	6%
1	1.0100	1.0200	1.0300	1.0400	1.0500	1.0600
2	1.0201	1.0404	1.0609	1.0816	1.1025	1.1236
3	1.0303	1.0612	1.0927	1.1249	1.1576	1.1910
4	1.0406	1.0824	1.1255	1.1699	1.2155	1.2625
5	1.0510	1.1041	1.1593	1.2167	1.2763	1.3382
6	1.0615	1.1262	1.1941	1.2653	1.3401	1.4185
7	1.0721	1.1487	1.2299	1.3159	1.4071	1.5036
8	1.0829	1.1717	1.2668	1.3686	1.4775	1.5938
9	1.0937	1.1951	1.3048	1.4233	1.5513	1.6895
10	1.1046	1.2190	1.3439	1.4802	1.6289	1.7908
11	1.1157	1.2434	1.3842	1.5395	1.7103	1.8983
12	1.1268	1.2682	1.4258	1.6010	1.7959	2.0122
13	1.1381	1.2936	1.4685	1.6651	1.8856	2.1329
14	1.1495	1.3195	1.5126	1.7317	1.9799	2.2609
15	1.1610	1.3459	1.5580	1.8009	2.0789	2.3966
16	1.1726	1.3728	1.6047	1.8730	2.1829	2.5404
17	1.1843	1.4002	1.6528	1.9479	2.2920	2.6928
18	1.1961	1.4282	1.7024	2.0258	2.4066	2.8543
19	1.2081	1.4568	1.7535	2.1068	2.5270	3.0256
20	1.2202	1.4859	1.8061	2.1911	2.6533	3.2071
25	1.2824	1.6406	2.0938	2.6658	3.3864	4.2919
30	1.3478	1.8114	2.4273	3.2434	4.3219	5.7435
35	1.4166	1.9999	2.8139	3.9461	5.5160	7.6861
40	1.4889	2.2080	3.2620	4.8010	7.0400	10.2857
45	1.5648	2.4379	3.7816	5.8412	8.9850	13.7646
50	1.6446	2.6916	4.3839	7.1067	11.4674	18.4202

7%	8%	9%	10%	11%	12%	13%
1.0700	1.0800	1.0900	1.1000	1.1100	1.1200	1.1300
1.1449	1.1664	1.1881	1.2100	1.2321	1.2544	1.2769
1.2250	1.2597	1.2950	1.3310	1.3676	1.4049	1.4429
1.3108	1.3605	1.4116	1.4641	1.5181	1.5735	1.6305
1.4026	1.4693	1.5386	1.6105	1.6851	1.7623	1.8424
1.5007	1.5869	1.6771	1.7716	1.8704	1.9738	2.0820
1.6058	1.7138	1.8280	1.9487	2.0762	2.2107	2.3526
1.7182	1.8509	1.9926	2.1436	2.3045	2.4760	2.6584
1.8385	1.9990	2.1719	2.3579	2.5580	2.7731	3.0040
1.9672	2.1589	2.3674	2.5937	2.8394	3.1058	3.3946
2.1049	2.3316	2.5804	2.8531	3.1518	3.4785	3.8359
2.2522	2.5182	2.8127	3.1384	3.4985	3.8960	4.3345
2.4098	2.7196	3.0658	3.4523	3.8833	4.3635	4.8980
2.5785	2.9372	3.3417	3.7975	4.3104	4.8871	5.5348
2.7590	3.1722	3.6425	4.1772	4.7846	5.4736	6.2543
2.9522	3.4259	3.9703	4.5950	5.3109	6.1304	7.0673
3.1588	3.7000	4.3276	5.0545	5.8951	6.8660	7.9861
3.3799	3.9960	4.7171	5.5599	6.5436	7.6900	9.0243
3.6165	4.3157	5.1417	6.1159	7.2633	8.6128	10.1974
3.8697	4.6610	5.6044	6.7275	8.0623	9.6463	11.5231
5.4274	6.8485	8.6231	10.8347	13.5855	17.0001	21.2305
7.6123	10.0627	13.2677	17.4494	22.8923	29.9599	39.1159
10.6766	14.7853	20.4140	28.1024	38.5749	52.7996	72.0685
14.9745	21.7245	31.4094	45.2593	65.0009	93.0510	132.7816
21.0025	31.9204	48.3273	72.8905	109.5302	163.9876	244.6414
29.4570	46.9016	74.3575	117.3909	184.5648	289.0022	450.7359

14%	15%	16%	17%	18%	19%	20%
1.1400	1.1500	1.1600	1.1700	1.1800	1.1900	1.2000
1.2996	1.3225	1.3456	1.3689	1.3924	1.4161	1.4400
1.4815	1.5209	1.5609	1.6016	1.6430	1.6852	1.7280
1.6890	1.7490	1.8106	1.8739	1.9388	2.0053	2.0736
1.9254	2.0114	2.1003	2.1924	2.2878	2.3864	2.4883
2.1950	2.3131	2.4364	2.5652	2.6996	2.8398	2.9860
2.5023	2.6600	2.8262	3.0012	3.1855	3.3793	3.5832
2.8526	3.0590	3.2784	3.5115	3.7589	4.0214	4.2998
3.2519	3.5179	3.8030	4.1084	4.4355	4.7854	5.1598
3.7072	4.0456	4.4114	4.8068	5.2338	5.6947	6.1917
4.2262	4.6524	5.1173	5.6240	6.1759	6.7767	7.4301
4.8179	5.3503	5.9360	6.5801	7.2876	8.0642	8.9161
5.4924	6.1528	6.8858	7.6987	8.5994	9.5964	10.6993
6.2613	7.0757	7.9875	9.0075	10.1472	11.4198	12.8392
7.1379	8.1371	9.2655	10.5387	11.9737	13.5895	15.4070
8.1372	9.3576	10.7480	12.3303	14.1290	16.1715	18.4884
9.2765	10.7613	12.4677	14.4265	16.6722	19.2441	22.1861
10.5752	12.3755	14.4625	16.8790	19.6733	22.9005	26.6233
12.0557	14.2318	16.7765	19.7484	23.2144	27.2516	31.9480
13.7435	16.3665	19.4608	23.1056	27.3930	32.4294	38.3376
26.4619	32.9190	40.8742	50.6578	62.6686	77.3881	95.3962
50.9502	66.2118	85.8499	111.0647	143.3706	184.6753	237.3763
98.1002	133.1755	180.3141	243.5035	327.9973	440.7006	590.6682
188.8835	267.8635	378.7212	533.8687	750.3783	1.05e+03	1.47e+03
363.6791	538.7693	795.4438	1.17e+03	1.72e+03	2.51e+03	3.66e+03
700.2330	1.08e+03	1.67e+03	2.57e+03	3.93e+03	5.99e+03	9.10e+03

Appendix A–2

FUTURE VALUE OF AN ANNUITY OF $1

$$FVIFA = ((1+k)^n-1)/k$$

Periods	1%	2%	3%	4%	5%	6%
1	1.0000	1.0000	1.0000	1.0000	1.0000	1.0000
2	2.0100	2.0200	2.0300	2.0400	2.0500	2.0600
3	3.0301	3.0604	3.0909	3.1216	3.1525	3.1836
4	4.0604	4.1216	4.1836	4.2465	4.3101	4.3746
5	5.1010	5.2040	5.3091	5.4163	5.5256	5.6371
6	6.1520	6.3081	6.4684	6.6330	6.8019	6.9753
7	7.2135	7.4343	7.6625	7.8983	8.1420	8.3938
8	8.2857	8.5830	8.8923	9.2142	9.5491	9.8975
9	9.3685	9.7546	10.1591	10.5828	11.0266	11.4913
10	10.4622	10.9497	11.4639	12.0061	12.5779	13.1808
11	11.5668	12.1687	12.8078	13.4864	14.2068	14.9716
12	12.6825	13.4121	14.1920	15.0258	15.9171	16.8699
13	13.8093	14.6803	15.6178	16.6268	17.7130	18.8821
14	14.9474	15.9739	17.0863	18.2919	19.5986	21.0151
15	16.0969	17.2934	18.5989	20.0236	21.5786	23.2760
16	17.2579	18.6393	20.1569	21.8245	23.6575	25.6725
17	18.4304	20.0121	21.7616	23.6975	25.8404	28.2129
18	19.6147	21.4123	23.4144	25.6454	28.1324	30.9057
19	20.8109	22.8406	25.1169	27.6712	30.5390	33.7600
20	22.0190	24.2974	26.8704	29.7781	33.0660	36.7856
25	28.2432	32.0303	36.4593	41.6459	47.7271	54.8645
30	34.7849	40.5681	47.5754	56.0849	66.4388	79.0582
35	41.6603	49.9945	60.4621	73.6522	90.3203	111.4348
40	48.8864	60.4020	75.4013	95.0255	120.7998	154.7620
45	56.4811	71.8927	92.7199	121.0294	159.7002	212.7435
50	64.4632	84.5794	112.7969	152.6671	209.3480	290.3359

7%	8%	9%	10%	11%	12%	13%
1.0000	1.0000	1.0000	1.0000	1.0000	1.0000	1.0000
2.0700	2.0800	2.0900	2.1000	2.1100	2.1200	2.1300
3.2149	3.2464	3.2781	3.3100	3.3421	3.3744	3.4069
4.4399	4.5061	4.5731	4.6410	4.7097	4.7793	4.8498
5.7507	5.8666	5.9847	6.1051	6.2278	6.3528	6.4803
7.1533	7.3359	7.5233	7.7156	7.9129	8.1152	8.3227
8.6540	8.9228	9.2004	9.4872	9.7833	10.0890	10.4047
10.2598	10.6366	11.0285	11.4359	11.8594	12.2997	12.7573
11.9780	12.4876	13.0210	13.5795	14.1640	14.7757	15.4157
13.8164	14.4866	15.1929	15.9374	16.7220	17.5487	18.4197
15.7836	16.6455	17.5603	18.5312	19.5614	20.6546	21.8143
17.8885	18.9771	20.1407	21.3843	22.7132	24.1331	25.6502
20.1406	21.4953	22.9534	24.5227	26.2116	28.0291	29.9847
22.5505	24.2149	26.0192	27.9750	30.0949	32.3926	34.8827
25.1290	27.1521	29.3609	31.7725	34.4054	37.2797	40.4175
27.8881	30.3243	33.0034	35.9497	39.1899	42.7533	46.6717
30.8402	33.7502	36.9737	40.5447	44.5008	48.8837	53.7391
33.9990	37.4502	41.3013	45.5992	50.3959	55.7497	61.7251
37.3790	41.4463	46.0185	51.1591	56.9395	63.4397	70.7494
40.9955	45.7620	51.1601	57.2750	64.2028	72.0524	80.9468
63.2490	73.1059	84.7009	98.3471	114.4133	133.3339	155.6196
94.4608	113.2832	136.3075	164.4940	199.0209	241.3327	293.1992
138.2369	172.3168	215.7108	271.0244	341.5896	431.6635	546.6808
199.6351	259.0565	337.8824	442.5926	581.8261	767.0914	1.01e+03
285.7493	386.5056	525.8587	718.9048	986.6386	1.36e+03	1.87e+03
406.5289	573.7702	815.0836	1.16e+03	1.67e+03	2.40e+03	3.46e+03

14%	15%	16%	17%	18%	19%	20%
1.0000	1.0000	1.0000	1.0000	1.0000	1.0000	1.0000
2.1400	2.1500	2.1600	2.1700	2.1800	2.1900	2.2000
3.4396	3.4725	3.5056	3.5389	3.5724	3.6061	3.6400
4.9211	4.9934	5.0665	5.1405	5.2154	5.2913	5.3680
6.6101	6.7424	6.8771	7.0144	7.1542	7.2966	7.4416
8.5355	8.7537	8.9775	9.2068	9.4420	9.6830	9.9299
10.7305	11.0668	11.4139	11.7720	12.1415	12.5227	12.9159
13.2328	13.7268	14.2401	14.7733	15.3270	15.9020	16.4991
16.0853	16.7858	17.5185	18.2847	19.0859	19.9234	20.7989
19.3373	20.3037	21.3215	22.3931	23.5213	24.7089	25.9587
23.0445	24.3493	25.7329	27.1999	28.7551	30.4035	32.1504
27.2707	29.0017	30.8502	32.8239	34.9311	37.1802	39.5805
32.0887	34.3519	36.7862	39.4040	42.2187	45.2445	48.4966
37.5811	40.5047	43.6720	47.1027	50.8180	54.8409	59.1959
43.8424	47.5804	51.6595	56.1101	60.9653	66.2607	72.0351
50.9804	55.7175	60.9250	66.6488	72.9390	79.8502	87.4421
59.1176	65.0751	71.6730	78.9792	87.0680	96.0218	105.9306
68.3941	75.8364	84.1407	93.4056	103.7403	115.2659	128.1167
78.9692	88.2118	98.6032	110.2846	123.4135	138.1664	154.7400
91.0249	102.4436	115.3797	130.0329	146.6280	165.4180	186.6880
181.8708	212.7930	249.2140	292.1049	342.6035	402.0425	471.9811
356.7868	434.7451	530.3117	647.4391	790.9480	966.7122	1.18e+03
693.5727	881.1702	1.12e+03	1.43e+03	1.82e+03	2.31e+03	2.95e+03
1.34e+03	1.78e+03	2.36e+03	3.13e+03	4.16e+03	5.53e+03	7.34e+03
2.59e+03	3.59e+03	4.97e+03	6.88e+03	9.53e+03	1.32e+04	1.83e+04
4.99e+03	7.22e+03	1.04e+04	1.51e+04	2.18e+04	3.15e+04	4.55e+04

Appendix A–3

PRESENT VALUE OF $1
$FVIF = (1/1(1+k)^n)$

Periods	1%	2%	3%	4%	5%	6%
1	0.9901	0.9804	0.9709	0.9615	0.9524	0.9434
2	0.9803	0.9612	0.9426	0.9246	0.9070	0.8900
3	0.9706	0.9423	0.9151	0.8890	0.8638	0.8396
4	0.9610	0.9238	0.8885	0.8548	0.8227	0.7921
5	0.9515	0.9057	0.8626	0.8219	0.7835	0.7473
6	0.9420	0.8880	0.8375	0.7903	0.7462	0.7050
7	0.9327	0.8706	0.8131	0.7599	0.7107	0.6651
8	0.9235	0.8535	0.7894	0.7307	0.6768	0.6274
9	0.9143	0.8368	0.7664	0.7026	0.6446	0.5919
10	0.9053	0.8203	0.7441	0.6756	0.6139	0.5584
11	0.8963	0.8043	0.7224	0.6496	0.5847	0.5268
12	0.8874	0.7885	0.7014	0.6246	0.5568	0.4970
13	0.8787	0.7730	0.6810	0.6006	0.5303	0.4688
14	0.8700	0.7579	0.6611	0.5775	0.5051	0.4423
15	0.8613	0.7430	0.6419	0.5553	0.4810	0.4173
16	0.8528	0.7284	0.6232	0.5339	0.4581	0.3936
17	0.8444	0.7142	0.6050	0.5134	0.4363	0.3714
18	0.8360	0.7002	0.5874	0.4936	0.4155	0.3503
19	0.8277	0.6864	0.5703	0.4746	0.3957	0.3305
20	0.8195	0.6730	0.5537	0.4564	0.3769	0.3118
25	0.7798	0.6095	0.4776	0.3751	0.2953	0.2330
30	0.7419	0.5521	0.4120	0.3083	0.2314	0.1741
35	0.7059	0.5000	0.3554	0.2534	0.1813	0.1301
40	0.6717	0.4529	0.3066	0.2083	0.1420	0.0972
45	0.6391	0.4102	0.2644	0.1712	0.1113	0.0727
50	1.0000	0.3715	0.2281	0.1407	0.0872	0.0543

7%	8%	9%	10%	11%	12%	13%
0.9346	0.9259	0.9174	0.9091	0.9009	0.8929	0.8850
0.8734	0.8573	0.8417	0.8264	0.8116	0.7972	0.7831
0.8163	0.7938	0.7722	0.7513	0.7312	0.7118	0.6931
0.7629	0.7350	0.7084	0.6830	0.6587	0.6355	0.6133
0.7130	0.6806	0.6499	0.6209	0.5935	0.5674	0.5428
0.6663	0.6302	0.5963	0.5645	0.5346	0.5066	0.4803
0.6227	0.5835	0.5470	0.5132	0.4817	0.4523	0.4251
0.5820	0.5403	0.5019	0.4665	0.4339	0.4039	0.3762
0.5439	0.5002	0.4604	0.4241	0.3909	0.3606	0.3329
0.5083	0.4632	0.4224	0.3855	0.3522	0.3220	0.2946
0.4751	0.4289	0.3875	0.3505	0.3173	0.2875	0.2607
0.4440	0.3971	0.3555	0.3186	0.2858	0.2567	0.2307
0.4150	0.3677	0.3262	0.2897	0.2575	0.2292	0.2042
0.3878	0.3405	0.2992	0.2633	0.2320	0.2046	0.1807
0.3624	0.3152	0.2745	0.2394	0.2090	0.1827	0.1599
0.3387	0.2919	0.2519	0.2176	0.1883	0.1631	0.1415
0.3166	0.2703	0.2311	0.1978	0.1696	0.1456	0.1252
0.2959	0.2502	0.2120	0.1799	0.1528	0.1300	0.1108
0.2765	0.2317	0.1945	0.1635	0.1377	0.1161	0.0981
0.2584	0.2145	0.1784	0.1486	0.1240	0.1037	0.0868
0.1842	0.1460	0.1160	0.0923	0.0736	0.0588	0.0471
0.1314	0.0994	0.0754	0.0573	0.0437	0.0334	0.0256
0.0937	0.0676	0.0490	0.0356	0.0259	0.0189	0.0139
0.0668	0.0460	0.0318	0.0221	0.0154	0.0107	0.0075
0.0476	0.0313	0.0207	0.0137	0.0091	0.0061	0.0041
0.0339	0.0213	0.0134	0.0085	0.0054	0.0035	0.0022

14%	15%	16%	17%	18%	19%	20%
0.8772	0.8696	0.8621	0.8547	0.8475	0.8403	0.8333
0.7695	0.7561	0.7432	0.7305	0.7182	0.7062	0.6944
0.6750	0.6575	0.6407	0.6244	0.6086	0.5934	0.5787
0.5921	0.5718	0.5523	0.5337	0.5158	0.4987	0.4823
0.5194	0.4972	0.4761	0.4561	0.4371	0.4190	0.4019
0.4556	0.4323	0.4104	0.3898	0.3704	0.3521	0.3349
0.3996	0.3759	0.3538	0.3332	0.3139	0.2959	0.2791
0.3506	0.3269	0.3050	0.2848	0.2660	0.2487	0.2326
0.3075	0.2843	0.2630	0.2434	0.2255	0.2090	0.1938
0.2697	0.2472	0.2267	0.2080	0.1911	0.1756	0.1615
0.2366	0.2149	0.1954	0.1778	0.1619	0.1476	0.1346
0.2076	0.1869	0.1685	0.1520	0.1372	0.1240	0.1122
0.1821	0.1625	0.1452	0.1299	0.1163	0.1042	0.0935
0.1597	0.1413	0.1252	0.1110	0.0985	0.0876	0.0779
0.1401	0.1229	0.1079	0.0949	0.0835	0.0736	0.0649
0.1229	0.1069	0.0930	0.0811	0.0708	0.0618	0.0541
0.1078	0.0929	0.0802	0.0693	0.0600	0.0520	0.0451
0.0946	0.0808	0.0691	0.0592	0.0508	0.0437	0.0376
0.0829	0.0703	0.0596	0.0506	0.0431	0.0367	0.0313
0.0728	0.0611	0.0514	0.0433	0.0365	0.0308	0.0261
0.0378	0.0304	0.0245	0.0197	0.0160	0.0129	0.0105
0.0196	0.0151	0.0116	0.0090	0.0070	0.0054	0.0042
0.0102	0.0075	0.0055	0.0041	0.0030	0.0023	0.0017
0.0053	0.0037	0.0026	0.0019	0.0013	0.0010	0.0007
0.0027	0.0019	0.0013	0.0009	0.0006	0.0004	0.0003
0.0014	0.0009	0.0006	0.0004	0.0003	0.0002	0.0001

Appendix A–4

PRESENT VALUE OF AN ANNUITY OF $1
$FVIFA = (1 - 1/(1+k)^n)/k$

Periods	1%	2%	3%	4%	5%	6%
1	0.9901	0.9804	0.9709	0.9615	0.9524	0.9434
2	1.9704	1.9416	1.9135	1.8861	1.8594	1.8334
3	2.9410	2.8839	2.8286	2.7751	2.7232	2.6730
4	3.9020	3.8077	3.7171	3.6299	3.5460	3.4651
5	4.8534	4.7135	4.5797	4.4518	4.3295	4.2124
6	5.7955	5.6014	5.4172	5.2421	5.0757	4.9173
7	6.7282	6.4720	6.2303	6.0021	5.7864	5.5824
8	7.6517	7.3255	7.0197	6.7327	6.4632	6.2098
9	8.5660	8.1622	7.7861	7.4353	7.1078	6.8017
10	9.4713	8.9826	8.5302	8.1109	7.7217	7.3601
11	10.3676	9.7868	9.2526	8.7605	8.3064	7.8869
12	11.2551	10.5753	9.9540	9.3851	8.8633	8.3838
13	12.1337	11.3484	10.6350	9.9856	9.3936	8.8527
14	13.0037	12.1062	11.2961	10.5631	9.8986	9.2950
15	13.8651	12.8493	11.9379	11.1184	10.3797	9.7122
16	14.7179	13.5777	12.5611	11.6523	10.8378	10.1059
17	15.5623	14.2919	13.1661	12.1657	11.2741	10.4773
18	16.3983	14.9920	13.7535	12.6593	11.6896	10.8276
19	17.2260	15.6785	14.3238	13.1339	12.0853	11.1581
20	18.0456	16.3514	14.8775	13.5903	12.4622	11.4699
25	22.0232	19.5235	17.4131	15.6221	14.0939	12.7834
30	25.8077	22.3965	19.6004	17.2920	15.3725	13.7648
35	29.4086	24.9986	21.4872	18.6646	16.3742	14.4982
40	32.8347	27.3555	23.1148	19.7928	17.1591	15.0463
45	36.0945	29.4902	24.5187	20.7200	17.7741	15.4558
50	39.1961	31.4236	25.7298	21.4822	18.2559	15.7619

7%	8%	9%	10%	11%	12%	13%
0.9346	0.9259	0.9174	0.9091	0.9009	0.8929	0.8850
1.8080	1.7833	1.7591	1.7355	1.7125	1.6901	1.6681
2.6243	2.5771	2.5313	2.4869	2.4437	2.4018	2.3612
3.3872	3.3121	3.2397	3.1699	3.1024	3.0373	2.9745
4.1002	3.9927	3.8897	3.7908	3.6959	3.6048	3.5172
4.7665	4.6229	4.4859	4.3553	4.2305	4.1114	3.9975
5.3893	5.2064	5.0330	4.8684	4.7122	4.5638	4.4226
5.9713	5.7466	5.5348	5.3349	5.1461	4.9676	4.7988
6.5152	6.2469	5.9952	5.7590	5.5370	5.3282	5.1317
7.0236	6.7101	6.4177	6.1446	5.8892	5.6502	5.4262
7.4987	7.1390	6.8052	6.4951	6.2065	5.9377	5.6869
7.9427	7.5361	7.1607	6.8137	6.4924	6.1944	5.9176
8.3577	7.9038	7.4869	7.1034	6.7499	6.4235	6.1218
8.7455	8.2442	7.7862	7.3667	6.9819	6.6282	6.3025
9.1079	8.5595	8.0607	7.6061	7.1909	6.8109	6.4624
9.4466	8.8514	8.3126	7.8237	7.3792	6.9740	6.6039
9.7632	9.1216	8.5436	8.0216	7.5488	7.1196	6.7291
10.0591	9.3719	8.7556	8.2014	7.7016	7.2497	6.8399
10.3356	9.6036	8.9501	8.3649	7.8393	7.3658	6.9380
10.5940	9.8181	9.1285	8.5136	7.9633	7.4694	7.0248
11.6536	10.6748	9.8226	9.0770	8.4217	7.8431	7.3300
12.4090	11.2578	10.2737	9.4269	8.6938	8.0552	7.4957
12.9477	11.6546	10.5668	9.6442	8.8552	8.1755	7.5856
13.3317	11.9246	10.7574	9.7791	8.9511	8.2438	7.6344
13.6055	12.1084	10.8812	9.8628	9.0079	8.2825	7.6609
13.8007	12.2335	10.9617	9.9148	9.0417	8.3045	7.6752

14%	15%	16%	17%	18%	19%	20%
0.8772	0.8696	0.8621	0.8547	0.8475	0.8403	0.8333
1.6467	1.6257	1.6052	1.5852	1.5656	1.5465	1.5278
2.3216	2.2832	2.2459	2.2096	2.1743	2.1399	2.1065
2.9137	2.8550	2.7982	2.7432	2.6901	2.6386	2.5887
3.4331	3.3522	3.2743	3.1993	3.1272	3.0576	2.9906
3.8887	3.7845	3.6847	3.5892	3.4976	3.4098	3.3255
4.2883	4.1604	4.0386	3.9224	3.8115	3.7057	3.6046
4.6389	4.4873	4.3436	4.2072	4.0776	3.9544	3.8372
4.9464	4.7716	4.6065	4.4506	4.3030	4.1633	4.0310
5.2161	5.0188	4.8332	4.6586	4.4941	4.3389	4.1925
5.4527	5.2337	5.0286	4.8364	4.6560	4.4865	4.3271
5.6603	5.4206	5.1971	4.9884	4.7932	4.6105	4.4392
5.8424	5.5831	5.3423	5.1183	4.9095	4.7147	4.5327
6.0021	5.7245	5.4675	5.2293	5.0081	4.8023	4.6106
6.1422	5.8474	5.5755	5.3242	5.0916	4.8759	4.6755
6.2651	5.9542	5.6685	5.4053	5.1624	4.9377	4.7296
6.3729	6.0472	5.7487	5.4746	5.2223	4.9897	4.7746
6.4674	6.1280	5.8178	5.5339	5.2732	5.0333	4.8122
6.5504	6.1982	5.8775	5.5845	5.3162	5.0700	4.8435
6.6231	6.2593	5.9288	5.6278	5.3527	5.1009	4.8696
6.8729	6.4641	6.0971	5.7662	5.4669	5.1951	4.9476
7.0027	6.5660	6.1772	5.8294	5.5168	5.2347	4.9789
7.0700	6.6166	6.2153	5.8582	5.5386	5.2512	4.9915
7.1050	6.6418	6.2335	5.8713	5.5482	5.2582	4.9966
7.1232	6.6543	6.2421	5.8773	5.5523	5.2611	4.9986
7.1327	6.6605	6.2463	5.8801	5.5541	5.2623	4.9995

Appendix B

BANK VALUATION SOFTWARE

Bank Valuation Software is available to support the valuation process. The first component is market valuation of assets and liabilities—that is, the bank's balance sheet equity. The valuation of balance sheet items includes variable-rate loans (with embedded options of interest rate caps and floors) and mortgage-related assets (with embedded prepayment options).

Also included in this valuation is fee income from deposit accounts, non-deposit services, trust activities, bank cards, loan origination activities, asset sales, and underwriting activities. These elements of fee income are valued as assets of the bank being evaluated. In addition, noninterest expense is valued and the result is considered a liability of the bank.

The fourth component of Bank Valuation Software is off-balance sheet positions. In terms of interest rate derivatives, Bank Valuation Software prices swaps, forwards, futures, and options. The swaps are valued using the theoretical zero-coupon yield curve. Values for forward and futures contracts are determined by reference to market conditions and attributes of the underlying assets. Option contracts are priced using Black Scholes option pricing model and Black's futures option pricing model. Other off-balance-sheet positions that are valued include unused loan commitments, letters of credit, loans transferred with recourse, and when-issued securities.

These four areas of analysis—balance sheet, fee income, noninterest expense, and off-balance-sheet positions—provide a comprehensive, objective assessment of the value of a commercial bank.

Bank Valuation Software also includes a module for branch valuation. This feature supports management in determining the optimal branch network. Branch valuations are based on objective variables that measure sales productivity and efficiency.

Bank Valuation Software also can be customized to incorporate other features that may be required by the bank.

Bank Valuation Software is PC-based and user-friendly. The system is installed on-site by highly trained professionals. On-site training sessions are conducted for all key officers of the bank. For more information, call Global Bank Research at 502-423-0760.

Index

About the Author

Hazel J. Johnson, Ph.D., is a professor of Finance at the University of Louisville. She has worked as a C.P.A. and auditor for a Big Six accounting firm, as a bank financial analyst, and as manager of internal audit for a national insurance company. She was formerly on the finance faculty of Georgetown University. Her research has been published widely in the United States and abroad. She has acted as a consultant to more than 35 of the largest U.S. banks and as an advisor to the International Trade.

She has most recently published *Banking Without Borders: Challenges and Opportunities in the Era of North American Free Trade and the Emerging Global Marketplace* (Probus, 1995), *The New Global Banker* (Probus, 1993), The Banking Keiretsu (Probus, 1993), *The Bank Valuation Handbook: A Market-Based Approach to Valuing a Bank* (Probus,1993), *Bank Regulation Today* (Probus, 1994), and *Bank Asset/Liability Management* (Probus, 1994).

Other books of interest to you from Irwin Professional Publishing . . .

BANK MERGERS, ACQUISITIONS AND STRATEGIC ALLIANCES
Hazel J. Johnson, Ph.D.

Bank Mergers, Acquisitions and Strategic Alliances reviews all sides of M&A activity in this new era of interstate banking. While market and acquisition strategies are fundamental issues, this management guide also reviews the often overlooked "back room" steps that are critical to successful mergers.
ISBN: 1-55738-746-X $60.00

THE BANKER'S GUIDE TO INVESTMENT BANKING
Securities & Underwriting Activities in Commercial Banking
Hazel J. Johnson, Ph.D.

The Banker's Guide to Investment Banking is the premier source for providing you with the insight on participating and underwriting various securities. Updated with timely information on this ever-changing industry, the *Guide* gives you an edge to accessing this profitable market.
ISBN: 1-55738-747-8 $50.00

THE BANKER'S GUIDE TO THE SECONDARY MARKET
Security Trading, Derivative Instruments, and Mutual Fund Services
in Commerical Banking
Hazel J. Johnson, Ph.D.

This insightful guide provides an expanded knowledge of the explosive secondary market. Designed to help you stay ahead in today's financial services industry, *The Banker's Guide to the Secondary Market* offers you a competitive edge and keeps you apprised of your customers' changing needs.
ISBN: 1-55738-922-5 $50.00

BANK ASSET/LIABILITY MANAGEMENT
The Concept and the Tools
Hazel J. Johnson, Ph.D.

Bank Asset/Liability Management is a comprehensive treatment of all the issues related to management bank portfolios of liquid assets, securities, loans, liabilities, and capital. The book examines bank profitability and its components, discussing the customary measures that form the basis for bank-to-bank comparisons.
ISBN: 1-55738-709-5 $32.50

STRATEGIC CAPITAL BUDGETING
Developing and Implementing the Corporate Capital Allocation Program
Hazel J. Johnson, Ph.D.

Strategic Capital Budgeting helps financial managers make better decisions about longterm, fixed asset investments by using the sound financial concepts presented in this straightforward and concise guide to the capital budgeting decision.
ISBN: 1-55738-426-6 $42.50

COST ACCOUNTING FOR FINANCIAL INSTITUTIONS
The Complete Desktop Reference Guide
Revised Edition
Leonard P. Cole

Cost Accounting for Financial Institutions is a guide for bankers to compile, analyze, and act upon that critical information. Focusing on the two key areas of cost and pricing, this book sums up the information retrieval and management process that has a direct impact on an institution's success.
ISBN: 1-55738-739-7 $60.00

MANAGEMENT ACCOUNTING FOR FINANCIAL INSTITUTIONS
The Complete Desktop Reference Guide
Revised Edition
Leonard P. Cole

Today's banker needs reliable and consistent information for making decisions. *Management Accounting for Financial Institutions* gives financial managers the whole picture from the accounting and finance side. This guide provides information in a timely, clear, and concise manner that allows the manager to formulate strategic planning for a bank.
ISBN: 1-55738-738-9 $60.00

THE TREASURER'S HANDBOOK OF FINANCIAL MANAGEMENT
Apply the Theories, Concepts, and Quantitative Methods of Corporate Finance
Treasury Management Association

The Treasurer's Handbook of Financial Management provides today's practitioner with step-by-step applications to the theories, concepts, and quantitative methods of treasury management.
ISBN: 1-55738-884-9 $69.95